COME
MY CUP

Linda

All the best —

happy reading

[signature]

COME *Fill Up* MY CUP

JEAN MURRAY MUNDEN

1603 Capitol Ave., Suite 310 Cheyenne, Wyoming USA 82001
1-888-980-6523 | admin@urlinkpublishing.com

URLink Print and Media is committed to excellence in the publishing industry.

Book design copyright © 2018 by URLink Print and Media. All rights reserved.

Published in the United States of America
ISBN 978-1-64367-111-6 (Paperback)
ISBN 978-1-64367-110-9 (Digital)

Fiction
30.10.18

Chapter 1

ROBIN AND JAMES 1996

James stood at the window and watched the storm approach. A black curtain of rain had obliterated the soft green hills to the west and was now rapidly moving toward their side of the valley. A sudden gust of wind rattled the window pane, and lightning flashed in the distance, followed by a rumble of thunder. Another flash, much closer, followed, and more thunder reverberated. He marveled how fast the weather could change in the Highlands. Just yesterday morning when he left his home south of Inverness the sky had been blue, a few wisps of cloud caressing the tops of the mountains—a perfect autumn day.

"As my sister would say, this is going to be a real humdinger of a storm," he remarked to his aunt, who was sitting in her big easy chair by the fireplace.

Sarah Donaldson smiled at him.

"You and Katharine always did enjoy a thunderstorm," she remarked.

"I remember once when Kath and I were small, and we were at the nursery window, noses pressed against the glass, watching the lightning. Nanny kept telling us to come away, that it was dangerous, but we just scoffed, and counted the seconds between the lightning and the thunder. Then there was a huge bolt that must have hit something close by because it made a tremendous crash, and lit up the whole sky. You never saw two kids move so fast across the room to Nanny's lap!" He smiled reminiscently.

"With this wind we're bound to have a power outage," Sarah said, putting aside her knitting and getting to her feet. "I had better hunt up candles and torches. I think the paraffin lamp is in the back porch. Would you mind fetching it for me, Jamie, please?"

Out on the porch, James shuddered at the deafening noise the rain was making on the metal roof. He found the lamp, and a tin of fuel, and was no sooner inside when there was a bright flash of lightning and a simultaneous crash of thunder. A moment later the lights flickered and went out.

"Talk about famous last words," he said, as he fumbled with the lamp. "Are you a female Prospero and have magicked up this storm? That must have hit something nearby."

Sarah was peering out the front window. "I think it must be the old oak tree that Thomas planted all these forty years ago," she said slowly. "It could have brought down the lines."

By the firelight she lit candles, and then went into the kitchen, blessing her big old coal burning cooker, which would keep the room warm as well as the supper hot. She stirred the soup, and then ladled out two bowls, sliced bread, and put out cheese and pickles. Calling her nephew, they sat down at the kitchen table and enjoyed the simple meal. Afterwards they went into the sitting room where James poured her a small single malt whisky—for digestion, he said with a smile.

"I am going to wash up the dishes, check Kelly and the horses, and then get ready for bed," she announced when she had finished her drink. "You stay up and enjoy the storm. I have a feeling there will be some tidying up to do in the yard tomorrow."

She lingered over the few dishes they had used, this time blessing the extra large hot water tank she had installed when she opened her bed and breakfast. As she wiped the dishes carefully and put them away, she thought of James and his visit. He didn't get out this way very often; he was kept busy with the farm and the distillery. Her brother Robert, James' father, had run the whisky business in the past, but the last few years Sarah thought that he'd been depending

2

more and more on James. She sighed. Since their troubles eight or nine years ago, James had immersed himself in the family business, and hadn't had much time for socializing, with family or otherwise. Therefore, he had surprised her the other day when he had telephoned and offered to spend a couple of nights with her provided she wasn't busy with her paying guests. He had business in Fort William, he said, and was she free? Sarah welcomed him; she was fond of her nephew, and continued to worry about him as though he were the son she had never had. He seemed to be recovered from his losses after all these years, but sometimes she wondered. Katharine had remarked once that her brother had buried all those awful memories with his mother and his wife; he never discussed that time with her. It wasn't as though they weren't fond of each other, she had continued. They were the best of friends, but that part of his life he had shut away. As for Sarah, she missed Fee dreadfully. Her sister-in-law had been her best friend, and also her best support when Thomas died so unexpectedly fifteen years ago. While she had become accustomed to being without Thomas—her horses and her guests kept her busy and happy—she was still not used to life without Fee on the end of the telephone line. They phoned each other at least once a week, and several times a year Fee would drive over in the Mini to spend a day gossiping, riding, or simply to be a shoulder to cry on. She remembered how Fee had escaped a visit from Claire's mother one time ("Can't abide that woman," Fee had declared.) and another time Fee had whisked her off to Edinburgh for a few days of shopping and spa visiting after Thomas had gone. Sarah sighed.

James told her last night that Janet had suggested he visit his aunt. "Somebody has need of you," she'd said. Janet was the family housekeeper, and had been brought up with James and Katharine, and at times it seemed she had "the sight". Sarah had smiled and said lightly that she always needed him, but privately wondered what on earth Janet had meant.

She rinsed and wrung out her dishcloth, put on her roomy sou'wester that had belonged to Thomas, and dashed across the cobbled yard to the stables. All was well as she thought it would be, but as she went in and passed through the sitting room on her way to the front hall stairs, James remarked,

"I thought I saw headlights out there, across the valley. Nobody but a fool would be out in this weather!"

⸎

"What a fool I am!" exclaimed the woman in the car. "How on earth did I get myself into this predicament?"

Robin was alone; there was no one to comment so she answered herself. "Well, I know very well: I stayed too long at that pub, mislaid my map somewhere, and then when I did ask for directions, I couldn't understand a word that the man was saying. And did I ask him to slow down and repeat himself? Oh, no, I just smiled like an idiot and drove off!"

And missed that all important first turn.

Tim, who had joked about the "wee daft roads" when they had visited Scotland before—and this was certainly one of them: the narrow, twisty *damned* thing—he would have understood the man; and if by chance he hadn't he would have smiled his charming smile and asked for a map. Why couldn't Tim be here to help her? She hadn't realized how difficult it was to be both driver and navigator, especially after dark, and on the wrong side of the road. *Damn* this right hand drive car, *damn* this horrible road, *damn* this storm, *damn* all Scots who couldn't speak proper English, and *damn* Tim for dying in that ghastly way.

Tears of grief and fright were running down her cheeks unchecked; Robin's hands remained clutched to the steering wheel. She stopped the car and tried to collect herself. Her stomach was churning with fear; the evening suddenly had become pitch dark, and there was not a light to be seen. She told herself that a car was probably the safest place to be in a thunderstorm, but it didn't make her feel any better. Where could she have left her map? She had traced her route with a bright pink marking pen, and she should have been nearly to Oban by now, not lost in the wilds of Scotland. After taking a few deep breaths she put the car in gear and commenced to crawl

4

along, looking for a place to turn around. She would make her way back to Speam and find a room for the night. As she turned a rather sharp corner, she saw by the headlights the large tree which was lying across the road, completely blocking it. She slammed on the brakes, and came to a halt only a few feet away. Well, she'd have to turn around now. She put the car in reverse and promptly backed into the ditch. Her rear wheels spun in the soft turf as she tried to go forward. The rain had made a mire of the area. Robin's heart sank.

"Now, what the hell do I do?"

She turned off the ignition and the headlights, and peered out the rain-washed window. The bank rose quite steeply away from the road, but she thought she could see a faint light above her. Was there a house up on the hill? She struggled into her jacket, found the flashlight and her shoulder bag, and got out of the car. She gasped as the wind grabbed her. There was another flash of lightning, and it lit up a sign that was swinging madly in the wind. She crossed the road and shone her flashlight on it: "Braeside Stables Bed and Breakfast". Maybe her guardian angel was looking out for her after all. She moved the flashlight up the slope of the hill, and sure enough, there was a set of stone steps leading up through the trees.

Robin felt like the Ancient Mariner when he cried, 'A sail, a sail!'

She started up the steps, slipping once, and falling to her knees. The wind had abated somewhat, but the rain continued to pour down, soaking her and chilling her to the bone. When she reached the porch, she smelled wood smoke and saw that indeed there were faint flickering lights inside. Someone was home. It took both hands to hold the flashlight because she was shaking so much, but she managed to illuminate the big oak door and was rewarded with the sight of a large thistle-shaped knocker. With stiff fingers, she lifted it and knocked as loudly as she could. A few moments later there were steps inside, and the door opened, silhouetting a man in the doorway. He held his lamp high.

"There's a tree down, and my car is stuck," she began.

She heard a woman's voice. "Who is it, Jamie?"

"A drowned rat, I'm thinking," he called back in an amused voice. Then he said to her impatiently, "For heaven's sake, don't just stand there. Come in and drip off inside."

She came in and closed the door behind her as an elderly woman entered the hall. She was dressed in a voluminous robe and was wearing huge fluffy bedroom slippers, the kind that Robin hadn't seen in twenty years. A kind face beneath graying hair regarded her with concern.

"Why, you're soaked to the skin, lassie! Come away with me and let's get you into some dry clothes! Thank the Dear we've still got plenty of hot water."

She led Robin up a set of steep stairs into a large old fashioned bathroom with an enormous tub under the window. She set down the lantern on a small stool next to the tub, and turned on the taps. From a narrow, white painted cupboard she brought out a large thick towel, a wash cloth, and a large cake of lavender soap. Its soothing fragrance filled the room.

"I can't thank you enough for taking me in like this," began Robin, but her hostess waved her remarks away with a smile. "Och, it's nothing. Now just put those wet clothes outside the door, and I'll see to them."

A short while later Robin found herself immersed in the steaming water, and thought to herself that she didn't even know the woman's name. Less than an hour ago she had been out on an unknown road, weeping for her husband and terrified of the storm; now here she was in a warm house bathing by lamplight. There was a knock on the door, and her hostess said from the hallway, "I've brought you a robe and pajamas—they belonged to my husband. I'm thinking that you are tall enough to wear them."

"How kind of you. He won't mind, then?"

"Bless you; he's been gone these fifteen years. I gave away most of his things, but kept a few things—in case. They were a comfort and also useful." She went away quietly and closed the door.

Robin understood. After Tim had died, she had refused to get rid of his clothes for months. Sometimes when misery enveloped her she would go into his closet and bury her face in his things. The smell of him had lingered, and for a moment she could pretend that he was there. On cold nights when her big bed was even wider and emptier that ever, she would climb into his pajamas and robe and cuddle down with his pillow. Looking back, she realized that it was all a part of the grieving process, and gradually she got on with her life.

A half hour later she came downstairs wrapped in the huge tartan dressing gown and was met by the man who had opened the door.

"Come on in and sit down and warm yourself." He paused and extended his hand. "I'm James Maclachlan, by the way, and you have found the hospitality of my aunt, Sarah Donaldson."

Robin shook his hand. His hand was warm and he had a firm grip. "I'm Robin Lindsay, and I feel like the biggest fool in all of Scotland."

"How on earth did you happen to be wandering away out here?"

Robin blushed with embarrassment. "Well, I took several wrong turns and got myself completely lost." She paused. "You know, I tried to thank your aunt, but she seemed to think it quite ordinary to take in a complete stranger." She sat down in the big overstuffed sofa under the window where the rain continued to splatter the pane. James sat down opposite her.

"We have a code here in the Highlands," he said rather shortly. "The door is always open to someone in trouble." He regarded her curiously. "Where were you supposed to be going?"

"I was on my way to Oban. I must have missed that first turn." She paused. "Are your phones down, too? My landlady was expecting me tonight."

"Aye, they are; would you like to try my mobile? It may not work in here, though."

Robin tried to use his telephone, but sure enough, she couldn't get through. And there was no way she was going back out in the rain to try it from the middle of a field.

"The land lines should be working again sometime in the morning." He sat back and smiled at her a trifle sardonically. "There's nothing you can do about it. Don't waste your time and energy worrying about a situation that you can't change. Let me pour you some whisky instead."

"Good advice on both counts," smiled Robin, deciding to ignore his manner, and over her drink she studied her companion. He was probably in his mid-forties like herself, had dark red curly hair that was liberally threaded with grey. His eyes were blue, deep set and widely spaced; there were lines around them, made by laughter or worry she wasn't sure.

"You're traveling alone," he remarked.

"Yes," said Robin. "My husband died three and a half years ago, and this is a bit of a pilgrimage, I guess. We enjoyed a trip here ten years ago, and had always meant to return. I'm revisiting some of the places we saw together, and seeing some new sights as well. I had planned to be back in Oban as I am supposed to visit my cousin who is staying on Iona. I joined a walking group when I first arrived, and did some hiking around Loch Lomond, then came up to this area. I've just been visiting Skye. The weather was lovely until this afternoon."

I'm babbling. I must be nervous. Why am I nervous?

"Where are you from, Mrs. Lindsay?" he asked.

"I live in Victoria, B.C. This I my second visit to Scotland—but I told you that, didn't I?"

She had arisen and was studying some photographs on the mantelpiece. One had been enlarged from a black and white snapshot and it was of a man and two children.

"This is you," she said. "Are these your children?"

"Yes," he answered. "It was actually taken on the Isle of Mull. I took the children to the island on a camping trip a few years ago. I haven't been there since."

"And their mother?"

"She died over eight years ago," he said.

"I'm sorry," Robin said. "It isn't easy raising children on your own."

"I've been fortunate to have family to help me," he replied.

The tone of his voice told Robin not to do any probing. She studied another picture. It was an old studio portrait of two children.

The boy was perhaps six or seven and the girl a curly haired toddler. They were staring solemnly at the camera, and the boy's arm was protectively around the little girl. James picked it up and smiled. "This is my Aunt Sarah, and my father, her older brother," he said. "Do you see the resemblance to my son in the photo there?"

Robin compared the two. "It's remarkable, isn't it?"

"Their coloring is quite different, but in the black and white photos that doesn't show up." He sat down and finished his drink. "Another wee dram?"

"It's very good, but no more on an empty stomach, thank you. Tim taught me to appreciate single malt Scotch. We did the Whisky Trail when we were here together. It was so much fun and so interesting to taste the different whiskies."

Mrs. Donaldson came in at that moment, bearing a large tray on which was a bowl of steaming soup, bread and tea.

"Come and have a wee bite. Jamie here thinks that whisky is the cure-all, but to me there is nothing like soup."

Robin put her glass down and realized that she was ravenous. With expressions of pleasure and gratitude, she sat down at the table and enjoyed her supper.

Later, Mrs. Donaldson showed her a small bedroom upstairs. "You'll be snug here," she said kindly. "I overheard you telling Jamie about your husband," she added. "What did he tell you about his wife?"

"When I asked about her he told me she had died," Robin replied.

Mrs. Donaldson nodded. "It was a terrible time. His mother was killed in a car crash about three weeks before that. He doesn't often talk about it."

"I don't blame him. How dreadful for them all!"

Mrs. Donaldson wished her goodnight, cautioning her to make sure the candle was out before she went to sleep, drew the curtains, then went out and shut the door behind her.

Robin awoke the next morning to a world washed shiny and clean. It was just before six and the fiery rim of the sun was emerging from behind the eastern hills as she opened the casement and looked out. She sniffed the air appreciatively. It was cool, and there was the smell of damp earth, dead leaves and pine. There were sounds below her, out of sight around the other side of the house. She heard horses neighing, the slam of a door, and a clatter of hooves on stone. She opened the bedroom door, and saw that someone had thoughtfully fetched her suitcase from the car. It meant she could brush her teeth and get into clean clothes.

A half hour later she stood on the front porch and watched as two trucks drove up from the opposite direction from which she had come, stop, and four men emerge. The spent a few minutes conferring with one another, then one pair started working at clearing the tree. The other two were soon at work with ladders and other equipment. Cheerful men's voices drifted up to Robin's ears, and the sound of axes and saws.

<hr/>

Out in the yard Sarah Donaldson came out of the stables with Kelly, her stable lad and general man of all work. The little Irishman was bow-legged and balding, his face seamed with lines from years of exposure to the sun and wind, but he had a brilliant smile and the friendliest eyes imaginable. He cocked his head and squinted as he looked up at his employer.

"The horses were fine, Ma'am," he assured her. "The thunder startled them, and they were very uneasy, but other than that, there were no problems." He looked down the road and remarked, "We're after having a visitor."

Sarah smiled as she saw a small figure riding a bicycle madly along the road and careen into the driveway that led up to the house.

"I thought perhaps we'd see Sheena this morning. I'm sure she fretted about her Rufus all night."

They both watched her pedal furiously up the hill and around to the stable yard, where she jumped off her bicycle, leaving it on its side, wheels spinning.

"Good morning, Sheena. Rufus is just fine," smiled Sarah.

"Oh, Mrs. Donaldson, are you sure? It was a dreadful storm. Our phone is still out, and we have no electricity. I couldn't telephone, so I came along before school just to make sure. Did you know your old oak tree has fallen down? I think it must have taken down the electric wires and the telephone lines. There are men working down there already." She turned to the little Irishman who was grinning broadly at her. "Kelly, are you sure Rufus is all right?"

"Bless you, miss, it would take more than that to worry Rufus. I was just about to begin exercising the horses. Do you have time to come along? I've saddled him this very minute."

"Oh, thank you, Kelly! I will!" And she rushed by them into the stable.

Sarah went into the kitchen, warm from the roaring fire in the wood stove, where James and Robin sat sipping their coffee. She smiled a good morning to them.

"Thanks to whoever brought up my suitcase," Robin said. "What a comfort to brush one's teeth. Last night I was too tired to even think about it."

"That was Jamie. I found your keys in the pocket of your trousers. They are in the scullery sink soaking, by the way. They'll have to be washed, after the electricity comes back on and we have hot water again." Sarah brought over two bowls of steaming oatmeal, and put them down in front of her guests.

They were still sitting talking when Sheena returned thirty minutes later. She came into the kitchen, cheeks red and eyes sparkling from her ride, and Sarah introduced them, and then asked, as Sheena was washing her hands, "Did you have breakfast, dear?"

"Well, no...Mummy made me take an apple, but I gave that to Rufus."

"Sit down then, and, since we still have no power, I'll make you some toast the old-fashioned way."

"Rufus is a lovely name, "remarked Robin. "Is he reddish-brown?"

Sheena smiled warmly. "Most people don't know what 'rufus' means," she said. "Are you American?" she asked. "You have an accent."

"I'm Canadian," Robin replied. "I live in Victoria, which is on Vancouver Island, away over on the West Coast." Her eyes twinkled. "And we all think that it's you folks that have the accent."

Sheena smiled, showing her even white teeth. "I guess it depends how you look at it." She took the toast that Sarah had made and was spooning marmalade onto it. Four mouthfuls and the toast had disappeared.

"You're the lady whose car is in the ditch?"

Robin nodded. "I was trying to turn around and got stuck."

"It was a horrible storm last night. We must have a hundred tree branches littering our garden."

Sarah nodded. "We've been picking up branches here as well."

Sheena glanced at her wristwatch, drank down the milk that Sarah handed her, threw on her jacket, thanked her hostess profusely, smiled at James and Robin and flung herself out the door. "I'm going to be late! I'll be back after school!"

"She makes me tired just watching her," Robin remarked. "What energy!"

"Sheena is a nice child," Sarah said. "Her father is the local doctor. They live in the village which is about four miles down the road. They have no room for the pony, so they board him here." She turned as they heard hum of the refrigerator. "Ah, there's the electricity back on. We'll have hot water soon and I'll do a washing. Would you like to see the stables, Mrs. Lindsay?"

Later, James and Sarah took Robin around the stables and inspected the horses. She told them how after her husband had died she decided to take up something completely new, and chose to receive riding lessons. She said her children thought she was crazy.

"I had been on a horse perhaps a half-dozen times before in my life, and it was always in the back of my mind that I would learn to ride properly some day. I am really enjoying it. I have a friend who has retired to the country, and raises horses. She says I am doing very well. And Deborah and Denis are now quite proud of me."

"Then shall we go for a ride this morning?" asked James. "I'll get Kelly to saddle up old Bonnie for you. She's gentle and sure-footed and knows the hills better than I do."

A short time later Sarah watched them ride out and up the winding trail that led over the hill. It was a glorious September morning, and she spent the next two hours weeding her garden and picking up the last of the broken branches. Around noon the men working at clearing the road and repairing the fallen lines came up the driveway to say they were finished. She offered them lunch, but they all shook their heads and said there were other calls to make. She was preparing lunch when Robin and James returned, and she could hear Robin talking animatedly, and James deep rumble in answer. They were laughing uproariously over something. Sarah shook her head. Well, well. She hadn't heard Jamie laugh like that for a long, long time. Oh, he would laugh, but in a mirthless sort of way, and he might be amused, but at the expense of others. The two came in, Robin flushed and still laughing, and James with a sparkle in his eyes, demanding lunch. It made Sarah smile, just watching them. Jamie needed a friend, and she liked Robin immensely.

"Do you know, Sarah, that Robin is the mother of twenty year old twins? One of each and both at university."

Sarah Donaldson looked from one to the other with interest. She nodded and said, "The telephone is working now, Mrs. Lindsay. You were concerned about your landlady in Oban. Why don't you put in a call to her, while Jamie lays the table here in the kitchen?"

"Oh, thank you, Mrs. Donaldson." And she disappeared into the hall. A few minutes later her clear voice came to them. "Mrs. Millar, this is Robin Lindsay....yes, I'm fine, thanks. I got lost last night and got stuck in a ditch, and some kind people took me in, but the telephone was out until now. I'll be back tomorrow sometime, but if you need my room, that's not a problem. Oh, that's very kind of you. I'll have to see to my car this afternoon. Yes, I'm still planning to go to Iona... Thank you again. Good-bye, Mrs. Millar." She came back into the kitchen, saying, "I hope it's all right, I said I wouldn't be back until tomorrow. Mrs. Millar is holding my room for me, and won't even charge me for the two nights I'll miss. Isn't that kind of her?" She breathed in with a smile. "Something smells delicious. The fresh air has made me very hungry."

Over lunch, Robin expressed her pleasure in their ride into the hill, and the beauty of the day. James had shown her a glimpse of the sea and then, studying her map, had explained just where they were located.

"I don't know how I could have gone so wrong in my directions," she confessed. "It isn't as if this area is crisscrossed with roads."

Sarah thought that perhaps it was meant to be, but she didn't voice her opinion. "You know you are welcome to stay as long as you want. We aren't far from Glenfinnan. It's a pleasant drive and there is an interesting display there."

"My cousin Celine is expecting me on Saturday," explained Robin. "I have appreciated your hospitality, and I don't want to wear out my welcome."

"You'll like Mull and Iona," James remarked. "I think I said last night that the last time I was there is when I took Nell and Malcolm camping two or three summers ago."

Impulsively Robin said, "Would you care at all to join me on Saturday? If you have the time, that is." Afterwards she wondered how she had had the nerve to ask a comparative stranger to join her on a weekend jaunt. It hadn't occurred to her at all; the words had just slipped out.

James hesitated and glanced at his aunt.

"If you don't have to be home, Jamie, do go ahead. We've had a good wee crack. Why don't you see about freeing Mrs. Lindsay's car while I iron her trousers?"

Jamie had already looked at the car and thought that he'd need Mac Smith's tow truck from the village. Now that the road was cleared, he would be able to bring his lorry and pull it out of the ditch. During the drive to the village they discussed the visit to Iona, and Robin explained that her cousin would be free from her duties for only two or three hours.

"I would be grateful for company while visiting Mull," she added, "and you'd enjoy meeting Celine. She's a very interesting person. I just love her."

"If you are sure that I'm not interfering with your reunion with her, I would love to show you Mull. Are you planning to take the early ferry? I could easily be in Oban before eight in the morning."

"Come for breakfast at seven-thirty," suggested Robin. "Mrs. Millar won't mind, and that would give us plenty of time to catch the ferry. Would you do the driving? I've rather lost my self confidence these days."

James smiled sympathetically at her. "Anyone would have gotten lost in that storm last night, but I'll gladly drive."

"And we share the expenses," said Robin firmly.

Chapter 2

IONA AND MULL

The mist lay on Oban Harbour like a thick grey blanket, obliterating the fishing boats bobbing up and down at the quay, covering the houses that clambered up the hillside, and dampening the sounds of the morning traffic. Only McCuaig's Folly, that bizarre structure on top of the hill, was visible, poking out from the fog bank like an ancient Roman ruin on a cloudy island. Robin and James stood on the deck of the ferry as it negotiated its way through the narrows between Kerrera and the mainland, and so out into the Firth of Lorne. The sun, with the aid of a stiff breeze, soon burned the fog away; the sea birds wheeled and cried over the blue sea, while the boat churned its way through the choppy water, leaving behind a silver wake that led back into the misty harbour. Robin's eyes shone with pleasure as she breathed in the cool salt air, and watched the spume flying off the tip of the waves. Her hair had come undone and was being whipped around her face, curls bouncing and blowing.

James regarded her with interest. She wasn't beautiful as Claire had been, but she glowed and sparkled, and her face was alive. "Tell me about your cousin," he suggested. "I've been meaning to ask you what she is doing on Iona."

"Celine is a social worker, and she took early retirement last spring. She says that she has always wanted to go to Iona and join the community there, and this is what she has done."

"Did you grow up with her?"

Robin hesitated. "Well, yes and no. You don't really want to hear my life history, do you?"

James grinned and replied, "As long as it's finished by the time we get to Craignure."

Robin smiled. "I guess I can condense it a little." She paused, gazing at the retreating mainland. "I was born in Abbotsford, B.C. It's a farming community in the Fraser Valley, and my father was a pharmacist. Chemist, I think you would call him here? We lived out in the country. It's very pretty there, green fields and mountains all around in the distance. I'm an only child, but my best friend lived just across the road where her family grew corn. You know, sweet corn, the kind you eat. Their corn was fabulous. Marilyn's house was my second home." She paused again and frowned slightly. "It's curious how children take situations for granted. I knew my parents were different, but that's the way it was."

"How were they different?"

"Well, they were totally wrapped up in each other. Sometimes I felt quite an outsider. My friend Marilyn's family did things together, and they actually talked to each other! I once asked my mother why my father didn't play games with me like Mr. Innes did with Marilyn, and my mother just said that he didn't enjoy children. Don't misunderstand me, I wasn't neglected or abused. I had good food and warm clothing and lived in a nice house."

"You had everything except what you needed most," observed James.

"I remember thinking that Mr. and Mrs. Innes liked me, and Marilyn wanted me to be her best friend. I just couldn't figure out why I couldn't please my father.

"When I was thirteen, my mother was diagnosed with breast cancer. My father was absolutely beside himself. He wouldn't accept the doctors' opinion that she was dying. He took her to clinics, and even to a faith healer. Nothing worked, of course, and we watched her grow weaker and weaker. She was in constant pain. They gave her morphine, but it was not enough. My father was afraid to give her more because he thought she would become addicted," she added bitterly. "Can you imagine such muddled thinking from a pharmacist?"

Robin was gripping the rail, and her knuckles were white. "He wouldn't let me visit her in the hospital at the last. It was a Sunday, I remember, the day she died. He came home and said that she was gone. I felt as though someone had punched me in the stomach. He hadn't even thought that I would want to say goodbye to her. When I asked him why he didn't allow me to say goodbye to her, he just shook his head and said she didn't ask for me. He went away into their room, and I could hear him weeping. I telephoned my Aunt Julia in Montreal, and she and Celine flew out immediately.

"My aunt was furious with my father. She took him aside and asked him why he hadn't let her know just how ill my mother was. 'Every time I phoned you told me she was the same. Didn't you think that I would want to see my sister before she died? I'll never forgive you for this, Frederick Marsh.' She and Celine took me back to Montreal for a visit, and I wound up living with them for the next seven or eight years.

"Celine was older sister, mother, and friend," Robin said. "Her brothers were good to me, and Aunt Julia and Uncle Jean were kindness itself, but Celine seemed to surround me with love and caring. I was a prickly teen, unsure of myself, grieving for my mother, bewildered at my father's defection, and landed suddenly in a strange city and culture. Celine was my rock that I clung to."

Aunt Julia had insisted that they should all be fluently bilingual, and there were French days and English days, when only one language was spoken, and Robin soon was speaking French like a native Francophone, though Aunt Julia would probably have been horrified at the gutter French that the boys taught her.

She grew up in Montreal, went to McGill University, and it was there she met Tim Lindsay at a party. Tim was a pilot for Canadian Pacific Airlines (as it was called then), and after that, every time he was in town, he called on her. They were married in 1973, and went back to Vancouver to live. The twins were born three years later, and she lived happily ever after.....

"Until Tim was killed in a plane crash in the Pacific in 1993. He was on his way back from Japan and the airplane just disappeared off the radar. It went down with everyone aboard, and they never found anything. Not a scrap of wreckage. That was the awful thing—not to be able to actually see his body. For the longest time I could not believe it. Celine flew out immediately that she knew of it. It was really strange. I found it difficult to make decisions. Even on ordinary things. I would start something, forget what I was doing, and then do something else. I thought I was having a breakdown. The twins had each other, were able to cope, and they pityingly would urge me to pull myself together. Celine was my rock again and I really don't know what I would have done without her."

James regarded her with compassion.

"So you were not only grieving his loss, but all those people too, and the guilt that goes with being a survivor.......and also the wife of the pilot."

Robin was silent, and her eyes filled. He understood. No one except Celine had really seemed to comprehend the wracking guilt that she had felt. Her physician had given her sleeping pills, but she had been afraid of becoming dependent on them, and she endured nightmares of trying vainly to pull people out of black water. She saw their white faces and she would weep in frustration and awake to a pillow wet with her tears. Sometimes she felt that she had fallen into a deep, dark hole out of which that she could not climb. She would lie in bed tears running down the sides of her face, wondering how she was going to survive without him. Little things would set her off. Waves of would sadness would wash over her and fill up the hole she was trapped in. She felt that she was drowning. She had never felt such pain in her life. She hadn't realized that the pain of grief was physical. Even when she was grieving her mother it hadn't been like that.

"Everyone was kind, and good to me, but as soon as the twins graduated from high school I decided to put the house on the market. I think I just wanted to have a new start somewhere else." She paused, looking out over the water toward the approaching shoreline. "When the twins were small, Tim inherited his grandfather's house out near the

University of Victoria. It was a good-sized house that his grandfather had converted into two flats. He lived on the ground floor and rented the upper floor. After he died we even considered relocating there— it's a lovely city to raise a family—but about the same time the airline gave him a promotion, so we stayed in Vancouver and rented the Victoria house. When Deb decided to attend U Vic she took over the house and I moved with her. At first I thought about sharing the house with her, but I decided that wouldn't be giving her enough space, so I looked around for a small house in the area. I found this nice little house that I've been renting."

James reached over and squeezed her hand briefly. "It was a nightmare, too, when my wife died, so I can understand a little of what you went through. Let's leave that and enjoy the day. I'm looking forward to meeting Celine and showing you the island. Look, you can see Duart Castle."

He pointed to the large structure on a rocky promontory brooding over the bay.

"Isn't it spectacular? Torosay Castle is across the bay, and there are beautiful gardens there, best in spring, though, but Duart is a real medieval fortress. It was the headquarters of the MacLean Clan, but fell to the Campbells. They really left it to rot until the MacLeans bought it back before the First World War. I have MacLean cousins and I feel sympathetic to their cause. We Scots have long memories. If we have time we should stop on the way back from Iona."

It wasn't long before the ferry was docking at the quay in Craignure, and they were through the village and on their way to Iona. A few miles past the village there was a turn-off and a sign saying "Lochbuie—6mi" and James remarked that that also was a must see. "We'll certainly stop there this afternoon on the way back. It's a lovely spot. A quiet beach and some stone circles, if you are interested in that sort of thing."

It was close to an hour's drive on the narrow road to Fionphort, where they left the car and boarded the foot passenger ferry. James said that there were days when the weather was such that the ferry couldn't run, and Iona was isolated completely. Today was beautiful, a light wind blowing from the north, making a little swell. It was just over a mile to the tiny island across the Sound of Iona, and as they neared the quay at Baile Mor they could see a tall woman waiting, her hand shading her face as she looked at the ferry coming in.

"There's Celine!" Robin said, waving.

"Go ahead and meet her. I'll join you in a few minutes."

Robin made her way off the ferry and dodging tourists ran to meet her cousin. James saw Celine's arms open wide and envelop the younger woman in a warm embrace. He followed slowly along the quay, and Robin, her face shining with happiness, beckoned him.

"Celine, this is a new friend, James Maclachlan. He and his aunt literally rescued me from the storm the other night. James, my cousin Celine la Roche."

Celine was very tall and thin, with a bony mobile face untouched by makeup, a generous mouth with sensuous lips, high cheekbones and two piercing black eyes. She wore her long, dark brown hair pulled back from her face and a thick braid fell almost to her waist. Her hair was threaded with grey, but her face was relatively unlined, except for frown lines on her forehead and laughter wrinkles around her eyes. She wore baggy trousers, a rusty red tunic, and had pinned a large tartan shawl around her shoulders. She came forward and took James' outstretched hand in both of hers, and for a moment looked into his face. James had the extraordinary feeling that she was looking straight into his soul and finding him lacking. In that moment he wanted to be wrapped in that warm embrace she had just given her younger cousin, and to lay his head on her shoulder and tell her all that he was unable to tell Robin. Then she spoke, and the spell was broken. She had an unusually deep voice.

"Welcome to Iona, James Maclachlan. It's a pleasure to meet you."

Celine and Robin made their way to the Community buildings, while James set out on a walk up Dun I, the hill behind the village. He had excused himself after a few minutes, and Celine suggested they meet at the Community Coffee House for lunch in an hour. He watched them go off arm in arm, the dark head bent toward Robin's ash brown curls. James reached the top of the hill and sat and enjoyed the view. He had climbed up here with Nell and Malcolm four years ago. Malcolm had run ahead on his sturdy five year old legs while he and Nell followed more slowly. They had been camping on Mull and had taken a day, as he and Robin were now doing, to visit Iona. He remembered how peaceful Nell thought it was. "This is a nice place, Daddy," she had said. "Almost as nice as Glen Rannoch." This was high praise indeed, for as far as Nell was concerned, her home was the center of the universe. Today, at seventeen, she hadn't made any signs of changing her opinion.

James eventually arose and walked down the path to the Abbey, and met Celine and Robin for lunch. They enjoyed home cooked soup and fresh bread and cheese, all made there by the community. Tea, strong and black, with a jug of milk on the side, was served with cakes for dessert. The three walked down to a sunny part of the island and sat on the rocks. Celine talked about the community and the possibility that she might stay on for the foreseeable future.

<hr />

Afterwards Robin remembered that day and the day that followed as a series of snapshots: Celine sitting in the sun, squinting in the bright light, James leaning against the rock, mahogany curls blowing in the wind; her farewells to Celine, and the promise to come again before she went home; their drive to Lochbuie and the walk on the beach there, with a visit to the stone circle; the setting sun on Loch na Keal; the amusing play they saw that evening in Dervaig, and their stay in charming Ardbeg House. (Separate rooms, of course.) The next day they visited Calgary (it was a must to see the namesake of a Canadian city), then back to Tobermory to explore that town on foot; they looked in on the museum, and even were able to watch a diving crew, one of many who searched for the Tobermory Treasure in the Harbour; they drove around the other side of Loch na Keal on their way back to Craignure, and had time to stop and see Duart Castle. They arrived back in Oban in time for dinner, and spent a leisurely evening enjoying each other's company, and talking over the events of the last two days.

"James, thank you for the time on Mull."

They were walking along the Esplanade on their way back to the guest house. It had started to rain, and James had taken her arm, saying that the cobbles would get slippery. He stopped and looked at her seriously.

"Robin, lass, bless you for asking me. I hadn't realized how much I needed to get away." He paused and frowned slightly. "Your cousin is an extraordinary person. Does she have Scots ancestry? I felt for an instant when we met that she was reading me, deep down."

She was silent for a moment. Celine had made a few comments about him when they were by themselves, and they had disturbed Robin.

"Our mothers' people are all of Scottish descent."

They came into the guest house lounge where a fire was burning cheerfully. No one was about except Mrs. Millar who put her head in and said that she had just made coffee, and would they like some? They settled themselves in front of the fireplace, sipping Mrs. Millar's excellent brew in silence. Finally James asked, "What are your plans for the next week or so?"

Robin thought a moment. "I have tickets for the Edinburgh Festival and had planned to spend a week or so there, then go on to St. Andrew's for another few days." She looked at him questioningly.

"Would you consider coming to stay at my home the weekend after next? It's my birthday on the Saturday and there is a dinner planned."

"I wouldn't want to intrude on a family gathering..."

"There will be others as well as the family," he said. "Mhoira and Fraser Smith, who lease the sheep farm; it's called Crickletop, God knows why, and Margaret and Hugh Rennie who is the local doctor. My father has an old navy crony coming for a few weeks. I'm going to persuade Aunt Sarah to come as well. She'd love to see you again."

"I'm not sure..."

He reached over and took her hand, and for Robin it was as though an electric shock went through her. "Robin, I have enjoyed your company immensely these last few days and frankly, I don't want to say good-bye! Somehow you seem to make the past irrelevant. I've been happy with you! I don't know where this is going, but I want you to come and meet my family and see my home before you leave my country. Please accept."

Robin's heart was beating very quickly and her cheeks were flushed. She caught her breath and said quietly, "James, I would like very much to see your home, and meet your family."

He smiled a smile that started in the corners of his mouth and spread to his eyes, and lit up his whole face. "Now," he went on, "I have a confession to make. I've not been entirely truthful with you." He laughed at the expression on her face. "My father is an earl."

Robin's round eyes grew even rounder. "An earl? Good grief, what on earth do I call him?"

"His official title is Robert Earl of Rannoch. He usually dispenses with the title except on formal occasions, but 'my Lord' when you meet him or 'Lord Rannoch' in general. We've always been rather informal about the family titles; in fact Sarah refuses to use it."

"Of course, she would be....Lady Sarah Donaldson, wouldn't she?"

He nodded. "I think the only person Sarah would accept calling her by her title would be the Queen herself. She actually was a Lady-in-Waiting to the Queen Mum years and years ago. She disliked court life immensely and when she met Thomas Donaldson she couldn't wait to get married and raise horses and children. To their sorrow, there were no children, but they had a very happy marriage. Tom had a heart attack about fifteen years ago. My sister and I loved to visit them when we were small. Tom bought that property forty years ago, and it really was isolated. There was no electricity, water came from a well, and he built the road to the village himself. My parents were very fond of them both."

"What do I call you?"

"Just go on calling me James," he answered. "The family calls me Jamie, as I sure you've guessed, and they won't break the habit."

"I think Jamie is rather nice," she said shyly. "You shouldn't mind. My cousins always called me Robbie. I liked it." She paused for a moment. "Will you tell me about the rest of your family?"

He paused and smiled a little.

"My sister Katharine is two years younger that I am, and she lives nearby. Her husband Roger Perry is the minister of our local church. They moved back nearly ten years ago. Their son Simon and my son Malcolm have grown up together, really, just like twins, born only a few weeks apart. It is wonderful having them so near. I really dread the day that Roger will be sent somewhere else. Malcolm and Simon go to the same school near Inverness. One weekend a month they get a long weekend. One of us picks them up after lunch on Friday, and they don't have to be back until Sunday evening. We usually make a big deal out of Fridays and have a huge family tea about five or five-thirty. It gives them time to run about that evening and get rid of excess energy. They're both fine boys; everyone looks forward to the long weekends." He paused. "Nell. Nell is seventeen, and going in her grandmother's footsteps. She and the head lad really run the stables together, and she gives riding lessons. She has left school and doesn't want to leave home—she's always said she's going to stay and look after me in my old age. My mother was a great horsewoman. She had Katharine and me astride a pony when we could barely walk, and did the same for Nell." He gazed past her into the flames. In the silence, Robin said tentatively,

"Your aunt told me very briefly about the deaths of your wife and mother. I am so very sorry. It must have been a dreadful time for all of you."

His face had gone quite still, but there was pain in his eyes as he replied, "Thank you. It almost killed my father. He is still grieving for my mother, after almost nine years."

So are you, she thought.

After a few moments he continued. "My young cousin Iain Maclachlan lives in a house on the estate, and he runs the dairy farm. He came to live with us when I was about Nell's age. His parents had been killed in a plane crash—he was about three, I guess. He was such a sturdy wee lad, with his dark hair and black eyes. My mother just took him to her heart. Katharine and I were practically grown, and he filled a void for her and she for him. I used to carry him around on my shoulders, and he has done the same with my children. They both love him like an older brother instead of second or third cousin or whatever he is. We have a small distillery which my father and I run. It actually employs quite a lot of people. You will have to have a tour of it and sample our single malt. You'll like my father. Janet Stevens runs the castle; she's practically family. She grew up with us because her mother was housekeeper for my parents."

"Castle?" queried Robin faintly.

"Och, it's not really a castle, just a big house. The original structure was used for defense, so it's officially called Rannoch Castle."

"Whew! You really know how to impress a girl."

"You will come?" he asked anxiously. "Come for tea Friday week."

"I won't get lost again and be wandering in the wilds?"

He smiled and shook his head. "Give me your road map, there, and I'll mark the route."

At the first opportunity Robin had replaced her missing map. Now she retrieved it from her carry-all and handed it to him. He balanced it on his knee and with a pen began tracing the route. She watched his hands as he wrote. The fingers were long and sensitive looking, and fine reddish hairs visible on his wrists. "You'll be coming from St. Andrew's, won't you...the easiest way is to go to Perth and up the A9 via Pitlochrie, Glen Garry, and toward Inverness. You can leave the A9 and take the 8970 here; it's a bonny drive up the valley, then turn here at Inverdruie. It's only a few miles to Nethy Bridge, then watch for the road to Glen Rannoch Village. We're up in the hills where the River Rannoch starts its run down into the Spey." She looked away from his hands to his face, and found him watching her. She blushed and took the map and put it away. "So," he said, getting to his feet, "you'll be with us Friday week?"

"Yes," she answered, also rising. For a moment she thought he was going to kiss her, but instead he held out his hand.

"*Au revoir,*" he said carefully, turned and let himself out of the hotel. From the window she watched him stride to his car, get in and drive away, not looking back. She went slowly up the stairs, a little dazed at the events that had rushed her way. *I have a date with an earl's son!* James had mentioned, while they were picnicking with Celine, a little bit about his wife Claire. They had met when he was taking two or three business and accounting courses at Oxford twenty years ago. He had met her through her sister Eleanor who was boarding with the aunt and uncle of a friend of his whose singing group he had joined.

"Eleanor played the piano very well, and accompanied us on one occasion," he had said. "Her father was in the American ambassador's office, I forget in what capacity, and Eleanor was studying music and art history. When I met Claire, I was completely bowled over."

Celine had studied him intently, and asked the question Robin would have like to. "She was beautiful, then?"

"The most beautiful girl I had ever seen."

He had said very little more, and nothing of her death and the 'nightmare' that he had gone through. Celine hadn't asked. When she and Celine were alone, Celine had said seriously, "There's a darkness in him, Robin. Take care. Though," she added with a twinkle, "I can see the attraction."

I really don't know anything about him, she thought, as she prepared for bed. Then she remembered Sarah Donaldson, with her clear blue eyes, all gold clean through, and her affection for her nephew. And Celine liked him, in spite of her reservations. Her last conscious thought was *what will be, will be,*

Chapter 3

ELEANOR AND JAMES 1976

The beautiful old stone Church of St. Stephen rang with the mellow tones of the organ. The player was Eleanor Shaw, and she had just finished her practicing session. She sat for a moment on the bench, her long fingers still resting on the keys, and absorbing the atmosphere of this lovely old place of worship. She was here nearly every day, and she never failed to look around and admire the sanctuary. The choir with its polished mahogany benches, the altar draped with a hand brocaded silk and the huge plain Cross suspended above it. There were some fine stained glass windows, and she especially liked the large rose windows in the transepts. The brass lectern, lovingly polished by members of the altar guild, stood below the pulpit. Peter Fleming, the Vicar, rarely preached from the pulpit. He preferred to be on level with the congregation, and gave his thoughtful, sometimes amusing, always interesting sermons, standing at the lectern, or at times striding back and forth. The congregation was varied; long time residents of the neighborhood, some elderly, some middle-aged, and some with children attended, but a large portion were students at the various colleges in Oxford, as was Eleanor, and they were young and enthusiastic. They were for the most part traditional young people, although some wore weird clothes and had strange hairdos, according to the older folk in the congregation, but they all came to hear Peter and listen to the fine music that St. Stephen's offered.

Eleanor, who was eighteen, was a music and art history student, and boarded at the Vicarage with the Flemings. She attended lectures during the week, did her practicing on the church organ and the Vicarage piano, and most weekends she went to stay with her family in their large furnished suite in London, where her father worked in the office of the American Ambassador. Occasionally she played the organ for services when the organist, Miles Renshaw, was going to be absent, and she always sang in the choir for Wednesday Evensong. She was thinking of her family now, and how uncomfortable it was for her to spend time with them. She wondered if there was something the matter with her. She shared a room with her older sister Claire, who was in the throes of preparing for Court Presentation next month. Her mother had a friend in Baltimore, who knew Lady Pilkington, and she was sponsoring Claire and hosting parties and introducing Claire to similarly involved young persons in the frantic rounds of receptions, dances and teas. Eleanor was rather scornful of all these activities, and her mother's encouragement of them. Her mother was always complaining that her husband had been passed over for advancement, and would have done anything to be an ambassador's wife, but her father pointed out that they wouldn't be enjoying the amenities of London if he were to be promoted to that high post.

"I'd be in some obscure country, and either you would be battling mosquitoes, or home in Baltimore," he observed dryly.

Eleanor's younger brother Billy, who was fourteen, was forever scrapping with Claire who rose to the bait every time. She shuddered when Billy said that in Saudi Arabia she would be stuck in the American compound. "And you couldn't even be seen with Daddy or me," he went on. "In Papua New Guinea they are still head hunters, and you couldn't even leave the house in Port Moresby, it's so dangerous. I'd like to go to India, but you couldn't stand the beggars in the street. And you couldn't take your car with you either."

For her twenty-first birthday her parents had given Claire a lovely, long, red TR 4, and Claire drove it everywhere in her spare time. Her friends admired it immensely, and even if Claire hadn't been very pretty, the boys would have still gathered around.

Eleanor sighed. She didn't care about not having a car of her own, but it seemed that Claire got whatever she wanted. Eleanor was a sensible girl, and knew that having one's heart's desire did not always make one happy, but she wouldn't have been human if she had not resented her parents' obvious preference for their first-born. Claire was small and delicately built, with dark blue, almost violet eyes set in a heart shaped face. She had a smooth complexion, fine arched eyebrows, a small red mouth that fell open over a row of perfect teeth, and a cloud of black hair that framed her face. Eleanor was tall and even at eighteen was still "all arms and legs", as her mother said. Billy called her Spider. Lately she had put on weight, and she had to endure sisterly remarks about being fat. Claire had taken ballet lessons as a small child, and had been a dainty graceful fairy princess in the Christmas pageant. Eleanor could hardly wait to follow in her footsteps, but found that it didn't come easily at all. She remembered demonstrating for her mother and a group of her bridge ladies, and wound up in a heap of arms and legs on the floor after a pirouette. "About as graceful as an O-X," was her mother's laughing remark. Eleanor could spell and knew that an ox was a big clumsy animal, so she had crept away and hid, red faced and humiliated.

Eleanor sighed again, and gathered up her music and put it in her case. On her way out of the church she paused in the doorway to the Lady Chapel. St. Stephen's, which was Church of England, wasn't particularly high church now, and certainly in Peter Fleming's theology devotion to the Virgin was not stressed. But it was a popular spot in the church to meditate, and Eleanor often found her way there. Other students, especially girls, would find it amenable in which to consider their love life, or exams, and from time to time one or two people could be observed sitting quietly. Today it was empty. The chapel had been commissioned by a family nearly 200 years ago when they donated a very fine statue of the Madonna and Child. It was sculpted of marble, nearly life size, of the young mother cuddling her baby. In some lights the mother was smiling at her child, and in others she seemed to be gazing out over his head. The marble was a delicate pink, smooth and lovely, and the folds of her gown looked as though they would move, so realistic were they. Today she seemed to be smiling sympathetically at Eleanor.

"I know I shouldn't be thinking uncharitable thoughts about my sister," she said ruefully to the Lady. "But she can be a pain sometimes." Perhaps the Lady had had an elder sister, too, to whom everyone compared her. She did seem to understand.

Eleanor went out into the afternoon spring sunshine and started down the path to the vicarage. The spring flowers in Sally's garden were at their best. Spiraea and daffodils nodded to her in the breeze, and the early plum blossom petals were whirling about her like so much confetti.

Sally Fleming waved her teapot from the kitchen door. "Tea's nearly made," she called.

Landlady and boarder sat in companionable silence at the kitchen table and sipped their tea.

"How was the Garden Party?" asked Sally presently. The Shaws had been invited to Buckingham Palace (along with thousands of others) for the annual affair.

"It was a great crush of people, but Mom and Claire were in their element, and even Billy was impressed, except about dressing up in a shirt and tie! Claire bought a gorgeous new outfit for it and looked super. She always manages to make me feel dowdy and clumsy," she added.

Sally had met Claire and didn't care for her very much. Oh, she had felt the charm (and Claire had set out to charm her) and she admired the talent that Claire possessed of making the person to whom she was speaking feel as though he or she were the most important person in the world. And she *was* a beauty. "She keeps all her goods in the shop window" was an expression her mother had used, and Sally thought that it fitted Claire perfectly. She considered Eleanor to be attractive now and thought that in a few years she would be beautiful. One of Eleanor's best features was her hair. It was long and straight and the color of ripe corn, and it swung back and forth when she walked. She had blue eyes, a rosy complexion, and a generous mouth that curved deliciously upward when she smiled. And when she smiled it was with her whole face. Eyes lit up and crinkled delightfully, and dimples appeared in her cheeks. Eleanor didn't know that she was beautiful, she was only aware of extra pounds, and legs that were too long. Sally thought that those long legs were quite shapely and would soon turn heads. All Eleanor needed was self confidence, and she was rapidly gaining that through her music. Here was one area where Claire could not compete. Even her mother admitted that Claire could not carry a tune, and piano lessons had been a lost cause.

Eleanor was beginning to feel a little guilty of complaining about her sister so she said,

"Did I tell you that Claire has a super new car? Daddy and Mom gave it to her for her twenty-first birthday last month. It goes like the wind." She paused and went on, "You know, Claire not only is an expert driver, but she really knows what goes on under the hood."

Sally raised her eyebrows in disbelief.

"No, honestly. When we lived in Baltimore she had a boyfriend who actually drove racing cars. He taught her how to drive and how to change the oil, and all the mechanical stuff that I would never understand in a hundred years. She never lets on much, though. I think she prefers to let guys think that she's not that smart. You'd never guess though, would you?"

Sally thought privately that she wouldn't put anything past Claire, but said nothing and merely changed the subject.

"My nephew Colin and his group are going to perform at the church in a few weeks," she began. "They sing mostly *a capella*, but need an accompanist for a couple selections. I told him I would ask you."

"What! Me?" exclaimed Eleanor. "I couldn't do that. It's not the same as playing a solo."

"I know," answered Sally quietly. "But you've played for the choir when you've filled in as organist. You've got a light touch on the piano. I think you would do very well."

"What sort of music do they do?"

"Not rock. Ballads and some contemporary gospel, old fashioned spirituals, that sort of thing—nothing highbrow. Nice stuff, I think," added Colin's aunt.

Eleanor considered. "Well, I guess I could try, and if I'm hopeless they'd have to find someone else."

"You won't be hopeless," said Sally firmly with a pleased smile. "I've asked them all to tea on Saturday. Can you stay here this weekend instead of going up to London?"

Eleanor was pleased to have the excuse of not going to her parents' flat. Weekends could be tedious with Claire and Billy bickering, her mother complaining, and her father buried in his books. At the vicarage there were sensible conversations about subjects that really mattered, and a warm, caring atmosphere.

———⟩◦⊙◦⟨———

When Eleanor entered the large old fashioned vicarage dining room on Saturday afternoon, it seemed to be full of people. There were only Colin and two large young men, but they seemed to fill the room. They all stood up as she came in, and Sally, pouring tea at the head of the table, waved Eleanor to a seat. The boys were all talking at once, discussing music, politics, and university, while at the same time passing plates of sandwiches and cakes around and consuming large amounts of both. Sally introduced them all around, and Eleanor questioned, "I thought Sally said there were four of you?"

Colin shook hands with her and said, "Old Mac is late. He had to pick up his guitar that was being restrung. He'll be along soon. He's our temp while George is recovering from measles. Can you imagine getting the measles a month before our concert?"

Eleanor sat down and accepted a cup of tea from Marcus (or was it Kirk?) and said, "Measles can be quite serious in an adult, can't they?"

Colin nodded. "George is all right, though. He'll be a few weeks getting his strength back. Lucky for us old Mac could jump in at a moment's notice. Oh, there he is. I'll let him in, Aunt Sally."

Through the window Eleanor could see a young man toiling up the walk carrying a large instrument case. A few moments later Colin was ushering him in, and introducing him to Sally and Eleanor. He had dark red hair, and a delightful Scottish accent, and with impeccable manners first acknowledged his hostess, then turned to gravely shake hands with Eleanor. His handshake was firm and the skin around his blue eyes crinkled as he smiled at her. He was of medium height, for Eleanor's eyes were nearly on level with his. His teeth were white, but slightly uneven, and his nose was straight except at the very end, where it turned up just a little. He seemed a few years older than Colin and his friends, and was certainly more reserved, for he sat down and quietly accepted a cup of tea and an egg sandwich, which he eagerly bit into with strong white teeth.

"I've no' had my dinner," he remarked to no one in particular, and when offered the plate of sandwiches again, selected two, which he put on his plate, then politely asked to have the pickles passed.

"It's probably not a good idea to eat too much before singing," remarked Colin, taking a large slice of pound cake, and in two minutes demolishing it to crumbs.

"Well, we're really not rehearsing," said Kirk (or was it Marcus?), holding out his cup for a refill.

"I thought we were auditioning for Miss Shaw," the newcomer said quietly, finishing his tea.

Eleanor was silent. She knew this wasn't true, but she was touched by his remark.

Their hostess got up and excused herself, saying that they could help themselves to the piano in the drawing room any time, and for goodness sake finish the food.

They soon moved into the drawing room, and Eleanor sat down at the piano and looked at the music which they had brought with them. She was a good sight reader, and soon was skillfully rippling through the accompaniment. Colin and his friends nodded to each other in delight, and the young Scot began one of the songs, and soon they all were happily singing. They rehearsed their two numbers needing the piano, then launched into an *a cappella* arrangement of a song unfamiliar to Eleanor. She listened in delight, and when they began a version of "Deep River", joined in with her clear contralto voice. Mac played his guitar, and hummed in harmony.

"Say, she's got a fab voice," Kirk declared.

"What about taking the lead in "Were You There", and we could do the background in harmony without the piano..."

"Old Mac could just give a few chords, it would be more dramatic."

"How about it, Eleanor, would you like to sing, too?"

"Then we'd be Three Lads, an Old Man and a Girl," joked Marcus.

They spent the rest of the afternoon and early evening planning, revising and experimenting with several numbers. At one point when there was a lull, Mac took his guitar, and in a quiet baritone began to sing "Scarlet Ribbons"....'*I peeked in to say good night, and I found my child in prayer. Send, dear God, some scarlet ribbons, scarlet ribbons for my hair.*'... Eleanor sat transfixed. He sang it so tenderly and with such emotion that she said quietly when he finished, "That was simply lovely, Mac. Do you have children of your own?"

He smiled at her, and said lightly, "No, I'm not married. And please call me James. It's James Maclachlan. These Philistines don't even know how to make a proper introduction."

At seven, the group got ready to leave, and Colin asked Eleanor if she wanted to join them for a pint and a bite of supper at the local pub. Eleanor hesitated, then refused, saying that she had studying to do, and when was the next rehearsal so she could plan her work?

"Now, there's a lass with a purpose. The rest of you young Sassenachs could take a lesson here."

Eleanor blushed, and saw them all to the door. "Tell Aunt Sally I shall phone her. We should probably meet at the church next time. Wednesday all right for you, Eleanor?"

<hr />

"It was such fun," she told Sally later. "Colin is very clever at leading the group, isn't he? I felt a part of it all, somehow, and they liked me!"

Sally gave her a hug, pleased with her experiment, remarking that she wasn't surprised that they liked her; she was a very likable person.

⊷◉◉◉⊶

For the next few weeks Eleanor lived and breathed The Oxford Lads, and felt as though she had known them forever. They continued to develop the program for the concert, rehearse in the church twice a week, and she was able to juggle her lectures and lessons and practicing. She would get up early and do her scales and finger exercises on the Vicarage piano, then rehearse the concert music, and in the afternoon after classes practice for her organ lesson. When Sally asked her if she had invited her family to the concert, Eleanor shook her head, saying that her parents already had plans for that weekend, Billy was going on a school outing, and Claire was going to a party; besides they wouldn't have been interested, anyway. She continued to refuse the Lads' invitations to join them at the pub after each rehearsal until one evening when Marcus announced that his girlfriend would be joining them. She enjoyed the time with them as they relaxed and drank a few pints, while she sipped a lemonade. She wasn't quite sure why she had not accepted their previous invitations. Was it because she didn't feel comfortable as a girl alone in a pub with a group of young men, or was it because James had never tried to persuade her to come?

As the days drew nearer the concert, she felt knots of apprehension in her stomach. She was surprised at herself, because rehearsals had been going smoothly, and she was confident that everyone would do well. She had not thought beyond the concert, and when she did, the knot was bigger than ever. In a few short weeks these people had become a part of her life, and she hadn't even considered everything coming to an end. George would rejoin the group, James would be off to Scotland, and life would never be the same.

Cross that bridge when you come to it, she thought.

The concert was a complete success, of course. All the tickets were sold, so extra chairs had to be set up in the aisles, always keeping fire regulations in mind. There was a standing ovation, and the church rang with shouts of 'Bravo!' and 'Encore!' They wound up with a rendition of the Beatles' "When I'm Sixty-four", with Colin wielding a pair of crutches borrowed, on the spur of the moment, from a man in the front row. After the money was counted, and put away safely in a locked cupboard in the vicarage study, they all trooped down to the pub by the river, the vicar and his wife included. Eleanor walked between Colin and James, arm-in-arm, her feet scarcely touching the ground.

"My old Nanny would say you're a bit above yourself," said James with a smile.

"Is this what being high is like?" she asked, doing a little skip. "Who needs alcohol anyway?"

"*I get no kick from champagne,*" Colin hummed. "You're hooked after one performance, Eleanor!"

"I shall probably have a hangover tomorrow," she said laughing.

"We should seriously think about another concert, maybe in the university theater," he said.

After an hour of laughter, jokes and talking over the evening's performance, they all walked back to the vicarage. One by one they all kissed Eleanor goodnight on the cheek, except James, who took her hand and kissed it gravely. Eleanor was too excited to sleep; she thought to herself that she felt just like Eliza Doolittle and certainly 'could have danced all night'. She lay in her bed and went over the whole evening, each scene in her mind she gathered and strung like pearls and held to herself. She hoped that Colin had been serious about another concert. Life would be flat without The Oxford Lads in her life. And James.

———◦◦◦———

Colin called a week later saying they had booked the university theater for May 19th, and the Lads had been unanimous in asking Eleanor if she would join them again.

"George, too. He was in the audience, you know, and thought you added a super dimension to the group. You will, won't you? You know we made over 800£." It had been agreed that 25% would go to the church, and the rest to UNICEF.

Eleanor wanted to ask about James, but couldn't get the words out. Instead she agreed to join them and asked them to come to the vicarage for the first rehearsal. "I'll make sure it's all right with Sally. Phone me back tonight," she said.

Sunday morning she played the organ, as Miles Renshaw, the organist was away, and her heart leaped when she saw James in the congregation. She made herself concentrate through the rest of the service, and when the final hymn was announced, she banged out the music triumphantly. *"And did those feet in ancient time/Walk up England's mountains green? And was the Holy Lamb of God /On England's pleasant pastures seen?"* Those words by William Blake went so well with Sir Hubert Parry's magnificent music, and as the crashing chords died away, and Peter pronounced the benediction, she peeked out into the congregation. James was still there, talking to Sally, and when Eleanor had gathered up her music and put away the hymn book, she came down into the sanctuary. Sally had gone and James was waiting for her.

"I've come to take you to lunch," he said with a smile. "How about our pub by the river?"

Our pub! Eleanor thought that she would burst with happiness as they walked down the road to the river.

"Colin says that you have agreed to join them for the concert in May. That was a great experience last week, wasn't it?"

"I've never had such a wonderful time, even the rehearsals, and the concert, well—I can't find the words to express myself," she confessed.

"Colin asked me to join them, too," he said, "but I don't know if it will work. I'm thinking about it seriously. George is back, so they don't really need me; exams start about that time, and then I'm off back home."

Eleanor felt a chill come over the day, but she reminded herself that he had said at the beginning of rehearsals that he would be finishing his courses earlier than the rest of them, and going back home to Scotland to put his new knowledge to work.

Over coffee after lunch, James said, "I've been asked to a dance Saturday at the home of friends of the family. It's actually a twenty-first birthday party for their eldest daughter Bridgett. Their name is Maddingsly, and they live near Eynsham, a few miles west of here. I should go, as I haven't seen them since I've come down from Scotland, and they said to bring a friend, if I liked. Would you come?"

Eleanor accepted eagerly, and, gathering her courage, then asked him if he would come to tea at her parent's flat in London two weeks from that day. "I have to be in London on the Saturday; I'm going with my class to the Victoria and Albert Museum, so I will be at my parents' on Sunday. Could you come about four?"

He accepted warmly. "And I'll pick you up at seven o'clock next Saturday. It's formal," he added, as an afterthought.

⊳⊚⊛⊚⊲

"Oh, why did I say I'd go?" she wailed to Sally later that afternoon. "I haven't a thing to wear!"

Sally considered. "I saw a pair of beautiful evening trousers in the window of Debenhams in the High Street the other day. I'm sure they would fit you. You have that lovely white cotton and lace blouse, and I'll lend you my velvet blazer. You'll look perfect."

"Oh, but I can't afford...."

"It will be a gift from Peter and me. An early birthday present."

"My birthday's not until September," she said, "but thank you very much."

Friday was one of those fine spring days that poets write about, with the warm air filled with the scent of cherry blossoms. The sun was setting, leaving in the western sky faint streaks of pink, mauve and grey, and above the chestnut tree, which was just beginning to show a trace of white, the evening star had appeared. James sniffed the air appreciatively as he came up the path to the front door. He was looking particularly splendid in his evening dress, which, of course, was full Highland regalia, right down to the dagger in his stocking. Eleanor opened the door to his knock, and her eyes widened in admiration.

39

"Come in, James. You look absolutely super! Is this what a Highland chief wears?"

James came in and regarded Eleanor with pleasure. "You're looking no' so bad yourself!" he returned. He produced a lovely tartan shawl. "This is my mother's. I found it when I was getting out my kilt. Dear knows how it got mixed up with my things. I thought you might like to borrow it for the occasion. The colors will be all right, I'm thinking."

Eleanor beamed with pleasure and allowed him to put it over her shoulders. "It's beautiful! Is the Maclachlan tartan?"

James nodded as Sally and Peter came in to say goodnight. She regarded Eleanor fondly. "You look lovely, dear. Take good care of her now, James. Enjoy the party, both of you."

Eleanor and James drove in the gathering twilight out of the city into the country. After a little thought James found the right road and soon they were driving up to a large country house. It was all lit up, other cars were arriving, and they could hear orchestra music coming from the open windows. There was a reception line, and as they approached their host and hostess, the young woman who was certainly Bridgett, smiled in welcome.

"Mrs. Maddingsly, may I present Eleanor Shaw. Eleanor, may I introduce Mr. and Mrs. Maddingsly, and Bridgett Maddingsly, the birthday girl."

Eleanor shook hands and murmured how glad she was to be there, and presented her hostess with a bouquet of flowers that Sally had arranged from her garden. James produced a small package from his pocket and gave it to Bridgett with a flourish, wishing her a happy birthday. Bridgett was not a shy girl, and gave James a big hug and kiss.

"We haven't seen you at all," she declared reproachfully, "and I suppose you'll be going back to Scotland any time now. Is Katharine in London still? Is it true that she made the equestrian team?"

"Yes, no, and yes," James replied, after a momentary pause. "She is training in Edinburgh at the moment."

"There is punch and champagne in the small drawing room, and dancing will begin shortly in the ballroom," said their hostess kindly. "Just follow the crowd."

"Save me a dance, James," called Bridgett, as they moved away.

"I don't think I have ever been in a house that has a ballroom," whispered Eleanor, as they made their way to the small drawing room. "And I suppose there is a large drawing room somewhere."

The rest of the evening went by in a blur. Eleanor danced, sipped punch, and danced some more. James waltzed with her, but he sat out the rock'n'roll numbers, saying that he was too old to do the twist and the mashed potato, whatever they were. Several young men asked her to dance, and soon she was swinging with all the young fry. During the orchestra's interval Bridgett coaxed James to the piano to sing and James insisted on Eleanor's playing for him. She shyly agreed, and James sang several Scottish ballads. She joined in with him singing "When I'm Sixty-four" as they had done at the concert. Several people approached her and said that they had been at the concert, and congratulated her on the group's success. Eleanor was pink with pleasure, reminded them that James also had taken part, and mentioned the date of the next concert in the University Theater.

"It's a good cause, and the music will be good. Other groups are taking part as well."

At supper Eleanor found herself surrounded by admirers. Only one incident marred her pleasure. She was in the powder room combing her hair and powdering her nose shiny from her exertions. She had sat down to take her shoes off for a moment, and was hidden from the door. Several girls came in, and one said,

"Whoever is that big blond kid with James Maclachlan? Bridgett's nose is certainly out of joint."

"She's just a baby. No need for Bridgett to get her knickers in a twist."

The third remarked scornfully, "You two are just green with envy that all the boys are fighting to dance with her. I think she's rather attractive."

Eleanor shrank down in the chair and waited for them to leave. She returned to the dance floor rather hesitantly, but immediately another young man took her arm and asked her to dance. She put the two spiteful remarks out of her mind, and enjoyed the music. There was more dancing, and when James found her for the final waltz, and swept her on to the floor, Eleanor's face glowed with happiness. They drove back to Oxford and the Vicarage in the moonlight, and when James saw her to the door, he leaned over and kissed her gently on the cheek.

"I'll be talking to you before next Sunday," he said. "You can tell me how to get to your parents' flat. Good night, Eleanor."

Eleanor went in on a cloud. Sally had waited up for her, and was eager to hear the details.

"It was wonderful, Sally, thanks to you. The evening trousers were just right. I danced all evening and James is coming for tea in London next Sunday. Oh, he forgot to take the shawl. No matter, I'll be seeing him soon." And she floated off to bed.

Sally watched her go upstairs, frowning a little. The next morning over coffee with Peter, she remarked, "I hope James Maclachlan is careful with Eleanor's heart. I think she's quite smitten with him."

Peter was philosophical. "The young folk will always manage their own affairs. I'm as fond of Eleanor as you are, darling, and I would hate to see her hurt. There isn't much we can do except to stand by and pick up the pieces, if needs be."

Sally sighed. She knew Peter was right, and she hoped that she was worrying needlessly. It occurred to her that it was because of her machinations that Eleanor had met James.

I need a baby of my own to worry about, she thought.

Chapter 4

JAMES AND CLAIRE

"Did you say someone was coming for tea?" Mrs. Shaw asked Eleanor. It was the following Sunday and Eleanor was in the kitchen making cookies and a cake. She wiped her floury hands on her apron, and replied,

"Yes, mother, at four o'clock. I did tell you last week when I telephoned."

"What a pity that Claire is away for the weekend."

Eleanor didn't reply, but busied herself mixing the dough. She had known very well that Claire would be away and wasn't planning to return until Monday afternoon. She had picked this weekend for that very reason. Claire had had all the attention lately, with parties and new outfits and the grand climax of being presented at court last week. She rolled out the dough, cut the cookies and placed them on her baking sheet. The timer rang, and she checked the cake already in the oven, pronounced it done, and removed it. The kitchen was filled with the delicious aroma of spice cake. She turned off the heat in the oven, and proceeded to start tidying up.

"Did you tell me who this person was?" queried Mrs. Shaw.

Eleanor rinsed her dishcloth thoroughly, and began wiping down the counter.

"I told you about the singing group I was playing for, and the concert a couple of weeks ago, when you and dad were away for the weekend, didn't I? Well, this is one of them."

"But what's her name?"

"It's not a her, it's a him," Eleanor replied. "His name is James Maclachlan, and he's from Scotland."

"From Scotland!" exclaimed Mrs. Shaw, in tones that placed Scotland on a par with deepest Africa and all Scots cousins to the Hottentots.

"Mother, he's just a friend. He invited me to a birthday party and I have reciprocated and invited him to tea." Which was true on the surface, and certainly true as far as James was concerned, she thought to herself. She didn't dare let herself dream too much. She finished tidying the kitchen, took the cookies out of the oven, and hurried away to change her clothes.

When she came into the sitting room a few minutes before four o'clock she was surprised to see that James had already arrived, and that he and Billy were chatting cheerfully together.

"I hope you don't mind my arriving early," he apologized, getting to his feet. "I gave myself more time that I needed, and I got here in no time at all."

"Eleanor, James has met the Beatles!" Billy exclaimed. "It would be so cool to meet the Fab Four," he added wistfully.

"Billy has every record that the Beatles have made," Eleanor remarked, smiling in welcome. "You sure know how to impress people, don't you? Have you met my parents?"

"We introduced ourselves," James replied. "What a wonderful smell! Have you been baking?"

"Eleanor has been baking all afternoon," remarked her mother, who had thawed considerably. "Shall I put the kettle on, Eleanor?"

Eleanor served the tea, and cake and cookies were passed around. They continued their discussion about the Beatles; James and Mr. Shaw discussed diplomacy and world economic conditions, and Mrs. Shaw chattered cheerfully about the Palace garden party, while Eleanor sat back and listened, and occasionally made a few remarks. She was content to sit and glow in James' presence, sipping her tea and nibbling her cookies. It was nearly six o'clock, and James was gathering himself to depart, when the door flew open and Claire came breezing in.

"Such a bore, Melanie came down with the flu this morning and Tommy wouldn't stay, so I had to drive him home...oh I didn't know you had company." She advanced to James who had risen to his feet and was gaping, dumbstruck, at the young woman. "I'm Claire Shaw," she said, holding out her hand.

Claire was a picture in her elegantly cut dress; she had a graceful and curvaceous figure, slim legs, small hands and feet, a beautifully shaped mouth with even white teeth that curved into a welcoming smile. She pulled off the red silk scarf which she had been wearing gypsy-like over her hair, and shook out tumbled curls. With cheeks flushed from the wind, her black hair like a cloud around her heart-shaped face, and her violet blue eyes sparkling, she was an irresistible sight. Eleanor immediately felt frumpish in her carefully selected outfit. She watched Claire draw James down onto the sofa, saying he couldn't go just yet, as she had just arrived, and soon they were chattering away like old friends. Eleanor felt an icy hand close around her heart as she watched Claire, with practiced charm, weave her magic. She made herself get up, and with trembling hands remove the tea things from the table and take them into the kitchen. Billy followed her in, and whispered fiercely,

"Talk to them, Eleanor. Do something."

She shook her head dumbly. "I can't."

"James likes you, Eleanor."

"You saw how he looked when she came in. He's never looked at me like that."

"Eleanor!" Claire's voice came from the sitting room. "I'm going to show James my car!"

"Go with them!" Billy whispered.

Eleanor reluctantly went out back and James said, "Claire has offered to drive me home. I've told her it's a long way, but she insists."

Billy was at her side, his elbow in her ribs, silently urging her to accompany them to Claire's garage in the next street, but she resisted, and shook hands with James, saying hesitantly,

"Will you be coming to rehearsals?"

"I haven't made up my mind yet, but most likely. I'll see you next week."

He said good-by to the others, and turned to go with Claire.

"Rehearsals?" they could hear her inquire as they went down the hall.

"Eleanor played and I sang as a substitute in a group for a concert recently."

"Oh, how exciting! Eleanor never told me. What kind of music?" her voice died away as Mr. Shaw gently closed the door. He looked with concern at his younger daughter. Eleanor's face was stiff with misery. She shook off his proffered hand and disappeared into the bedroom she shared with her sister. Face down on her bed; she shed bitter tears of anger and humiliation. Later when Billy came in softly and said that dinner was ready, she shook her head mutely.

"Oh why didn't you say something?" he asked.

"I couldn't. You saw his face, Billy."

"You'll be seeing him again."

"Maybe." At that moment she remembered that she had again forgotten to give him his mother's tartan shawl. Surely he would call her. Surely he'd come back to the Oxford Lads. She got up, washed her face, and readied herself for bed. She lay awake for a long time, waiting for Claire to return, but at midnight she still hadn't come home. Finally at two am her sister crept in. and after a short time got into bed. Eleanor lay with her eyes closed, feigning sleep. In five minutes Claire was asleep, and Eleanor turned her face into her pillow and shed more tears. Finally she fell into an exhausted sleep.

The next morning Eleanor awoke to see Claire sitting cross-legged on her bed, smoking a cigarette, and looking at her with a peculiar expression.

"Phhhf! How can you smoke those foul things?" Eleanor said, and reached to open the window. "I sure wish you wouldn't do it here."

Claire ignored her comment and blew a cloud of smoke to the ceiling.

"You are a sly one," she said. "An earl's son for a boyfriend and not a word to us."

An earl's son! Eleanor didn't know what to say, so she said nothing.

"He lives in a castle in the Highlands and they have a farm and a distillery. We are meeting tomorrow for lunch and I've asked him to one of the parties next weekend. You don't mind, do you? I mean he said you were just friends. You do know he's twenty-five, don't you? He was surprised to find out that you were only seventeen."

Now Eleanor couldn't let *that* pass. "Claire, how could you! You know I was eighteen last September!"

She was suddenly very angry at James and disgusted with herself. She watched Claire pick up the tartan shawl which had been folded up on the chest at the end of Eleanor's bed and examine it.

"Where did this come from?"

"James lent it to me. I forgot to return it to him."

"Oh, in that case, I'll be seeing him tomorrow, and I'll give it to him."

"Fine. I don't care if I see him again." And she disappeared into their bathroom and slammed the door.

Later, she made excuses for an early return to Oxford. Of course she hadn't meant it when she had said that she didn't want to see James again. Twice she saw someone that reminded her of him, and her heart leapt, then sank. Perhaps he'd come to see her at the Vicarage. Perhaps he'd come to rehearsals with the Lads. She got off the bus and walked the five blocks home and hoped that she wouldn't encounter Sally. She wanted to lick her wounds alone.

Sally knew, as soon as she saw Eleanor, that something was wrong. Eleanor's face should have been bright and smiling, instead it was stiff, and she wasn't walking with her usual bounce. She didn't ask any questions, merely put on the kettle and made tea. Her mother had always made tea in times of crisis. Sally could hear her mother's voice in her mind: *A nice cuppa is what you need, dearie.* She brought it upstairs; tapped on Eleanor's door, and when bid to enter went in and silently put down the tray. Eleanor had been sitting at the window, but turned to greet Sally.

"How kind of you, Sally. Some hot tea is what I need." Sally was about to leave, but Eleanor said, "Don't go, Sally. I thought I didn't want to talk to anyone, but I guess I do. It was a disaster, Sally." And she went on to relate yesterday afternoon's events. "I was angry at James at first, but it's not his fault. Claire was a gorgeous whirlwind and just swept him along. You should have seen his face. He never looked at me that way."

Sally hugged her fiercely. Eleanor was worth a hundred Claires, and as far as she was concerned. James was a fool.

"They're meeting for lunch tomorrow, and she's invited him to one of her posh parties."

Sally still said nothing, only squeezed her hand.

"Do you know his father's an earl and he lives in a castle in the Highlands? He told her things about himself in a few hours that he never told me in the two months since I met him. That really impressed Claire. Sally, if she hurts him, I'll kill her!"

Sally made soothing noises, and continued to hold her and stroke her hair. She remembered her first love, and how devastated she had felt when things went awry.

"What will I do, Sally?"

"You'll carry on and do what you have to do. You'll smile and pretend the world's a wonderful place. You'll make music with the Lads and go to classes and play the organ."

"You know, I've heard that expression 'the world crashing around you'. Now I know what it means."

Sally drew away a little and looked into Eleanor's face. The girl's blue eyes were filled with tears, and at that moment they overflowed and ran silently down her cheeks.

"He never, *ever*, looked at me that way," she repeated. "Oh Sally, I feel like dying!" And flung herself into Sally's arms and sobbed bitterly.

———⊙◊⊙———

The next day James traveled back down to London and met Claire in St. James Park. It was a beautiful day, and Claire arrived with a picnic basket and a blanket and they found a sunny grassy spot by the river and spread out their things.

"I thought it would be nicer than a restaurant," Claire said. "There's cold chicken, potato salad, and coleslaw. This is a real American picnic." She also produced cheese and pickles and crisps. "In America we call these potato chips, and what you call chips we call fries," she said. The English language is funny sometimes."

"Did you make all this? How clever of you. I see you have Eleanor's cake too. It was delicious."

Claire hadn't realized that Eleanor had made the spice cake. "That reminds me, James." And she brought out the tartan shawl from her bag. "Eleanor asked me to return this to you. She said you had given it to her, but she doesn't want it now. She was rather annoyed at you. I understood that you were just friends," she added carelessly.

James frowned. "She said I'd given it to her?" He was certain Eleanor knew that it was his mother's. Claire must have misunderstood. "We've been friends for about two months," he said.

"Well, she says she doesn't want to see you again." Claire's expression was of concern for her sister. "It will be awkward if you are singing together, won't it."

James had been half planning to rejoin the Lads for the concert, but now he reconsidered. "I really don't have time for rehearsals," he told her. And he certainly didn't want an awkward situation, either.

"Let's eat lunch, and then we'll go for a drive. I brought a small bottle of wine, too, James." She poured the wine and looked at him with a concerned expression. "I just wanted to clear the air."

Her dark blue eyes were guileless. How pretty she was!

"You're so beautiful. Claire!" He reached over and tucked a strand of dark hair behind her ear. "And so kind to be worried about your sister. Don't worry. We were just friends. She's a sweet girl."

Claire's beautiful lips curved into a slow, satisfied smile. "James!" she whispered, and raised her mouth to his.

Eleanor kept herself very busy during the next few weeks. She stayed in Oxford, practiced her music, rehearsed with Colin and the others, and went to her classes as usual. She didn't encounter James at all.

Sally had told Colin briefly that James was seeing Eleanor's sister. Colin was very annoyed at James, first for dropping the group without explanation, and secondly for treating Eleanor in such a callous fashion. To be sure, James had been temporary until George returned after his illness, and George was back and as fit as a fiddle. Still, he missed old Mac and his guitar, and his teasing ways. Eleanor was pale and distracted only for a few days, then seemed to deliberately put it all aside and threw herself into the rehearsals. He began to depend on her ideas and suggestions on how to present a number, and she even arranged a song herself. She went to the pub with them after every rehearsal, sipped her lemonade and listened to the conversation. She didn't discuss James and her sister, and Colin never asked. He had warned the others not to bother her with questions, and Eleanor, who was very sensitive to such things, knew they were treating her like glass. One evening as they were all walking back to the Vicarage she said lightly,

"You know, I wish you would all treat me just the way you used to. I'm all right, you know!" They gave a collective sigh of relief. The subject had been brought up, obliquely, perhaps, but it had been raised, and now it was closed. Old Mac was a fool to have dropped her, but his loss was their gain. They were all extremely fond of Eleanor.

The concert was sold out again to a large audience. Three other artists had joined them this time, and the selections were varied. Amongst the audience were Eleanor's family and James. He came up to them afterwards and congratulated them, bringing Claire with him. Colin was cool in response, and Eleanor had managed to slip away with Sally and Peter before James reached them.

"Where's Eleanor?" asked Claire, looking around. James had introduced her to the four young men, and she had bestowed her most charming smile on them. "How odd of her to scuttle away like that. You'd think she didn't want to see us."

Face like and angel and tongue like an adder, thought Colin. *Why can't old Mac see it?*

A few weeks later two important things happened. Mr. Shaw received his long awaited promotion, and James and Claire announced their engagement. Mr. and Mrs. Shaw and Billy would be traveling to Wellington, New Zealand, in August, so that meant Claire and James would not have to endure a long engagement. She grumbled, however, about the lack of time to plan, and the impossibility of having her wedding gown made. Why couldn't she stay with the Pilkingtons and put the wedding back until Christmas? There would be more time to plan, and her parents and Billy could fly back from New Zealand. Besides, this would seem a hasty wedding to a lot of people. They might think she 'had' to get married. For once Mrs. Shaw stood firm and didn't give Claire her own way. She pointed out the enormous cost of traveling from that distance, and what if Claire's father couldn't get away at that time? She also wanted to be a part of the planning and did not want to be just a guest at her daughter's wedding. With a rebellious sigh Claire set the date when St. Margaret's Church had an opening, and Lady Pilkington agreed to hold the reception at her very luxurious home in Mayfair. Mrs. Shaw didn't know which to boast about first—her husband acquiring an ambassadorship, or her daughter acquiring an earl's son.

"Just think," she gushed to Lady Pilkington as they sat in the Shaw sitting room making wedding plans, "my daughter will be a countess."

"Not just yet, Mom," Billy contradicted from the dining room where he was doing homework. "She won't be a countess until James is an earl, and that won't happen until James' father dies. She'll be Mistress Maclachlan when she's married. I looked it up. Scottish peerage is different from the English."

Claire came in from the telephone scowling. "Eleanor says she won't sing at the wedding. In fact she says she probably won't be able to come at all! My own sister!"

"I thought that she would be your bridesmaid," said Lady Pilkington. "And doesn't your fiancé have a sister? It's generally considered good taste to invite her to be in the wedding party."

James had taken Claire to Scotland to meet his parents, and his sister had happened to be visiting at the time. Neither had taken to the other. Claire hadn't even considered her. She had chosen four friends who would look 'good' together. Eleanor, tall and fair, would 'clash' with the others, and besides, she wanted her sister to sing "O Promise Me." It would look odd to have a member of the wedding party leave the group in the middle of the ceremony. However, Eleanor had just flatly refused this reasonable request.

"Mother, you'll have to talk to her."

Mrs. Shaw sighed and wondered if her daughters, so different in every way, would ever get along.

A week or so after this, Mr. Shaw traveled up to Oxford to visit his younger daughter.

"Daddy, I don't even want to go to the wedding. You know she won't let James wear his kilt! She wants all the men in morning suits. And St. Margaret's. What snobbery!"

Eleanor had allowed herself to dream a little before James had met Claire, and she had seen him in his Highland outfit in her lovely old St. Stephen's Church, with Peter presiding, and somebody looking very much like herself in white.....She mentally shook herself and gazed tragically at her father.

"Come and sit down, Norrie." He hadn't used his old pet name for her in years. He looked at her kindly. "I think that you'll have to come to the wedding. It would look mighty strange if you didn't."

"Couldn't I suddenly have a sick relative to go to? Somebody like Aunt Effie in Seattle."

Her father smiled in spite of himself. His aunt, who was only ten years older than he, was hale and hearty, and planning to come to the wedding.

"Eleanor, have you decided what you want to do? You have some options, you know. I am willing that you should stay on at Oxford until you get your degree, and board full time here with the Flemings."

"I love it here, and I would miss Sally and Peter. Claire would want me to visit, and I really don't want to. She doesn't understand."

"I know, dear. If you feel uncomfortable seeing James, then you should leave England. There are universities in New Zealand," he added tentatively.

Eleanor shook her head. That option was equally as unpalatable. She and her mother had no meeting ground whatsoever. Her father had expected the negative reaction, and was sorry, for he would miss her; but he had been thinking, and had talked to his aunt.

"Effie spoke to me some time ago and was wondering if you would be interested in going to Seattle, (actually it's Kirkland, a suburb), and sharing her house. The University of Washington has an excellent music program, and it isn't that far to travel to classes. You know she never married, and I think she is a bit lonely. She is much younger than her two brothers, an "afterthought" as we used to say, and has nothing in common with them. Besides, your grandfather, her eldest brother, is in Baltimore, as you know, and he's nearly eighty, and Uncle John is in a nursing home with Alzheimer's disease."

"I could go back with her after the wedding, couldn't I?"

"You may find your feelings will change for James, and it won't be too far to come to visit."

Eleanor, sitting beside her father, put her arms around him gratefully. "Thank you for understanding, Daddy," she said softly.

"You will come to the wedding, then, won't you? What can't be cured must be endured."

Her assent was muffled in his lapel.

"Will you consider singing?"

"Oh, Dad!" She sprang back and looked at him with an exasperated expression. "She wants me to sing that sappy "O Promise Me"! I told her flatly that I wouldn't."

"She'll agree to your choosing a suitable song."

"I couldn't. My throat will close up and....."

"Do it for yourself. I know you can."

Eleanor looked at her father and knew that he was right. "It'll be good for my soul, is that it?"

Mr. Shaw smiled. "All difficult tasks are good for your character. I also think that James would be pleased if you would."

Eleanor sighed. She knew when she was defeated.

James' and Claire's wedding took place at St. Margaret's on a warm August day. Claire looked cool and triumphant in her white gown and veil with orange blossoms entwined in her hair and pink roses for her bouquet. The bridesmaids were all in pink, with white roses in their bouquets. The men sweltered in their morning costumes. Mrs. Shaw alternated between pleased smiles and sentimental tears. The bride gave her vows in clear ringing tones; the groom's voice was low, but steady. There were many photographers present. The Earl of Rannoch might be an obscure Scottish title, but the groom was handsome and the bride, who had been recently presented to the Queen, was certainly a beauty. So it was News.

Eleanor had chosen simple hymn to sing, an old favorite of hers. She was wearing a simple dress of royal blue satin, with a corsage of white gardenias. She stood straight and tall and sang in her clear contralto voice:

> 'I would be true, for there are those who trust me,
> I would be pure, for there are those who care;
> I would be strong, for there is much to suffer,
> I would be brave, for there is much to dare.
> I would be friend to all, the foe, the friendless,
> I would be giving, and forget the gift.
> I would be humble, for I know my weakness,
> I would look up, and laugh, and love, and lift!'

At the reception, she was introduced to James' parents. His father was taller than James, dark red hair graying, and "eyes so blue you could swim in them," as she remarked to Aunt Effie later when they were traveling to the States. His mother was almost as tall as Eleanor, dark hair pulled back simply. She had black, fiercely intelligent eyes, and they gazed at Eleanor with an expression she couldn't read. His sister was as beautiful as Claire, only in a different way. She was dark like her mother, and elegant, and smiled with her eyes. James kissed Eleanor in a brisk, brotherly fashion.

"Eleanor! Thank you for that lovely song! It was beautiful. When will you come to visit us?"

Eleanor blushed, and said lightly, "Name me godmother to your first, and I'll be there for the baptism."

"Done!"

The Countess of Rannoch observed this tableau with interest. Later, after the luncheon was served and there was an interval before the speeches and toasts, she sought Eleanor out.

"I also wanted to thank you for your music. It was brave of you, in the circumstances."

Eleanor looked stricken. "Is it that obvious?"

The Countess shook her head firmly. "James mentioned that you were good friends. Sometimes I just sense things." She gazed at Eleanor, and added warmly, "What has my son done to you?"

"Please don't blame James," she said quietly. "He never said anything to me that he couldn't have said in front of a thousand people." She caught her breath. "I can't help what my heart feels. I guess I just love him," she added simply.

"What will you do now?"

"My aunt wants me to go and live with her in the States. I plan to apply to the University of Washington and continue my studies there."

"I will write to you," said the Countess firmly. She reached into her bag and produced a card. "Please write and send me your address. I would like to know how you get on."

"You're very kind."

"I want to hear from you," the Countess said, even more firmly. "My friends call me Fee. Shall I call you Eleanor? Oh, my dear, you'll be fine," she added, as Eleanor's eyes filled. She squeezed her hand affectionately. "Promise me that you will write."

Eleanor smiled, lips trembling. "I promise. Thank you for caring." And she turned, blinking away the tears, and made her way out of the room.

Fiona, Countess of Rannoch, watched her go, and gave a sigh for what might have been. There were men who were fools about women, and she was very much afraid that her son was one of them.

Chapter 5

ELEANOR AND EFFIE 1979

S pring comes early in the Pacific Northwest, and Eleanor Shaw sat in her Aunt Effie's garden reading her mail and enjoying the warm sunshine. Lake Washington sparkled in the afternoon sunshine, and in the garden forsythia was in full blossom, Spiraea nodded its white clusters, and daffodils were flaunting their golden blooms. Eleanor had an hour until she expected her next student, so she had made tea, sorted the mail, and was relaxing in the sheltered garden at the back of the house. She was pleased to see a fat letter addressed to her in the Countess of Rannoch's firm upright script. There were cheques from the parents of two of her students (the Tremblays and the Phelps always paid on time), and to counter that, a bill from J.C. Penney's, a local department store; there was also a notice of a music workshop, and, at the bottom, a thin missive in her sister's handwriting. Claire wrote rarely; occasionally James would drop Eleanor a note, and he had written the Christmas letter for the past three seasons; but she and James' mother had carried on a lively correspondence for nearly three years. Fee was one of those people that you could hear speaking as you read her letters. She had kept Eleanor apprised of the family's activities, and of the estate's business, while Eleanor had described, first her experiences at university, then her struggles to develop a small business teaching children to play the piano. She had been teaching for two years now, and had gained her degree last spring. To her astonishment, Fiona, Countess of Rannoch appeared at her commencement exercises at the university, stayed for a week, and then whisked Eleanor away for a short holiday spring skiing at Whistler, a mountain resort in British Columbia to the north. Neither women could ski, but they took lessons and had a hilarious time on the gentle novice slopes.

"I've always wanted to see what skiing was like," she had declared. "I have friends and acquaintances who flip off to St. Moritz or Innsbruck as though they were going to Edinburgh on a shopping trip. So now I can tell them I skied Whistler when it was small. This is going to be a major attraction." she said looking around her. "What a setting, and only two or three hours from Vancouver. Now they should get that highway in shape."

Eleanor smiled to herself as she thought about that time with Fee. She was a perfect mother-in-law. Lucky Claire. She put aside her sister's letter and picked up Fee's, reading it with interest.

> *"I expect that you've already heard from your sister; she said that she had written you, so you will know that we are expecting our first grandchild at last. I am afraid life is one long moan for Claire; you'd have thought no one had ever had a baby before. Though to be fair, she doesn't look so grand. I think that Claire is one of those women that pregnancy doesn't suit. The doctor has looked her over and pronounced her fit, so she will just have to thole it. I was out riding a few days before Jamie put in his appearance."*

Eleanor sat back and digested this bit of news. So that was why she had been honored with a letter from Claire! She was happy for James for she was sure he had wanted to start a family soon. Had he remembered her words at the wedding, she wondered.

> *"Jamie's ecstatic, of course, and coddles Claire dreadfully. I hope you will keep your promise and*

come for the christening. The baby is due toward the end of September, and God willing will be baptized when he or she is about six weeks old. So keep it in mind, my dear."

The countess went on to describe mundane things, her trip to London a few weeks earlier, and her quarrel with her brother in England. *"Sandy's a worthy man, but takes life far too seriously. No sense of humor. We have made up our differences, of course, for I cannot stay angry at anyone, especially Sandy. I think that is part of Claire's problems, that she cannot see the funny side of life. So different from her sister! I remember how we giggled on the ski slopes last year. Time surely passes quickly. It must mean that I am getting old. It just seems like a month or so ago that I was in Seattle with you.*

"Claire has written to your mother and hopes that she will come to visit. You won't be insulted, dear, if I make my escape to an unalterable commitment while she is there? Besides, it will allow Claire a good visit with her mother. We did have a cold winter, and several days in March were snowbound from the rest of the valley. Jamie, of course, was busy just keeping the cows fed and warm in the barn, and I my horses. So it was rather dull for her, poor dear."

Eleanor finished the letter, and then reread it. Then she picked up her sister's thin envelope and opened it, wondering about Claire's point of view. After the opening salutation and polite queries of her health and Aunt Effie's, she went on,

> *I am feeling wretched these days. I am going to have a baby in September. Don't believe anyone when they tell you that being pregnant is natural and wonderful. They haven't been heaving their guts out for four straight months. My hair is limp and dull, and Eleanor, I have zits!!! People look at me as though it's my fault I look and feel so horrible. We had a cold nasty winter, especially in December and last month. I thought that I was going to freeze to death at Rannoch so I made James take me away for*

a holiday, and we spent two weeks in Spain over New Years. It was glorious there, the sun so warm down on the coast. I guess that was when it happened. So now I am paying for my holiday throwing up and looking like a hag. I had my portrait painted by an artist while we were there, it is quite beautiful and I have it hanging over my bed.

James' mother is very unsympathetic. Tells me how she rode throughout her pregnancies and sailed through them with no troubles whatsoever. I don't believe it. She's just forgotten what it's like. I must say, James' father treats me as though I am made of glass. The coming of the heir and all that. God, I hope it's a boy, and I can forget about having any more.

James told me that you are to be the godmother—that you promised to come for the christening. If I don't die first, the wretched infant should be here toward the end of September. So perhaps we shall see you in October sometime. Mother is making noises about a visit in June or July, which would be good, and then we could take off and have a little break. Probably by that time I won't even be able to get behind the wheel of my car, let alone drive.... The doctor tells me this nausea should go away soon, but what does he know, the old grandmother.

It looks as though spring might actually come. The snow is melted off the hills and we've seen the sun once or twice this past week. How could I have known when I first visited this place in June how awful it could be in the winter? James spends all the time with the cows anyway and the days are so short.

And it was signed simply 'Claire'.

Eleanor sat back, frowning. She wondered just how many of Claire's complaints were exaggerated. She knew that some women had

had uncomfortable pregnancies, but Claire made it sound absolutely dreadful. And her remarks as though James was neglecting her. Fee thought he was 'coddling' her. As she was mulling over the news in the letters the doorbell rang and Molly Warner came in for her half hour lesson. Eleanor invited Mrs. Warner, who had accompanied her daughter, to sit in the garden and enjoy the sunshine while the lesson took place. Soon the little music room was ringing with the sounds of scales and canons.

<hr />

Eleanor and her great aunt took turns in making dinner when they were both going to be in. They got on well, in spite of the age difference, or perhaps because of it. They would share their respective days, even if it was only housework or golf on Effie's part and music lessons and shopping on Eleanor's. That evening it was Eleanor who was preparing the meal, and she had just put the small roast in the oven, and was peeling vegetables when Effie came in, windblown and weary from her round of golf with three friends. She came over and kissed Eleanor's cheek, took a look in the oven, then perched herself on the counter stool and pulled off her sweater.

"How was your day, dear?"

Eleanor, a piece of carrot in her mouth, reached over and handed Claire's letter to her. She continued to peel vegetables while the older women read and then reread the letter.

"So she's pregnant! Poor Claire, she sounds so wretched, but I can't help wondering if she's exaggerating a bit."

Eleanor nodded. "I was thinking exactly the same thing—though in Fee's letter which also came today she says 'Claire doesn't look so grand.' So perhaps she is having a bad time. It must be exhausting, throwing up every day."

"You're planning to go, of course. You should make a holiday of it, see London again and visit your friends in Oxford. You haven't had a proper holiday, only that week away with the Countess last year, since you arrived here."

Eleanor nodded. "I've put a bit by, and Daddy sent me a thousand last year, and I have some bonds that come due in the fall."

"Now don't dig too deep into your savings, dear. Will you let me buy your airline tickets and your hotel in London? I have no kith or kin except my brothers' grandchildren, and frankly, you are the only one I care about. I have more money than I'll ever need, and I'd like to do it for you."

Eleanor smile affectionately at her aunt. "You are so kind and generous. I know I'd insult you dreadfully if I refused"—this with a wicked grin—"so I'll say thank-you! And," she added in a serious vein, "perhaps I'd better add Claire and that wee bit of life she's carrying to my prayers from now on."

It was early morning August 12 and the telephone awakened Eleanor from her sleep. She struggled out of bed and made her way into the hall to answer it.

"Eleanor! It's James!" His voice sounded as though it was in the next county, not ten thousand miles away. "Did I wake you? Gosh, but I'm sorry; I always get the time change wrong. Eleanor, we have a little daughter."

Eleanor, her heart hammering, was instantly awake when she heard his voice. "James! It's so soon! Are they all right?"

"Yes. Claire has been very ill, more seriously then was thought. Her kidneys got involved, I don't know the details, but they did a Cesarean Section two days ago. It was touch and go, and the wee bairn weighs only four and a half pounds, but they are both going to be fine, the doctors say. They're both in hospital in Inverness. We thought not to phone until we knew for certain that all would be well. She was born August 10 at 6am. I've named her Katharine Eleanor after her two beautiful aunts, and I'm already calling her Nell. Can you hear me, Eleanor? . . . Eleanor, are you there?"

Eleanor found that her eyes had filled unexpectedly with tears, and there was a huge lump in her throat. "Yes I'm here, James. I can hear you very well. Congratulations! Are you sure they're all right?" she added anxiously.

"Aye, the doctors say they'll be grand, it will take a wee while though. Claire does look ill, but relieved that it's all over, and Nell is so very tiny. My old Nanny is coming to look after them when they come home. She's as excited as the rest of us! Eleanor, my mother wants to speak to you."

A moment later Fee's clear tones came over the wire. Eleanor congratulated her, and asked to have her best wishes passed on to James' father. "We almost had you come a few days ago, but Claire responded well to the treatment and they did the Section as I guess Jamie has told you. We waited a day to call you, just to be sure."

"It's been a dreadfully anxious time for you all, hasn't it? I'm so happy everything is all right."

"Jamie wants to say some more. Good-bye, my dear, I hope to see you soon."

"Eleanor! You will be godmother, won't you, and you did promise to come to the baptism."

"Yes, and yes," laughed Eleanor. "Just let me know when, and I'll be there with bells on."

"My, but it will be grand to see you."

Eleanor's heart was hammering again, but she managed to say calmly, "It will be wonderful to see you all." She paused, then added, "James, tell Claire to take care, and I will see her in a few weeks. My dearest love to you both."

"Good-bye, Eleanor."

Eleanor put down the phone, and went back into her bedroom. Streaks of light could be seen in the sky as she knelt and looked out her window. The hum of early morning traffic was just beginning along the shores of the lake. A robin in the garden began his beautiful song, and Eleanor breathed a prayer of thanks for a safe delivery. 'The valley of the shadow' had lightened for James. She thought that she should have known somehow that there had been trouble. She had been thinking of them all the past few days, but never dreamed that the situation had been so serious.

She got up, went into the kitchen, and put the kettle on. She was making tea, when Effie padded in, wearing her bedroom slippers, tying her dressing gown tie.

"You're a great-great aunt, Effie," she said gaily. "Four and a half pounds, born on the 10th by C- Section. Her name is Katharine Eleanor, James is calling her Nell, and she and Claire will be fine." She poured tea into two mugs and passed one to her aunt. "Claire has been quite ill, so I gather it was emergency surgery."

Effie sat down at the table. "Nearly eight weeks early. Was she toxic?" Effie had been a registered nurse for many years.

"James said her kidneys were involved."

"Sounds like pre-eclampsia. So she wasn't exaggerating her discomforts. I'm so glad she and the baby are all right."

Eleanor opened the doors to the garden, and wandered out on to the patio. "What a lovely warm morning. You know, I didn't ask if they had phoned mother and dad. Perhaps I had better phone New Zealand today. They may need some more reassurance."

"Your mother was there for a visit, wasn't she?"

"Yes, at the beginning of June. When she wrote she said that Claire had gained a lot of weight, but she didn't say they were especially worried about her."

They both stood in the garden and listened to the birdsong; robins, finches and chickadees were all in concert. Effie made a mental note to contact her travel agent and book a seat for Eleanor as soon as she knew when she was going. Eleanor was beginning to plan her trip in her mind. The baptism would take place probably at the end of September or early October. A few days in Oxford, a week or so in London, then perhaps the train to Edinburgh or Inverness. Autumn in the highlands, her birthday while she was there, the new baby Nell, and James!

<hr />

"Eleanor! Over here!"

Eleanor turned, her suitcase in one hand, and her large carryon bag slung over her shoulder, and broke into a brilliant smile as she saw the sturdy blonde woman waving energetically at her. She strode over to her and they embraced fondly.

"Sally! How kind of you to meet me!"

"You look absolutely marvelous, Eleanor. Not as though you've just been on an airplane for nine and a half hours."

"Aunt Effie, bless her heart, insisted on paying my airfare—executive class, no less. It's the only way to fly, Sally. I'm now completely spoiled. You're not looking too bad yourself."

"When you two stop admiring each other, do you suppose a poor vicar could get himself a hug?"

"Peter! How good to see you again!" exclaimed Eleanor, as he folded her into his arms. She regarded her two friends fondly. How she had loved boarding with them. They had seemed more like family than her actual one.

Presently the three threaded their way through the crowd and outside into the fine drizzle that was falling. Peter instructed the women to stay where they were, and he would bring the car around in a few minutes. It was closer to ten minutes later that he drove up, helped Eleanor put her luggage in the boot, and soon they were purring along the motorway. He negotiated the traffic at the outskirts of London, and then found the M-40, and they were speeding west toward Oxford. Eleanor, in spite of her restful flight, dozed in the back seat of Peter's car, and was surprised when they turned into the drive of St. Stephen's Vicarage.

"Are we here already? I must have slept most of the way. I'm sorry," she said sleepily. "I didn't realize how tired I was."

"Better not to sleep today, or you won't get into the time change," commented Sally. "I recommend lunch and a walk this afternoon. By the way, Eleanor, I mentioned to Miles Renshaw that you'd be here for a few days, and he asked me to tell you that he and the choir would welcome your joining them on Sunday. You will stay until Sunday?"

"I'd love to, Sally. They still have choir practice Thursday night?"

'Yes. Doesn't every church choir in the world practice Thursday nights?"

That evening Eleanor received a rapturous welcome when she walked into the choir room. It is always gratifying to find that you have been missed. There were several new faces who regarded her curiously and who looked pleased to make her acquaintance. Miles hugged her enthusiastically and showed her the music for Sunday.

"When Sally told me that you would be here this week, I immediately thought of 'Jesu, Joy of Man's Desiring'. The choir has sung it many times, and you can play the organ or the piano parts in your sleep, can't you. You are still pursuing a music career, aren't you?" he asked sharply.

"Yes," smiled Eleanor. "I would probably be more comfortable with the piano, if it doesn't make any difference."

"That'll work well. We can play the duet after the choral part. We'll go over that later. We're trying something new this Sunday, a recessional anthem. After the benediction the choir will recess, singing "As We Leave This Place'." He regarded her hopefully. "I guess you won't be staying until Wednesday. Our ranks are going to be severely depleted for Evensong."

"Wednesday I'll be in Edinburgh, Miles, I'm afraid," she replied regretfully.

After practice several of the women she had known best gathered around to visit with her.

"You are looking so very well, Eleanor. Are you really happy over there in America?"

"Oh yes, I really love the North-West. I'm living with my aunt, who is a retired nurse. She's got a fair amount of money of her own; her mother left her a pile, which didn't endear her to the rest of the family." Eleanor laughed. "Her eldest brother, who is my grandfather, still hasn't really forgiven her for his mother's favoritism. However, she has always been fond of my dad, her nephew, and I am reaping those rewards. She refuses to take rent from me, and she bought me business class tickets to England."

"Are you still in music?" asked another.

"Oh, yes, how could I do anything else? I have piano students, I actually get paid for being assistant music director at the church, so along with singing in the choir when I can, I direct the junior choir and this fall I'm going to start a hand bell choir. A long time member left us $5,000 in her will, and directed it to be spent on music. So the music committee decided to purchase hand bells and there has been a lot of interest expressed. I'm really looking forward to it when I get back in a few weeks."

"Are you just here on holiday, then?"

"My sister has just had her first baby, and as godmother, I'm going up to Scotland next week to the baptism. My brother-in-law's family is Church of Scotland; I don't know how it differs from C. of E."

"I don't know either," replied the first woman. "Aren't all baptisms just about naming the child and welcoming it into the family of God? What an exciting time for you. Is it a boy or a girl?"

"A girl, and they even named her after me, and her other aunt, James' sister Katharine. They're calling her Nell. I can't wait to see her. She was a preemie, and my sister was quite ill, but they are both fine now."

Eleanor spent the next three days with the Flemings. On Sunday she sang with the choir and played in church, and that evening Colin came to dinner. She was delighted to see him, and also to be presented with the first album by the Oxford Lads, which had just been produced.

"Colin, I am so proud of you!" she exclaimed, giving him an enthusiastic hug and kiss.

He looked at her admiringly. "It won't ever get gold status, but we enjoyed making it, and it's bringing in a small amount of money. It would have been even better with you in it," he declared. "Will you be coming south after your trip to Scotland? I'd love to see you again."

"Unfortunately not. My return flight is out of Prestwick to Vancouver, and then I fly down to SeaTac. I leave on the 25th."

He presented her rather shyly with a business card. "If you have time before you leave, call me."

The next day she and Sally went into London, and after checking into her hotel, attended a matinee performance of 'The Mousetrap' at St. Martins Theater. The theater fascinated Eleanor. It was small and intimate, with old fashioned paneling, a carved ceiling and boxes with curtains. Afterwards they walked over to Covent Gardens, and to Drury Lane, where they sat in a pub with a half pint of ale and people-watched. They said their reluctant good-byes, and Eleanor saw Sally to the train.

"Write to me, Eleanor!"

"I promise!"

Chapter 6

ELEANOR AND CLAIRE

Tuesday morning found Eleanor on another train, this one going to Edinburgh out of King's Cross Station. She found her first class compartment, and settled down to finish her copy of 'Greyfriars' Bobby' that she had picked up in WH Smith's in Oxford on Saturday. She also got out her map to follow their route and to see where they were. They passed Darlington, and York, where she looked for the towers of York Minster, but they were not visible from the station. They glided through rolling farmland with sheep grazing on the hills, and so out to the coast. The sea was in sight several times and they passed through one town which she thought must be Eyemouth. It was an attractive seaside village, with houses facing the sea and boats aground in the tidal river. When the train finally rumbled into Edinburgh station she had finished her book, blown her nose and wiped a tear or two away—it was a touching story— and made up her mind to go and look at the statue of the little dog, and the churchyard, before she went north.

When she disembarked with her luggage she was surprised to find that she was quite a distance below street level, and there was a series of staircases leading up to Princes Street.

"Are you Miss Eleanor Shaw?"

Eleanor turned to see a porter approaching her, a welcoming smile on her face.

"Yes I am."

"Welcome to Scotland, Miss Shaw. I'm from the North British Hotel. The Countess has sent me to meet you. She thought you might need assistance climbing yon stairs."

"The Countess is here? How thoughtful of her! Thank-you." And Eleanor tripped up the stairs while the porter followed with her suitcase. A smiling kilted doorman held open the door for them, and the first person she saw, ensconced in a large chair in the lobby, was Fee.

"Darling Fee! How wonderful to see you!"

"Forgive me for not meeting the train, my dear, but I couldn't face those stairs. I hope the porter suited you."

Eleanor hugged her affectionately. "He's not as pretty as you," she giggled, "but he's very efficient with the luggage."

"Come on up. I booked a suite for us, and I'm settled in. Let the man bring up your bags."

"I'll take this bag—there are gifts for everyone in it. I'd better not leave them to his tender mercies. Oh, it's wonderful to see you— 'Grandma!' How is everyone? Is Claire all right, and how about Nell?"

"Claire is doing all right, and you can practically see the baby growing. Nanny is just wonderful. James is quite silly about wee Nell, but so are we all."

The next day Fee took Eleanor on a walking tour up and down the Royal Mile, through the castle and Holyrood Palace. They also, at Eleanor's request, went to Greyfriars' Kirk, looked at the statue and the grave of the famous dog and strolled about the quiet green oasis in the center of the busy city. Friday they left for the north in Fee's efficient sedan and purred up the motorway to Perth, then north on the A-9. Just outside of Pitlochrie, a road branched off west.

"That's 'The Road to the Isles'—you know the ballad, don't you? Loch Rannoch has nothing to do with our River Rannoch. Ours is a small stream, really, that runs through our glen, down the valley, and into the Spey. Our glen is in the hills above the Spey valley, and can be quite isolated at times. I'm sure Claire told you about being snowbound for two weeks last March. But it's beautiful, and we love it."

When they reached the Spey Valley, Fee crossed over onto the east side of the river and continued up a secondary road. When they reached the village of Nethy Bridge, she turned up a narrow graveled road that led steeply up into the hills. The leaves had turned, and were beginning to fall, but the heather was still blooming. The sky was blue and the sunlight dappled the road in front of them. Glen Rannoch Village was a small hamlet tucked into what the locals called 'the lower glen'. It had a village square with old fashioned buildings around it, thatch-roofed houses in amongst the trees, and a church with a tall stone tower on the hill above overlooking the valley.

"It's what I imagine 'Brigadoon' should look like," sighed Eleanor in delight.

They drove by a farm with fields of grain golden in the sun, and turned up into the hillside again. Fee geared down as they negotiated two hairpin turns, and finally came out on to level ground. The road forked and led downward in another direction to more fields of grain, and Eleanor could see a blue stream dancing in the sun.

"That's the Upper Glen," said Fee. "Those are our barley fields, and you can see the distillery over there." She pointed to a group of low buildings on the other side of the small valley. They took the other fork and continued to climb somewhat, then the road turned and Eleanor saw a large gate in the roadway. It was open, and they sailed through. "This is our dairy farm that James runs, with the help of several men, all local. We employ quite a few people here." They passed a large cottage tucked in amongst some tall trees. "That's the Dower House. My mother-in-law lived there until a few years ago, when she died. She was a bonnie woman. She planted the garden around the Dower House. It will be my home eventually after my husband dies, and James succeeds to the title, and then Claire will be mistress of Rannoch Castle."

Nell glanced at Fee; there seemed to be an edge in her voice, but Fee was smiling and gazing ahead.

After about half a mile the road led into a grove of trees, turned a corner, and Fee stopped the car. Eleanor gasped in delight as she saw the scene before her. Rannoch Castle was a large manor house perched on the side of the cliff. Below were the fields of barley and the distillery. Fee explained that the stables were off to the right, behind grey stone walls. The Castle was built out of a stone that had mellowed to a pinkish gold. A great grove of trees framed one side. Her husband's grandmother had planted them over a hundred years ago, Fee continued. "She was a tartar by all accounts, but I bless her every day for planting the trees. There's a formal garden there, too, but it needs a lot of work. None of us is a gardener except Mrs. Stevens, who runs the castle, and she only has time for the kitchen garden. Her daughter Janet grew up here, and she likes to garden, too, but she's away at university at the moment. She's about your age, I think."

Fee started up the car and drove into the yard and parked the car. "I always stop at that spot and gaze at the castle. It's bonnie, isn't it?"

Eleanor nodded. "It is perfectly lovely."

They were met by a small dark haired woman with a silver streak in her hair. "Mrs. Stevens, this is Miss Shaw. Eleanor, as I mentioned, Mrs. Stevens runs the house and us with great efficiency. How's my darling granddaughter?"

"Not too grand. Nanny says she has fussed most of the morning."

"We'll go straight up to the nursery. Where are we putting Miss Shaw?"

"The Green Room, milady. I'll get Warren to carry the bags upstairs."

Fee led the way up the stairs from the ground floor to the first floor. "Our apartments are on this floor in the west wing," she said, nodding to double doors of polished wood on their left. "The guest rooms are in the opposite wing, with the gallery between. James and Claire have a suite of rooms on the second floor right above ours. My mother-in-law, bless her heart, when she married Robert's father, insisted that they have a separate set of rooms, and have the option of independent living. So they renovated upstairs across the landing from the old nursery and schoolrooms, and while they're not as elaborate as ours on this floor, they allow the young couple more privacy. Robert and I lived upstairs for the first ten years of our married life, and Katharine and Jamie's old rooms still have some of their stuff in them. Iain actually has Jamie's old room."

71

She continued briskly up the second flight of stairs, which came out on to a wide landing. To the left were closed double doors with a brass knocker on one side. In front of them was another door and the faint sound of a baby crying issuing from it. Fee pushed open the door and strode in. A tiny woman with grey hair was sitting by the fireplace rocking an old fashioned cradle. She arose when they entered, and exclaimed,

"Oh, milady, you're home at last. There's just no comforting wee Nell today. She won't finish her formula, and Lady Maclachlan has the migraine." Eleanor thought she heard a faint stress on 'Lady'.

"Nanny, meet Miss Shaw, Nell's auntie from America, and her godmother. Eleanor, this Nanny Markham without whom the world here would stop turning, and all would be chaos."

Eleanor shook hands with her warmly and said, "You looked after James, too, didn't you. What a pleasure to meet you."

Nanny bent over the cradle, and lifted up the wailing infant. "There, there," she crooned. "Here's your granny to cuddle you."

Fee took the baby and rocked it gently, then handed her to Eleanor. "Nell, meet your darling Auntie Eleanor from America. She's come to see you christened properly."

Eleanor took the baby and her heart turned over in her breast. She said wonderingly, "Oh, she's so beautiful. Now my sweet little one, don't cry. Your Auntie Eleanor has come all this way to see you." And she began to sing softly in her sweet contralto voice.

The baby, to everyone's surprise, stopped crying immediately. She opened up big blue eyes and gazed at Eleanor.

Nanny was astonished. "Did you ever see the like? She wanted her Auntie, that's what. Her formula's still warm; maybe she'll take it now. Sit down in the rocking chair, Miss Shaw, dear, and I'll bring it from the kitchenette." The little woman bustled away, and returned in a minute with a small bottle. Eleanor touched the nipple to the baby's mouth, and she was soon sucking hungrily. In five minutes Nell was sound asleep in Eleanor's arms. Nanny helped her lay the baby back into the cradle where she didn't stir.

"She's exhausted, puir wee lamb. You certainly have a knack with her," she said ungrudgingly to Eleanor. Eleanor was still bent over the cradle, lost in love and admiration. Her niece—James' daughter. She had not thought it possible that one could feel this way. The rush of love and tenderness that had come to her when first she held her sister's baby was astonishing. She looked up at Nanny, and smiled sweetly and sincerely.

"She's just lovely, Nanny, a tiny miracle!"

If Nanny had had any reservations about Lady Maclachlan's sister, they vanished at that moment. "She's that, Miss Eleanor, indeed she is. She had a bad start, with her mother so ill, and having to be born so early. Puir wee lamb, she just need lots of love and cuddles."

"How could anyone not love her?" Eleanor asked wonderingly. "She's just beautiful."

Fee suggested they go, and let the baby sleep. "Why don't you see how Claire is? Your room is one floor down, just turn left. The guest rooms are beyond the gallery, yours is the first door on your right, and there is a big bathroom right next door."

As they went out into the landing Fee said softly, "You handled Nanny exactly right."

Eleanor looked at her in surprise. "I don't think I 'handled' her. She's a delightful lady and she evidently adores Nell."

Fee regarded Eleanor ruefully. "You are quite right. I take back that word. I'm just used to the antagonism between her and Claire. Calling you 'Miss Eleanor' so quickly is a great tribute from Nanny. She's very reserved, and sometimes suspicious. Claire can't see that she could and should have a wonderful friend in Nanny, but they are mutually suspicious. "

With that, Fee disappeared down the stairs, while Eleanor, mind whirling, tapped on the door to her sister's and James' suite. There was no answer, so she pushed open the door and went in. The afternoon sunshine streamed in through long windows beautifully draped in brocade of a blue and pink pattern. The colors were echoed in the upholstery of a large sofa, two wing chairs by the fireplace, and the wall paper which covered the lower half of the walls. The rest of the walls and ceiling were plastered and painted in a soft off-white. There were floor to ceiling bookcases on either side of the fireplace, an antique desk, and a corner cabinet filled with Claire's wedding crystal. An open door led into a square hall from which several doors led; one was ajar, and led into a study, very masculine, likely James' office. Over the desk hung a portrait of Claire, obviously the one she had mentioned in her letter. Claire had been painted in a high-backed rattan chair, colorful flowers cascading about her, with a glimpse of a blue sea in the background. It was a beautiful portrait, and the painter had caught Claire's exquisite looks very well indeed. She had thought that Claire had said she had it hanging in the bedroom. But it looked very well in this room—a splash of color on the wall, and perhaps coincidentally, the reds of the flowers in the painting were in the same tones as the large upholstered chair by the desk. On the other side of the hall was a small kitchen and dinette. It would have the morning sun and be a cheerful place to eat breakfast. The last door was a handsome double door, with brass hardware, and it was tightly closed. She tapped tentatively on it, and called her sister's name softly.

"Eleanor? Is it you?" There was the sound of a key in the lock and the door opened. "You're here at last! I thought it was Nanny prowling around, and I didn't want to be disturbed. The baby has been crying all morning, and I've had such a headache." She regarded her sister critically. "You're looking very well, Eleanor. Did you just arrive?"

"I've been to see Nell, she's sleeping at last, and Nanny let me feed her the last of her formula. Oh, Claire! She's just gorgeous! How lucky you are!"

"Come on in and see my bedroom. You sound just like James," she went on. "He's besotted. He didn't have to carry her for nearly eight months and throw up every morning. Eleanor, I nearly died, you know. I still feel horrible and look even worse."

Eleanor gazed at her sister. "You are too thin, and you need a trip to the hairdresser, but other than that, you look just fine."

"I was so bloated, and my kidneys almost shut down. The doctor says I shouldn't have any more babies, and I am going to make sure I don't. I'm not going through *that* again."

"I peeked into James' office next door. Is that the picture you told me about in your letter? It is as beautiful as you said."

"I can't stand looking at it now." she said crossly. "I'll never be myself again. I told him it was his fault, and he could have the picture to look at and feel sorry how I've changed."

Eleanor was appalled. "Claire, it will take time to build yourself up and feel better. Sometimes your hormones get all mixed up and make you feel ill. Have you talked with your doctor?"

"That old grandmother! What does he know? He didn't even recognize toxemia. I insisted on going into Inverness to the specialist, or maybe I wouldn't be here." Her eyes filled with tears. "Nobody understands how I feel. I thought at least my sister would."

Eleanor said helplessly, "Claire, I'm sorry you aren't well. But you have to try for James' and Nell's sake. Come on, have a shower and wash your hair, and I'll set it for you. Then we'll go and see Nell, and you can show me the house. I'm going down to my room and unpack and change. I'll be back up in thirty minutes. Find one of your pretty outfits to put on. Go on, now, have your bath."

Eleanor went downstairs slowly and thoughtfully. She went through the gallery with barely a glance at the portraits on its walls. She found her room, her suitcase all unpacked; her clothes were neatly put away and hung up in the wardrobe. Her room was charming and she felt at home in it at once. The color scheme was green, of course, with the spread on the big bed in a tartan in soft shades of mossy green and earthy blue. The same long casement windows were present as in Claire's room upstairs, an upholstered window seat was a pleasant addition. There was a fireplace, clean and ready to be lit, a cozy reading corner consisting of a comfortable chair in soft blues and greens, a polished table on which a reading lamp stood, and several books thoughtfully had been placed. On the walls were prints of highland scenes, and beside the huge wardrobe a wash basin had been installed, gleaming brass faucets, and thick mossy green towels piled on the shelves below. There was a mirror over the basin and beside it a small table with an electric kettle and cup and saucer, a small canister of tea, and packets of sugar and creamer. A tin of biscuits had been added.

Eleanor washed her face and hands, and stripped off her travel weary clothes and changed into a soft tweed skirt and silk blouse. She brushed her hair until it gleamed, and clasped gold earrings on and a gold chain. A splash of perfume, and she headed back upstairs, first to see Nell again, and then her sister. Nell was still asleep and Nanny was dozing by the fire when she crept in.

Nanny must be exhausted, with Claire no help to her. Eleanor banished her uncharitable thoughts and retreated to Claire's rooms. He sister was wrapped in a fluffy robe and combing her wet hair.

"Here, let me blow dry it and style it for you. Your natural curls don't need much help."

Soon she had Claire's hair looking soft and natural. "There! That looks better. Now do your face and put that lovely yellow dress on while I go and visit your daughter again. I'll see you in the nursery in ten minutes."

Claire gave her a wan smile. Her hair did look better, and maybe a bit of makeup would improve her state of mind. Eleanor had been clever, doing her hair like that, so quickly and deftly. Why couldn't Mary the little maid do that?

Nanny was awake and bustling about when Eleanor returned. The baby was also awake, but content, waving her tiny hands.

"May I pick her up, Nanny?" she asked.

"Bless you, Miss Eleanor, of course you may. She probably wants another song."

Eleanor held Nell in her arms, and crooned that wonderful Gershwin tune to her:

> "Summertime, and the livin' is easy,
> Fish are jumpin', and the cotton is high
> Oh, your daddy's rich, and your ma is good-lookin'
> So hush, little baby, don' you cry.
> One of these mawnins you're gonna rise up singin'
> And you'll spread your wings and you'll take the sky,
> Until that mawnin', there's a-nothin' kin harm you
> With daddy and mammy standin' by."

James had come in and was standing by the door watching. Nanny had held up her hand for him not to disturb them. Eleanor was humming and murmuring sweet things to Nell as she put her back in the cradle. The baby was making cooing sounds.

"Clever Nell," she murmured, "telling me you like the song. What a clever, darling wee lady." She sensed another presence, and turned and saw James watching her. Her heart did some strange things in her breast, and she was suddenly tongue-tied. She got to her feet as James strode across the room and gave her a warm hug and a brotherly kiss.

"Eleanor, it's marvelous to see you. How do you like your goddaughter?"

"She's lovely, James. I'm so glad she's doing so well."

"I can practically see her growing every day," he declared.

They both were bending over the cradle when Claire came in.

"There you are, both doting over her," she said. "James, you smell foul! Straight in from the barns, no doubt. Why won't you ever change first?"

"I have to see my Nell first," he said gaily, ignoring Claire's cross tone. "I'll go shower and change now, and see you both down in the library for drinks. We have to celebrate Eleanor's arrival!"

"He didn't even notice that I had my hair done," she grumbled as they went down the stairs.

"Why would he compliment you if you snap at him like that?" her sister asked.

Claire was silent for a moment. "Oh, don't let's quarrel. This is the first floor. James' parents have those private apartments there. They are much grander than mine. By the way, how did you like my suite? I redecorated it myself last year."

"It's lovely, Claire. You always were clever with color schemes."

"What room has Mrs. Stevens put you in?"

"The Green Room. It's very comfortable. Did you choose the books? That was a thoughtful touch."

"Me? No, I left everything to Mrs. Stevens. She runs this house with an iron hand."

"She seemed very nice when I met her."

"She doesn't like me any better than James' mother does."

"Claire! I'm sure you're mistaken. Fee has been kindness itself to me."

"Oh, I'm sure she likes you well enough. She probably wishes you were here instead of me."

"Don't talk such utter drivel!" exclaimed Eleanor, suddenly angry with her sister. "You have to meet people halfway." She stopped suddenly and caught her sister's arm. "Look. You have a wonderful home, a husband who loves you, and the most delicious baby I've ever seen. For heaven's sake, count your blessings instead of grumbling all the time."

Claire stared at her sister in surprise. She had the grace to look a little shamefaced, but she raised her chin stubbornly, and said, "I refuse to quarrel." And shook off her sister's hand and continued down the stairs.

Eleanor followed slowly, her thoughts troubled. *I will have to ignore her tantrums. She did have a bad time after all, and everyone is obviously making allowances.*

She caught up with Claire, and said to her softly, "Sorry for being so sharp. I guess I must be tired, too."

"It was quite uncalled for," returned her sister coldly, "but I forgive you." Then, suddenly she thawed and she smiled at Eleanor. "Thanks for helping me with my hair."

Drinks were being served in the library when they went in; James' parents were already there, and the earl rose to greet them.

"Claire, my dear, you look lovely. And Eleanor! How nice to meet you properly at last. Fee has told me so much about you." He shook hand gravely, and once again Eleanor was struck by those very blue eyes.

"I think your granddaughter has your eyes," she commented.

"Isn't she a pet? We're all quite mad about her," he laughed, handing Eleanor a drink. "Or would you prefer sherry?"

"I'm not used to whiskey, but I'll try it." She took a sip and was pleasantly surprised. "It's like a brandy. Someone recently gave me some brandy to drink, and I didn't mind it at all. This is even better."

"It's ours," said the earl with a proud smile. "It's fifteen years old."

She sat back and looked around, admiring the room. What a lovely old home James had. How lucky to have grown up in this beautiful countryside with parents who obviously adored him and who were kind and pleasant and obviously adored one another. Claire should be counting her blessings, but perhaps it hadn't been prudent to have told her so.

Over dinner they discussed the plans for the weekend, and Fee asked Claire if she felt up to driving into Nairn and collecting Iain at his school the next day, which was Friday.

"I think so, perhaps Eleanor could come, and we could make a day of it, go into Inverness first, and do a bit of shopping and have lunch. We won't be able to use my car, though, if we're picking up Iain."

James' father was pleased to see Claire perking up. Eleanor's visit was just what she needed. He had felt that her mother's stay back in June did more harm than good. He had not taken to Mrs. Shaw the first time he met her, and after a week of her presence in his house he had been glad to see her leave. Fee deserted him after two days, finding that she had an unalterable commitment (as she put it) to be with his sister who lived over near Fort William. She returned in time to transport Mrs. Shaw to the train at Inverness, and came back sighing, and commenting tartly. "I'm surprised somebody hasn't murdered that woman before now." He smiled now, at the recollection.

"Why don't you take the Jag," he suggested.

"Oh thank you, Father-in-Law," she exclaimed. "That's an honor due to you, Eleanor! I've only driven it a few times. Let's go after breakfast tomorrow. Before he changes his mind," she added, with a bright little smile at the earl.

They also discussed the baptismal service on Sunday. It was to be part of the morning service which was at ten o'clock. Fee had arranged for a photographer to be present and to take pictures either in the church after the service, or outdoors, depending on the weather. Friends and family who planned to attend the service were invited to the castle for lunch afterwards, and more pictures.

"Mr. Dallas, the minister, asked me if we wanted special music," said Fee. "And I thought, if Claire and Eleanor agree, to have Eleanor sing that lovely hymn she sang at the wedding. What do you think, you two?"

Claire, of course, had no recollection of what Eleanor had sung at her wedding. She had been slightly miffed that her sister had refused to sing 'O Promise Me'. Eleanor nodded her agreement. "That is, if Claire agrees," she said, "and if I can rehearse it with the organist on Saturday."

After dinner, Eleanor produced gifts for everyone. She had brought smoked Sockeye salmon for James' father ("actually made in Canada," she confessed). She had bought it at the Vancouver airport, packed in a lovely wooden box with a Native Indian motif. For Fee she had selected some silver jewelry that she had admired last year while at Whistler. For James and Claire, there was a piece of their silver pattern.

"This is for Nell; I carried them in my luggage all the way from Kirkland." It was her complete set of Beatrix Potter books, all in their original jackets, and all first editions. The earl was very interested indeed.

"These are very valuable," he declared, examining them carefully. "Where on earth did you find them?"

"Oh, they were mine," she explained. "My father bought them years and years ago at a rummage sale. He had them appraised, but kept them for me. He explained to me what made books collectable, and how you should never write in good books. Only the author's signature, or perhaps if the owner was a famous person, that would increase the value. He explained that valuable books, like fine crystal, should be used, but with great care. He bought these book labels with *Ex Libris* on them, and they peel off. So you can identify your treasured books without marring them. You *never* turn down corners to mark your place, and you *never* turn them over and leave them open. It damages the spine. He drummed this into me from the time I was small."

"He was always on my case for doing just that," laughed Claire. "I guess I won't touch these. You had better take charge of them, Father-in-law. You certainly are the book lover in this family."

"I will," said the earl. "I shall teach Nell all that when I read to her. This is a magnificent and generous gift, Eleanor."

"All your gifts are lovely," said James.

"Two more! Aunt Effie and I bought this silver mug, and had engraved with her birth date and the date of the baptism. It's not so practical, and it has to be polished, but we thought it would be a memento for her later on." Fee examined it with interest, and remarked that this would be the first item that Nell would learn to polish.

Eleanor said, "This is the *piece de resistance,* and it's from Aunt Effie." She took, from layers of tissue paper, a delicate, hand sewn christening dress. "It was made by her grandmother for Effie's mother, so it is not really a Shaw heirloom. Curiously enough, her grandmother's name was Eleanor McLaughlin, (spelled differently from your name) and she came from Scotland. Eleanor McLaughlin's daughter Marianne married George Shaw, Claire's and my great-grandfather, and was the mother of Effie, my Grandfather Shaw, and my great-uncle. They all wore it, and it was given to Effie, who has kept it all these years."

"I wonder why it was never used for us," Claire said, as she examined it with great interest.

"Effie said she had it packed it away in an airtight package, and actually forgot about it until recently. I think, as the daughter of the family, she had it passed on to her. She, having no family, is now passing it on to the eldest granddaughter of her elder brother. And it comes from an Eleanor McLaughlin to another Eleanor Maclachlan six generations later. I think it is an absolutely fascinating story."

"And brought to us by another Eleanor," James reminded her.

"It is exquisite," Claire said, and passed it over for Fee to look at. "I shall write to thank her tonight."

James looked at Eleanor admiringly. "And you got that entire lineage straight. It is almost as bad as all those 'begats' in the Bible," he said with a smile.

"And perhaps one day Nell's children will be christened in it," Fee said dreamily.

<hr />

The next day Claire and Eleanor drove into Inverness, did some shopping, and had lunch at a hotel. It was not warm enough to sit outside, but they were given a table by the window with a view of the park across the street. Claire discussed her family life at Rannoch Castle, how she and James usually had their breakfast in their rooms, always dined *en famille* in the big formal dining room downstairs. Lunch was always an option if there weren't guests or a special occasion. Sunday breakfast was always with the family downstairs at eight o'clock precisely, "and," went on Claire, "consists of eggs, bacon, sausage, and those disgusting blood puddings, tomatoes, mushrooms and the whole bit."

Claire called for the bill, and said, "Now what do you want to do? There's the castle, but it's not very interesting. It might be closed for the season now, I'm not sure. Maybe you'd like go to the museum— there's an art gallery, too. Or there's St. Andrew's Cathedral across the river. We could walk there, and stroll along the river; it's quite pretty."

"Do you feel up to it, Claire?" Eleanor asked anxiously. "Remember, you had major surgery less than two months ago."

"I'm fine so far. It's such a relief to get out of the house. I've been doing nothing but rest ever since the baby was born. Look, you hauled me out of my room yesterday. Now you want to send me back."

"The Cathedral, then, and the river walk. We can always take a taxi back to where the car is parked."

They walked across the river to the Cathedral, and although there was nothing really remarkable about it, Eleanor enjoyed the atmosphere. Claire sat and rested while she strolled around, stopping once to offer prayers for her sister. Claire seemed fine today, but Eleanor couldn't forget her wild remarks about her looks and nearly dying and no more babies. Then they strolled down the river to the footbridge and walked back to the car park. Eleanor had been worried about her sister, but Claire seemed to have lots of energy and didn't pause until they got to the car. They threaded their way out of the city and drove a few miles east to Iain's school.

"Iain is James' cousin, isn't he?"

"Yes. Don't ask me the exact relationship, because I don't know. I could never get first and second cousins sorted out like you seem to be able to. James' parents are bringing him up because his parents died when he was small. He's about thirteen or fourteen now. I must say, he's not a bad kid, not nearly as unpleasant as Billy was at that age."

Eleanor opened her mouth to defend her brother, and then thought better of it. What was the point of arguing with her sister? So she ignored the remark and said, curiously, "You don't call James' mother 'Mom', or his father 'Dad', do you."

"I never could, you know, they aren't my parents! And she hasn't invited me to call her 'Fee,' either," she added, with a sidelong look at Eleanor. "I told you she really doesn't like me, so I really don't call her anything, and refer to her as James' mother."

Eleanor frowned and bit her lip. What on earth was a safe topic with Claire? So she sat and looked out of the window until they turned into a wide drive that led to Iain's school. Schoolboys of all sizes and shapes were noisily leaving for the weekend. Claire pointed out a tall gangly teenager walking toward them, and said that he was Iain. Eleanor saw a pleasant faced boy, taller than his peers, and feeling a bit awkward about it, with a shock of thick black hair and wearing horn rimmed glasses. He was busily shedding his jacket and tie, and he waved at them.

"Oh, it's you, Claire! I thought it was Uncle Robert. Because of the Jag, I mean." He blushed scarlet. "I don't mean that I'm not glad to see you...." His voice died away as he noticed Eleanor for the first time.

"This is my sister Eleanor Shaw from America," she said shortly. "This is Iain, James' cousin."

He was just as busily putting his jacket back on, and climbed into the back seat. "I'm glad you're feeling better, Claire. How is Nell?"

"Doing all the things babies do, and doing them just fine."

"That's good. I think she's a dear little thing." And to Eleanor said anxiously, "I'm afraid I didn't say how d'ye do properly. Did you have a nice trip over?"

"Yes, thank you. I spent a few days in Oxford visiting friends. That reminds me, Claire, you remember Colin, Sally Fleming's nephew whose group I played for? The group has just recorded an album. James will be interested to know that. Maybe he's missed fame and fortune."

"What kind of music do they do?" asked Iain politely.

"Rather a mixture, I should say. Gospel, folk, ballads, that sort of thing. I guess you prefer rock'n'roll?"

"Not really," he replied. "I like all kinds."

"Well, Colin gave me a record album, and I'll play it for you if you like. Do you have a record player?"

"Yes. That would be grand. You were in Edinburgh, weren't you? Auntie Fee said she was going to meet you there."

"That was one of the nice surprises on my trip. I hadn't expected her. She even sent a porter to meet the train and carry my bags up those hundreds of steps."

"It is a long way up," he remarked with a laugh. "I keep forgetting to count them whenever I've been there. Do you like Scotland?"

Eleanor waved her hand at the countryside. They were now climbing out of Rannoch Village to the upper glen. "I think it's beautiful."

"Tomorrow, I'll give you a tour of the Castle," he offered, "unless somebody already has."

"I've seen bits, but not officially. That would be fun. It's a date."

Iain blushed. "What should I call you? Miss Shaw sounds like a schoolteacher."

"Please call me Eleanor. We're almost cousins, aren't we?

"Aye. Oh, Claire, stop the car! I always like to look at the castle. Isn't it a bonnie sight?"

Claire stopped the car near the spot that Fee had the afternoon before. Was it only yesterday that she had arrived? Eleanor wondered.

"I think I'll get out here, and go back to the farm and see James. He's bound to be there. Then I'll walk back to the house. Is that all right? It was nice meeting you, Eleanor," he added politely. "Thanks for collecting me, Claire! See you later!" And he was away, jogging back up the road.

"Well that's a relief," said Claire. "He never stops talking. I don't know how James stands it. He's always following him about, asking questions about cows and things."

"I think that's good," Eleanor said stoutly. She had quite fallen for Iain. "James is a good role model, and who knows, maybe Iain will take over the dairy farm one day."

Chapter 7

NELL AND ELEANOR

That evening after dinner, Eleanor went up to see Nell. Iain was already there, hanging over the cradle and shaking a rattle at her. The baby cooed.

"I think she smiled at me," he remarked.

"Just gas, I fear," said Nanny indulgently. She had helped look after Iain when he was small and had first come to live with the family. When he went off to school, she decided to retire, but eagerly had returned to look after Mr. James' wee new daughter.

"Nanny," said Eleanor, "don't you take any time off? If you want to have a break, I'll be glad to help my sister with Nell."

Nanny beamed. "You are thoughtful, Miss Eleanor. I have a sister in Lossiemouth who hasn't been too grand lately. She would be glad of a visit from me the day."

"You should take as long as you need to. I'm sure Fee, I mean the Countess, wouldn't object, and I can help Claire. I could even sleep in the nursery."

"I'll ask for one night, if you can manage."

"There, it's settled. I'll talk to Claire." And to Iain she said, "I'll get that record, and play it for you, if you like. Oh also, I have a small gift for you from America."

"Super! We can use the record player in the library." On their way down to Eleanor's room, he commented, "Claire's been quite ill, hasn't she. Do babies always make their mothers ill?"

"No, I think Claire's is not common. It's called toxemia, I think, and the kidneys are affected. I'm not really sure how. My Aunt Effie could explain it better. She was a nurse. It can be very serious."

"How do you spell it?"

Eleanor spelled it for him, and he followed her into her room in thoughtful silence.

On their way downstairs he remarked, "I won't tell you anything about the house until the Tour tomorrow. It's better in the daytime."

They went into the library, and Iain put the record on. They sat in comfortable silence listening to it, and when one side was finished, Iain remarked, "I like it very much. Did you say you performed with them?"

"Three years ago when I was living in Oxford I was in two concerts with them. It was great fun. I'll never forget it. James was in the first one, too. He was subbing for one of the guys who had the measles."

"What did you play?"

"The piano and I sang a couple of songs with them."

"So you knew James then."

"Yes, we were good friends."

"I wish you were married to him instead of Claire."

Eleanor blushed. "Iain! What a thing to say!"

It was Iain's turn to be embarrassed. "I keep forgetting you're sisters. You are so different from each other. I shouldn't have said that, I'm sorry."

She reached over and ruffled his black hair. "Just don't say it in front of Claire."

He took off his glasses and polished them. "Maybe you'd wait for me and marry me when I'm older," he said gruffly.

Eleanor looked at him affectionately and said, "That's the nicest compliment I've ever had, Iain. Thank you. If you still feel the same in ten years, you come and see me, and ask me again."

Iain blushed again, got to his feet and turned over the record.

"I almost forgot about your gift, Iain. Here it is."

Iain opened the package and found a small framed print of killer whales swimming and leaping in the ocean.

"Orcas, they're called, aren't they. Thank you, Eleanor! I'm going to hang this over my bed at school. I'll think of you every time I look at it."

When she went back to her room, she found Claire waiting for her. "How dare you interfere?" Claire said furiously. "James' mother has just given Nanny two days off next week, and she said you suggested it!"

She had really erred in not talking to Claire immediately, instead of making friends with Iain. That could have waited. How was she to know that Nanny would go to Fee so quickly?

"I'm sorry, Claire. I should have talked to you before mentioning it to Nanny. She just looked so tired this evening."

"It's her job to look after the baby."

"I disagree, Claire. I think it's your job, and she's there to help you." She bit her lip. *Why can't I keep my mouth shut?*

"Well, since you offered to baby-sit, I'll take you up on it. She's going to be gone Monday and Tuesday."

"We can both look after her, you and I. It's just two days."

Claire flounced out of the room. "You interfered, you baby-sit."

Eleanor sighed. She had better go to Fee and talk to her.

Saturday it rained all day. It matched Eleanor's mood. Claire sulked; Nanny was upset because she thought she'd made trouble between the sisters, and the baby fussed. Eleanor had gone to Fee and apologized for interfering.

"I'm the one that should apologize," Fee said, patting her on the shoulder. "I should have noticed how tired Nanny was and made arrangements. I am afraid I have been taking dear Nanny for granted. And you are right. Claire should be taking more responsibility. It was too easy to get into that habit when she was ill. I shall wait until after your visit to sit down and have a heart to heart talk with her and James. Don't worry, my dear."

Iain took her on his grand tour of the house, and in spite of her blue mood she enjoyed seeing all the fine old rooms and the pictures in the gallery on the first floor. She played the piano in the drawing room, and then attempted to teach Iain the rudiments of Contract Bridge. Fee came upon them discussing hands and what to do with them. She paused in the library doorway and watched them for a moment. Iain's face was turned to Eleanor's worshipfully, and he was taking the lesson very seriously.

"My Aunt Effie taught me how to play," she was saying, "and I fill in sometimes in her bridge group. It's fun, and apparently it's a good way to keep your brain exercised, especially for the older folks."

Fee came in laughing. "I suppose Robert and I should play more. James can play, but it doesn't interest him that much. I was just talking to our organist, Eleanor, and he can rehearse your song for tomorrow's service now, if you can get away."

"Oh, thank you, Fee. Who can take me down?"

"James is outside with the car as we speak," she said. "Off you go, then."

Eleanor hadn't seen James alone since Thursday afternoon in the nursery. She began to explain what she had done to annoy Claire so, but he brushed off her apology.

"Dinna fash yourself, lassie," he said with a smile. "I have found that if I get into a lather every time Claire has a tantrum, I'd be that way forever. It bothers me, though, that she won't go and see the doctor. Something surely can be done for her mood swings. I'm trying to help her, but she won't let me."

"It probably will straighten itself out. I'm just sorry I made things worse last night interfering."

"She shouldn't be letting Nanny have the entire load. I shall take my turn, and let Nanny teach me how to look after Nell too." He reached over and took Eleanor's hand and gave it a squeeze. "Promise me you won't let this spoil your visit."

Eleanor's heart was hammering away, and she was afraid to speak. She just nodded and smiled at him.

James and Eleanor had been gone about a half hour, and Fee, walking across the stable yard, heard a car crunch on the gravel drive. Surely that couldn't be Eleanor and James back so soon. She came through the stone archway and out into the front drive and saw her daughter's small green car. Katharine was there, unloading two small bags. A tall, slim, bearded young man unfolded himself from the passenger seat and took the two bags from her. Fee hurried toward them, and Katharine, hearing footsteps on the gravel, turned and waved.

"Katharine, darling! How wonderful to see you! I thought you were in France or somewhere."

Fee hugged her daughter affectionately, and then looked questioningly at the Katharine's companion.

"Mother, this Roger Perry. Roger, my mother. We've come to talk to you and Dad. Is he down at the Still or is he in his office in the house?"

Fee didn't blink an eye. "As a matter of fact he is in his office. Let's go and see him now." To Roger she said, "You can put the bags down in the hall when we go in." And then with a smile she added, "I do wish Katharine wouldn't call it the 'Still'. It sounds as though we are making moonshine in the cellar."

Roger grinned, warming to this charming woman. He set the bags down inside the door as he had been instructed, then followed Katharine and her mother left past the large staircase down a hall which seemed to run the length of the house. They stopped in front of a door which was ajar.

Katharine sighed with relief. "He's available. When we were children Daddy drummed into us regarding his office door: 'Closed, I am busy and can't be disturbed; ajar, knock first; wide open, come on in!' "

Fee knocked, and the earl's deep voice bade them enter.

"Robert, dear, Katharine has brought a friend home with her and wants to talk with us."

The earl arose and came around his desk, and greeted his daughter with a warm embrace. Katharine made the introductions, her father asked them to all sit down, he went back to his seat, and looked at them quizzically. There was a long silence.

Roger cleared his throat. "Lord Rannoch, I've come to ask your permission to marry Katharine."

Katharine's father looked from one to the other, eyebrows raised. "Could you tell us about yourself, Mr. Perry?"

"I'm thirty years old, I'm a minister in the Kirk, newly ordained, I've just received a call, but I won't be making much money. I have a little money of my own which is invested in bonds, and I love Katharine very much."

"Daddy, it's more than just a little, and it was his idea to come and see you first. We really want yours and Mother's blessing."

"How long have you known each other?"

"We met six months ago, sir."

"What about the equestrian team and the Olympics?" This to Katharine.

"Roger is very much for it if I want to continue. I don't care if I continue. I want to marry Roger and start a family."

"Well, Roger, it looks as though you, my wife and I have no say in this matter." His eyes twinkled, and then grew serious. "Frankly, I trust her judgment. If you and she have chosen each other, I can't stand in your way. Congratulations, Roger. I hope you know what you're getting into."

Fee had sat there as if in a dream. With no warning whatsoever, Katharine comes home engaged to be married. She hadn't even formed an opinion about him. A minister! They would always be poor unless Katharine used the money that had come to her from her grandmother. She opened her eyes and looked at Roger. He was looking at Katharine with his heart in his eyes. Those eyes, Fee discovered, were clear and grey and intelligent. He also had a kind face. His hair was worn rather long, but it was clean and cut expertly, and his beard was trimmed neatly. She was glad to see that he was well-groomed and neatly dressed. Some might say that that sort of thing wasn't important, but Fee always felt that one's appearance announced to the world how one felt about oneself. Fee heard Robert saying to her, "Well, Fiona, what now?"

Fee jumped up and hugged her daughter again. "Darling, I am so happy for you!" To Roger, who had risen from his chair, she offered her hand gravely. "Welcome to the family, Roger."

"Where is everybody?" asked Katharine. "We should make the announcement right away."

"James should be home shortly. He took Eleanor down to the church to rehearse the song she is singing tomorrow at the baptismal ceremony. I expect Claire is upstairs with Nanny and the baby, and Iain is somewhere about. We should tell Mrs. Stevens there will be two more to dinner, and for lunch tomorrow."

"I'll run down to her rooms and speak to her," Katharine said. "And I want to see Nanny and Nell."

"Well, I'm neither fit for man nor beast, and especially not for dinner," commented Fee. "I had better bathe and change. I think jackets and ties tonight, Robert? It's a very special occasion. I'll leave you two to chat. Drinks in the library at six." And she went out and closed the door.

Meanwhile Katharine had found Mrs. Stevens in the dining room supervising dinner preparations. Mary Rose, who lived in the village, and worked as a maid at the castle, was setting the table. She loved the job, and had confided to Cook that one day she wanted to be in the hotel business. "Running the Castle must be very similar to managing a hotel," she had said. So she observed Mrs. Stevens closely and tucked away pertinent information in the back of her very agile brain. When Mrs. James was ill before the baby was born, she was sent up to their suite and looked after everything for Mr. James and his wife. She cleaned and cooked (though it wasn't very convenient in their tiny kitchen, and sometimes Mr. James had dinner downstairs with his parents), but she had enjoyed it in spite of his wife's moods. She made allowances for her. When Mary had confided in her mother that Mrs. James could be difficult at times, Mrs. Rose had told her that at times out of balance hormones could make you feel depressed and moody.

She and Mrs. Stevens looked up in surprise to see a smiling Katharine enter the room.

"Mrs. Stevens," she began, "I should have telephoned to say I was coming, but we were so busy that I forgot. I said, 'Let's just go!' And here we are. I'm sorry, but there will be two more for dinner, and breakfast and lunch tomorrow. And is there a guest room ready?"

"Miss Katharine!" Mrs. Stevens said reproachfully. "My guest rooms are always ready for such an emergency. And may I say it's lovely to see you home for wee Nell's christening."

"Thank you, Mrs. S. We're glad to be here and kill two birds with one stone. But I won't mess up another guest room. I'm not a guest—yet. I'll just take my things up to my old room."

"Oh, Miss Katharine, your room needs to be made up. Since we didn't expect you..."

"Mrs. Stevens, how were you to know, and goodness knows you've got enough work to do without people arriving unexpectedly. I'm on my knees to beg forgiveness. And I'll make up the room myself. No, no, I insist. I know where everything is. Which room shall I put Roger in?"

Mrs. Stevens thought a moment. "Miss Shaw has the Green Room, and I'm saving the Gold and Silver Room in case Lady Sarah and Mr. Donaldson stay tomorrow night. So either the Chinese Room or the King's Room."

"The King's Room it shall be. That's appropriate," she laughed, and whirled out.

"Mrs. Stevens!" Mary Rose was saying. "I'm going to have to put another leaf in the table. Everything will have to come off!"

"Well, Mary, let's get on with it. I'll help you with the crystal. Now I wonder..."

Mrs. Stevens shut her lips suddenly, and Mary never did know what she was wondering. Mary's thoughts, however, were also busy as she began to carefully remove the crystal.

Katharine came back into the hall in time to see her brother and a girl who had to be Eleanor come in the front door. James was looking curiously at the baggage in the hall. Katharine grinned at her brother and rushed over for a hug.

"I thought it must be your car in the yard! I thought you were in France or somewhere."

"That's exactly what Mother said." She held out her hand to the girl who was hanging back somewhat shyly. "Eleanor, I remember you very well from James' wedding. It is really nice to see you again. James, I've just been upsetting Mrs. Stevens' routine by making extra work for her, so I'm going to make up my room myself. She's mortified that it's not ready. How was she to know that we were coming? Look, will you please do me a favor? Roger's dress jacket and trousers are still hanging in the car. Will you take it and the brown bag here up to the King's Room? I'll take mine with me now. Drinks in the library as usual at six? Thanks, old dear. See you later."

"Just a minute, Kath," he called after her, but his sister was already hurrying up the stairs. "'We'? 'Roger'? What's going on?"

Eleanor hesitated a moment, then as James shrugged and turned to go outside again, she followed Katharine up the staircase.

"Katharine, may I help?"

James' sister stopped and turned and smiled in a friendly way. "Of course. That would be grand. Then we can go and you can introduce me to our niece. I haven't seen her since she was in an incubator in hospital."

"How do you find your sister?" continued Katharine, as they were making her bed a short time later.

"I'm worried about her, frankly. We have never been really close, but I can't seem to say anything, but she's offended." Eleanor went on to tell Katharine of how she had spoken out of turn to Nanny, and it had gotten back to Claire. "She's even forgotten that it's my birthday today." She paused and said ruefully, "I didn't mean to let it out. Don't say anything."

Katharine regarded the younger woman, and said sympathetically, "Mother did mention that Claire was having some serious mood swings, and I suppose you've been the brunt of them since you arrived. But Happy Birthday, anyway! We won't let it pass unmarked. That's just one more thing to celebrate." She paused and said in a conspiratorial tone, "Let me let another cat out of the bag. Roger and I just got engaged." She was gratified with Eleanor's reaction: "That is simply wonderful! May I wish much happiness?" Katharine took her arm and said, "Don't say a word until the official announcement tonight. Now, let's see, I have towels and soap, and I had better hang up my dress for tomorrow. Now let's go visit Nell."

It was a merry evening. The earl had put champagne on ice, and they all toasted the newly engaged couple. Katharine had taken James aside and told him it was Eleanor's birthday, and so there were more toasts and good wishes offered. Iain remarked that they should also be toasting Nell, and then Katharine remembered the case of fine sherry she had in the car.

"I've bought it to lay down until her nineteenth birthday, and give her a chance to appreciate something other than Scotch," she remarked with a giggle. "I'll put it in the wine cellar and mark it carefully with her name and the date it's to be opened."

Iain worked out that it would be August 10, 1998, and that he'd be thirty-three. Fee said she knew that seemed old to him now.

"Trust me, Iain, it won't be then. Your life will just be beginning."

After dinner, Mrs. Stevens brought in a cake with candles and they all sang 'Happy Birthday' to Eleanor. Claire was making an effort to be pleasant and friendly, chatting with Roger and quizzing him on where and when he and Katharine had met. Roger told her seriously that they had met on the steps of the church in Braemar, and it wasn't until quite a while after that that she told him she'd been a guest at Balmoral Castle.

"It would have completely demoralized you, wouldn't it?" laughed Katharine, overhearing the conversation. "Now we're headed for the Western Isles, which will completely demoralize me. He's to have a charge of three small congregations."

"I think it should be an adventure," said Eleanor.

"On your next visit to Scotland you'll have to come and see us," Katharine said, as they got up, and went into the library for coffee. She tucked her arm into Eleanor's. "How long are you staying?"

Eleanor hesitated. "Just a few more days," she said cautiously. "My flight leaves from Prestwick on the 25th, but I'd like to spend a day or two in Ayr, see the Robbie Burns house, so I thought I'd go down on Thursday and find a Bed and Breakfast for a couple of nights. I promised Claire I'd help her look after Nell Monday and

Tuesday while Nanny's away seeing her sister, and I also want to see Culloden before I leave."

Katharine nodded. "We could be going south on Thursday, too. I haven't been home for ages, and I want to do some planning with mother, and visit some friends in the area. I'll talk to you in a day or so and if it works out, we'd gladly give you a lift. It's a small car, but I think you could squeeze in."

"Thank you. I'd like that. I had intended to take the train from Inverness, but a ride with you and Roger would be lovely. Your mother met me in Edinburgh, and drove me here."

"She visited you in America, didn't she?"

Eleanor nodded, smiling in pleasure at the remembered visit. "Yes. She came to my commencement ceremonies last year and then took me skiing at a resort in British Columbia. We had a ball. Your mother is absolutely marvelous."

"She mentioned that Jamie met Claire through you, is that right?"

Eleanor's color receded, and then grew pink again. She looked at Katharine steadily, however, and briefly described her friendship with James. Katharine looked across the room at Claire who was flirting mildly with Roger, and, like her mother, thought that her brother had married the wrong sister. Eleanor was gold clear through; and beautiful and charming though Claire was, she couldn't hold a candle to her younger sister.

※

It was still raining Sunday morning, but by eight o'clock when they were all gathered around the dining room table for breakfast it had stopped. It was clearing as they drove down to the church, and by eleven thirty when they had come out, the sun had broken through, and the photographer was able to take some good family pictures in the garden. They were delighted to see Aunt Sarah and Uncle Thomas Donaldson.

"We'll come for lunch, and then must fly," said Sarah. "Is there room for us?"

"There is always room for my favorite sister!" exclaimed the earl, kissing her affectionately.

"It was a lovely service, Claire," she said, walking beside her to the car, "And Nell was perfectly behaved. She has grown so much since I saw her last. And you are looking splendid now." She smiled at Eleanor. "I enjoyed that song very much."

Claire smiled sweetly at James' aunt, but as soon as her back was turned, she muttered to her sister, "Old cat," and went to find Nanny to give her the baby.

Eleanor blinked at her sister's retreating figure. Surely Mrs. Donaldson was being sincere. Why couldn't Claire get rid of that chip on her shoulder? She could be so charming when she wanted to be.

Claire was perfectly charming the rest of the day. Nanny whisked away Nell for her nap, and Eleanor followed her upstairs saying that she wanted to take a picture of Nell and Nanny.

"I'll send you a copy if they turn out. I hope they all turn out. Don't the men look splendid in their kilts?"

Nanny posed with Nell, then put her down. She then showed Eleanor where all the baby things were, and showed her how to heat up the formula in the little kitchenette.

"I'll change the sheets on the bed if you should want to sleep upstairs tomorrow night," she said.

"Nanny," said Eleanor seriously, "I want to keep in touch with Nell, and be a proper godmother, even if it is from a distance. If I write to her, will you save the letters for her until she is able to read them? I'll send pictures and gifts, too. I want her to know that her aunt loves her and wants to get to know her."

"What a good idea, Miss Eleanor! I'll keep them in order and safe for her. And I'll stay here as long as Mr. James wants me."

Impulsively, Eleanor stooped and kissed her rosy cheek. "Nanny, you're a treasure!"

The next morning, Katharine took Nanny to Elgin, dropping Iain off at school on their way. He shook hands gravely with Eleanor before he left, and Eleanor thanked him again for her 'official' tour of the house yesterday afternoon after lunch.

"I can see why you love it here," she said to him. "It's a beautiful home in a beautiful setting, and your family is special, too."

He nodded. "May I write to you sometimes, Eleanor?"

"I would love that, Iain. Tell me about school, and everything. You can also let me know how Nell is doing. You can be her 'Lord Protector', and help look after her."

Katharine was calling him to get into the car, and saying that they he'd be late. "I have to go, Eleanor. Good-bye!" And impulsively he reached up and kissed her cheek.

Fee had been watching from the steps. "You've made a friend for life, Eleanor," she remarked, smiling.

"Iain is a remarkable boy," she answered.

That evening she took her sleeping things up to the nursery to be near to the baby. It had been an enjoyable, but exhausting, day looking after her niece. She had changed her diaper several times, and had gotten the hang of it; she'd fed her, and had taken her for a walk in the garden in the pram. At dinnertime she had insisted on bringing Nell down and putting her in the pram while they ate. The baby cooed and played with her rattle all through dinner, and even Claire was charmed by her little daughter.

"She's so wriggly," she commented, picking up the baby. "She wouldn't stay still when I was trying to put on the christening gown yesterday morning. I think Nanny was afraid I'd drop her. I wouldn't do that, now, would I?" she asked the baby. Nell answered by starting to cry. Claire looked helplessly at Eleanor. "What did I do?"

Eleanor laughed, got up, and took the baby from her sister. "Nothing at all. She's just not used to you. Come and help me get her settled."

Eleanor and Claire went upstairs, but Claire didn't have any better luck with Nell. She screamed while her mother attempted to change her diaper, and managed to wriggle even more than yesterday. Claire was frustrated and angry, and handing her over to Eleanor, she went away, saying that a headache was coming on. Eleanor soothed her charge, and began to prepare the evening feed.

James came in an hour or so later and found Eleanor sitting in the rocker, calmly feeding Nell. He stood at the door for a moment and watched them. Eleanor had lit a fire in the fireplace and the flickering flames gave highlights to her long blonde hair which was hiding her face as she bent over the baby. She was humming a tune softly, and talking to Nell. She looked up as he came in, smiling and indicating for him to draw up the other chair. He watched her while she burped Nell, holding her up on her shoulder, and patting her back.

"Claire's gone to bed with a headache. She says she's hopeless with Nell."

"If she spent some time with Nanny and watched and practiced with Nanny there, I'm sure she'd be fine. James, you *must* see that she gets to her doctor soon. These mood swings and migraines should be looked at. I'm quite concerned about her."

"Nell's due for another check up in a couple of weeks, I think. I'll make sure the doctor hears about Claire's problems. Maybe a specialist could help."

Eleanor put the baby into the cradle, and turned her on her side. "Insist on it, James. And be sure to let me know how she's doing. I'll try and talk to her tactfully as well."

She accompanied him to the door. "Don't worry too much, James, but do get Claire some help. I think Nell is doing splendidly! What a lovely daughter you have!" She smiled at him, and without thinking, kissed him lightly on the mouth. The answering look in his eyes was one of such despair and longing, that she kissed him again, her heart hammering wildly in her breast. For just a moment she stood within the circle of his arms, and then she drew away and gently pushed him out the door.

"Goodnight, James," she said softly, and closed the door firmly.

She sat down in the chair that was still warm from James' sitting in it. She felt quite weak at the knees.

What have I done now? She asked herself. *It's indeed time to go home.*

Thursday morning she said her good-byes to everyone. Nanny had returned, happy with her visit to her sister, and glad to be back with her Nell. Claire was surprisingly acquiescent when Eleanor cautiously brought up the subject of her seeing a specialist.

"James has been nagging me about it," she said shortly. "You too? I guess I had better keep the peace and have a chat with the man."

She put her hand out to shake hands with the earl, but he instead stooped and planted a warm kiss on her cheek. Fee hugged her affectionately and urged her to write often. James had made no reference to the episode in the nursery Monday night, and now he put his arms around her and firmly kissed her on the cheek.

"Thanks for the tour of Culloden yesterday," she said, rather breathlessly.

"I enjoyed taking you," he replied.

There was an awkward pause. She kissed her sister on both cheeks, and said with a smile, "Now, remember, you promised me to look after yourself. Good-bye, Claire. I'll keep in touch. Thank you, everybody, for all your hospitality!"

As Katharine's car went through the gates, Eleanor turned for a last look at Rannoch Castle. They were all still on the steps, waving their good-byes. Someone was waving a white towel furiously from a second floor window. It was Nanny, no doubt, and Eleanor smiled to herself. Dear Nanny! She would certainly keep in touch with her, and through her, Nell. She also was glad that Claire had seemed reasonable about seeing her physician. Perhaps, with better health, she would see the wisdom of making friends of Nanny and Fee. She sighed. Claire wasn't clever about seeing another person's point of view, but she should realize that it was in her best interests to have Nanny on her side.

There's nothing I can do but leave it in God's hands.

Years later she was to remember her departure and be grateful that her last encounter with her sister had been a pleasant one. On that final day in Glen Rannoch, with the smiling family gathered on the steps and the sunlight glinting on the surrounding hills, it seemed that all would be well. Eleanor, however, would never see Claire again.

Chapter 8

ROBIN 1996

The Balmoral Hotel, once called the North British Hotel, is located in central Edinburgh, just around the corner from the stairs leading down to the railway station, and within a few minutes' walk of the 'Royal Mile', Princes Street shopping, and the lovely old Princes Gardens below the Castle. Robin Lindsay had arrived from Oban the day before, and found herself glad to put the car in a garage for a few days. It had been a harrowing experience negotiating the city streets, finding the correct exit from the traffic circles (definitely designed by a sadist) and parking on the left hand side of the road. And her map of the city was flawed in that it showed streets going through which in reality ended in stone walls or shop fronts, and it didn't always indicate that some were one way. With much relief she found the rental car garage, and took a cab to the Balmoral. She unpacked at once (something she always did), hanging up her things in the closet, and folding other garments and putting them neatly in drawers. She carried with her a photo of Tim and the twins, which she placed on her bedside table, plus her alarm clock, book, and other reading material. With these small items she would make the room her home during her stay. She showered, and wrapped in her dressing gown, she stretched out on the bed and considered her activities for the next few days. She had a whole week in Edinburgh, so there was no need to rush about madly. She had tickets for the Festival, and planned to take a day coach tour to Peebles. She and Tim had stayed there for two nights at the Hydro Hotel, and had enjoyed the walks around this tranquil town on the Tweed. She smiled, remembering making love with Tim in the big four poster, then splashing around in the huge old-fashioned bathtub, and once or twice falling back into bed with him. Suddenly Tim's face faded in her mind's eye and another took its place: blue eyed and auburn haired, sensitive lips curving upward in a warm smile as they walked the beaches on Mull. She remembered seeing his head thrown back and laughing unrestrainedly at the theater in Dervaig, and later watching his hands as he marked the map for her, so she wouldn't get lost this time. What would it be like, with those hands touching her, and that mouth on hers making her shiver with anticipation?

Tim, am I being disloyal to you?

Celine saying, "There's darkness in him."

James saying, "You've made the past irrelevant."

But the past is never irrelevant. 'I am a part of all that I have met...'

Back to the matter at hand, my girl——planning this week.

Robin put her clothes on, firmly put James out of her mind, and got to the matter at hand.

That evening, because it was easier than searching out a restaurant, she dined at the hotel. She chose fish and chips, a green salad, and a bottle of cold Chablis. She was amused to see the fish and chips come in imitation newspaper, and the salad greens in an imitation wooden bowl. But the wine glasses were good crystal, and the wine was chilled to perfection. She spoke to the concierge about a coach tour to Peebles and Traquair House, with lunch at the Hydro Hotel, then on to a quick tour of the Tweed Valley and Jedburgh. She organized her tickets, and studied the list of preferred restaurants, and places to see.

Her week was beautifully filled with sightseeing, concerts, theater and dining, and though she was alone, she took pleasure in all these activities. It would have been perfect with a companion of any sort, just to discuss what they were seeing and to reminisce with afterwards. And though she consciously had put James firmly out of her mind he still managed to intrude at times. As she toured Traquair House she wondered whether Rannoch Castle was as old or as gracious as this and whether his father was as unassuming and welcoming as was the Laird of Traquair.

Monday morning found her carefully driving out of the city toward the Forth Bridge. She had taken her map to the concierge, and he had marked a route for her. His hands were broad, with short pudgy fingers, and Robin couldn't help comparing them to the long lean ones that had marked her map in Mrs. Millar's lounge in Oban. The directions he gave were spot on, however, and it wasn't long before the bridge came into view. At his suggestion, she stopped at North Queensferry, and paid a visit to Deep Sea World, which she found as fascinating as the aquarium at home, and then cut over to the A921, which was the roundabout coast route to St. Andrew's. It also took her through Kirkaldy where Ravenscraig Castle was located. She had read that the stairs that flanked each side of the castle were the inspiration for John Buchan's *The Thirty-nine Steps*. It had been one of the first 'adult' books she had read as a schoolgirl. She then had discovered *Greenmantle*, which she enjoyed even more, and soon became addicted to mystery thrillers.

She meandered her way along the coast, happy that she had no busy schedule to which to keep, and able to stop when she wanted, or take a different road if she chose to. Tim would have barreled to the motorway and been in St. Andrew's in less than two hours from hotel to hotel. It had been one area of contention between them, and when occasionally he relented and would take a longer route and stop at her whim, she always sensed his impatience, as if his mind was already at his destination. She always laughed and said it came from his being an airline pilot. It was rather difficult to meander in a 747. So she took most of the day. She stopped at Pittenweem for no other reason than that she was charmed by the name; and she discovered a tiny bake shop that made the most delicious meat pies she had ever tasted. She bought another for her dinner 'just in case'. Twice she made detours to points of interest, so it was late afternoon when she drove into St. Andrew's and found her hotel in North Street, near Murray Park. Aslar House was a modest guest house, and she was given a comfortable room overlooking the park. After unpacking, she went downstairs and was able to obtain a tray of tea and fruit and biscuits, and with her meat pie, now cold, she made her supper in her room. After a nightcap of whisky and water she crawled into bed, well satisfied with her day.

The next day she spent wandering the streets, absorbing the atmosphere of this attractive town, visited St. Andrew's Cathedral and climbed the 157 steps to the top of St. Rule's Tower for the magnificent view. She walked along the East Sands, and was surprised by the fine white sand of the beach. It was a sunny day with a brisk breeze off the North Sea, and it was pleasant walk, discovering hidden coves and caves. She visited the ruined castle, and finally found her way to The Old Course. Not a golfer herself, she was nevertheless aware that this was the Mecca of golfers, the roots of the game. She and Tim always watched the Open Championship and had seen it played here at least twice. She wandered over to the nearby woolen mills and was deciding between a red and a blue cardigan sweater, when she heard her name spoken in transatlantic accents.

"Robin Lindsay! Is it really you?"

She turned in surprise to see a tall, silver haired man striding toward her, a delighted smile on his face.

"Charlie Morrison! What on earth are you doing here?" She lifted her face and turned a cheek for him to kiss. "I guess that's a silly question, and I'll answer it myself: golf, of course."

Charlie and Tim had been fellow pilots, and also played golf together on occasion. While the Morrisons and the Lindsays were not close friends, they had encountered each other often at parties and golf gatherings. The Morrisons lived in the fashionable west side of Vancouver in a large house on South West Marine Drive, bought, so gossip said, by Charlie's wife Georgia. Robin liked Georgia, but wasn't so sure of Charlie. He was tall and extremely good looking, with a head of wavy, prematurely white hair, brown eyes liberally fringed by thick, curly eyelashes any woman would die for, and a mouth that was just a bit too red and soft looking. "Charlie's so very handsome," she remembered saying once to Tim, "and doesn't he know it!" However, he and Georgia had been very kind to her after

Tim's death, but she hadn't seen them for many months since she had moved to Victoria.

He was looking down at her with those eyes which in her youth she called 'bedroom eyes', smiling with the pleasure of seeing her.

"Yes, my buddy Johnny and I have been here several days here, playing the Old and New courses; I don't think you have met him, Johnny Eden?" She shook her head, and he went on, "He's just gone back to the hotel with an upset stomach. But I played a round of 87, not bad, huh?"

"Is Georgia with you?"

"We're meeting our wives on Friday in Edinburgh. They're in London at the moment. How long are you here for?"

"Friday I'm driving north to visit friends near Inverness."

"I didn't know you had Scottish friends."

"Tim and I were here before, you know. It's a sort of pilgrimage, visiting some of the places we saw together, and also seeing some new sights."

"Say, have you heard of the Peat Inn? It's a restaurant just a few miles south of here, and I hear it's just super. How about dinner tonight with me?"

Robin hesitated. It might be pleasant having a dining companion after a week of eating alone. "Thanks. That would be nice. Be sure to include Johnny, though, Charlie."

"Great! Sure, if he's feeling up to par. Get it, up to par?" and he laughed at his own pun.

Robin smiled politely, and told him where he could pick her up. He said he would make reservations for seven-thirty; if not, he would call her.

Charlie arrived a few minutes after seven, and he was alone.

"Johnny didn't feel up to coming out, he still has a queasy tummy," Charlie said, when Robin asked after him.

For some reason she suddenly felt reluctant, but she got in beside him, and they drove through the gathering dusk.

"You have twins, don't you," he remarked.

"Yes, Deborah and Denis. They are both at university. Den thinks he wants to go into medicine and Deb into physiotherapy.

They may combine their talents one day and practice together." Her voice trailed off as she realized that he wasn't listening.

He turned and apologized. "Sorry. University, you say? You sure don't look old enough to have two grown children. You're looking especially gorgeous, actually. A new man in your life, maybe?"

Taken aback by such an unexpected question, she blurted, "No! Whatever makes you think that?"

He grinned and patted her knee lightly. "Uncle Charlie always knows."

She changed the subject abruptly to two safe ones: his wife and golf. He was reiterating his glorious round of the day when they reached the restaurant. As they went in, Robin was immediately charmed by the atmosphere and equally startled by the prices when she studied the menu. The waiter had given them a quiet table by a window that in summer would have overlooked the garden, the lighting was soft and intimate, and the music coming from the speakers was pleasant and unobtrusive. Charlie looked around in satisfaction.

"This looks a bit of all right," he remarked, and to the hovering waiter he said, "Two dry martinis on the rocks." He smiled at her, showing his perfectly even white teeth. "I remember you like martinis."

She mentally shrugged. Tim had been the martini fancier, but she drank them on occasion. When the drinks came, Charlie raised his glass to her, said "Cheers!" and took a sip, and practically spit it across the table. "This isn't a martini! It's nothing but vermouth! Waiter!"

"Charlie, not so loud," she said, embarrassed that heads had turned.

He ignored her and when the waiter hurried over, said in an irritated voice, "Take this muck back to the bar. Tell him we want a dry martini, that's six parts gin to one part vermouth."

"Mine will do fine," she began, but Charlie again ignored her and handed the waiter her glass. He then studied the menu, seemingly not at all surprised by the prices. The waiter returned with the drinks, and waited politely for Charlie to taste his. He nodded brusquely and looked at Robin. "What do you fancy?"

"I thought perhaps you were going to order for me," she remarked lightly, but the irony was lost on Charlie. "I'll have the curried pumpkin soup and the noisettes of venison, medium rare," she told the waiter with a smile she hoped was apologetic.

"Very good, madam; and for the gentleman?" Robin wondered if the waiter also indulged in irony, or was his skin just thick and his words those he used for everyone?

Their dinners ordered, Charlie, leaned back, sipping his drink, and studied her through half closed eyes. "Tell me all about yourself, and how you are faring on your little lonesome."

Robin watched with distaste as his mouth folded itself greedily on his glass. She had never noticed that mannerism before, but she certainly had not forgotten his being full of himself and platitudes as well.

"I'm doing very well, thank you," she answered politely. "I've visited my cousin on Iona. She's in the community there."

"Do you mean she's a nun?"

"Oh, no, they're all lay people there, but Celine is going to commit some time there, perhaps five years, she says. I did some hiking and have been driving around sightseeing, and just spent a week in Edinburgh. I had some festival tickets, did a bus tour, and generally explored the city."

As their first course arrived, Robin was conscious of his knee pressing hers. She removed her leg, hoping devoutly that it had been accidental. The soup was delicious, lightly curried, and very hot and creamy. Charlie ordered some wine, again without consulting her. He leaned forward and patted her hand.

"You've been lonely?" he asked, with a half smile, and gazing again at her through those curly eyelashes. There was his knee again, and Robin thought with despair that he didn't take hints easily. Was he really coming on to her, or was it just his general manner he had with all the women? She recalled at parties that he had flirted considerably, but he had never tried it with her. She removed her hand and leg, and firmly shifted her chair.

"The food is delicious," she said, ignoring his question.

He tossed back a glass of wine and poured himself another, in spite of the waiter's being nearby. She shook her head when he went to fill her glass, but he filled it anyway, and signaled for another bottle. Robin gratefully accepted the main course when it came. She could hardly wait for this meal to be over and to get back to her hotel. She hoped he wasn't going to be a nuisance, and was annoyed that he knew where she was staying. But what could she have done? Refused the dinner invitation, of course, but there was really no reason to at the time. Good grief, the man had been a friend of Tim's; they had flown and had played golf together. Tim had never made any disparaging remarks about him. She chattered on about inconsequential things, and when coffee arrived, she relaxed a bit, only to stiffen when he brought out a cigar.

"Charlie, do you think..." she began, but the waiter was there in an instant, saying in his soft polite Scots voice that cigars were not permitted, for the comfort of the other diners, if you really don't mind, sir. Charlie began to argue, but met the bland but nevertheless steady gaze of the waiter's, and put it away.

"Sorry about that! Shall we have a liqueur? Two Drambuies, waiter."

When Robin protested that she didn't drink liqueurs, he blustered, "Nonsense! You have to have Bonnie Prince Charlie's drink when you're over here."

"No thank you, Charlie," she said firmly. "They give me a headache. Just a glass of water, please," she said to the waiter. He inclined his head and went silently away. Charlie finished off his wine. "The barman may not know much, but the chef here is certainly good," he remarked. "Nothing's too good for poor Tim's widow."

Robin frowned and was silent, and when the bill finally came, she gathered up her coat in preparation for leaving. He helped her on with it, hands lingering a little long on her shoulders. On the way to the car he took her hand and tried to kiss it.

"Charlie, this is nonsense!" she said, snatching her hand away.

"Oh, come on now, Robin," he said, his voice slurring a little. "Give us a little kiss. Haven't you been missing it, or have you been coming across with the new man?"

"Charlie, I don't know what you're talking about," she said with dignity, "I think that I had better drive."

"I'm fine. Come on Robin, I was just joking." He leered at her and got into the driver's seat, leaving her to climb in on her own. She was to wish many times later on that she had not and instead turned and gone back to the restaurant. She would have had to endure the waiter's pitying gaze, and perhaps Charlie would make more of a fuss than he already had. So she got in and fastened her seat belt, and prepared to endure his company for at least another fifteen or twenty minutes. He also ignored her suggestion that he fasten his.

"You're sure playing hard to get, Robin," he muttered as they drove back to town.

"I'm not playing at anything," she retorted with spirit. "You are being insufferable. I had forgotten how rude and boorish you are."

"You're beautiful when you're angry," he said with a grin.

Good grief, what other platitude would he come up with next, she wondered. As they neared her hotel, he made a turn the wrong way, and drove into a parking area of the nearby park.

"Charlie, please take me to my hotel."

"Not until you give a little. Come on Robin, you know you want it. You never minded when Tim had his fun."

"Whaaat! Charlie, what are you saying?"

"He always said you were an understanding wife."

Robin sat there, appalled. She couldn't believe what she was hearing. "Are you saying that Tim had affairs when he was traveling? If you are, I don't believe a word of it."

"We all have our fun," he said, reaching for her clumsily and trying to kiss her. She pushed him away, and said furiously, "That's about enough. Take me home."

"Don't get mad, Robin. God, you're beautiful."

She opened the door, then realizing her seat belt was still on, fumbled with the catch, and slipped out. She couldn't have believed how fast Charlie could move, drunk though he was. He was around the car in a flash, and caught her by the wrist. His grip was viselike, and for the first time, distaste and disgust turned to fear.

"Don't be so prim and proper. Tim always said you liked the wild stuff." She gasped as he grabbed her by the hair and bent to her face. "Caveman stuff. That's what you like, eh?" Wine soaked breath assaulted her, and his lips folded over hers as they had with the cocktail glass. His tongue was insistent, and forced her lips apart, and darted in her mouth. The other hand was on her breast, squeezing painfully. One of her arms he had pinned to her side, and she struggled furiously for a moment. Then instinct told her to relax, and she suddenly bit down on his repulsive tongue, and at the same time kicked him firmly in the shins. He gave a yell of pain and backed away. "You bitch! I'll have you..." He took a step toward her, she twisted away, and he tripped over something and fell headlong on the ground. She wheeled and ran as fast as she could out of the empty car park.

"You bitch! You'll be sorry!" he shouted again, and as she sprinted up the street, she looked over her shoulder and saw him struggling to his feet. She fairly flew around the corner, and she saw that she was perhaps two blocks from her hotel. A fine rain was beginning to fall, and the streets were empty. There was nobody in the reception area when she entered the hotel, and she hurried up the stairs to her room, went in and locked the door. She went to the window, half expecting to see Charlie stumbling after her, but there was no one in sight. She sat down on the bed, heart still racing from her run, appalled and disgusted with her encounter with Charlie. How could she have thought he was a friend of Tim's, he who had voiced those ugly insinuations about someone who could no longer defend himself? She thought she could taste blood in her mouth, so feeling almost nauseated, she rinsed it out with mouthwash. Turning on the shower, she stripped, and stepped under the spray. She made up her mind then and there that she wouldn't be here the next day. She wasn't taking any chances of another encounter with Charlie Morrison, no matter whether his mood was apologetic or angry. She packed her suitcase carefully, leaving out her toilet things, put her coat on over her nightgown and housecoat, slipped into her shoes and went down to the desk. She explained that something had come up, and that she had to leave very early in the morning, and could she settle her bill now? The clerk seemed to think that this was quite acceptable, and asked no questions, except would there be a forwarding address? She shook her head and mumbled that she wasn't sure where she would be, then realized how stupid that sounded. She hurried back upstairs, set the alarm clock for six am and crawled into bed. She'd leave as soon as it was light enough to see her way, and maybe go to Inverness or Nairn and hide for two days. She lay there for some time, the evening's events playing themselves in her mind. She knew she hadn't sent any signals to Charlie that he could have misinterpreted. He just couldn't believe she wouldn't fall into his arms. He had been rude and boorish and obnoxious. And the insinuations about Tim! Tears of anger came to her eyes as she lay there.

*I wish I had slugged him as well. I hope his shins hurt. How could Tim ever have been friends with him? God, I wish I had gone back into the restaurant and called a cab. Damn, damn, damn! Why do **I** feel guilty?*

Her thoughts raced, until she fell into an exhausted sleep.

Chapter 9

NELL

Wednesday was one of those perfect autumn days in the Highlands: blue sky, wisps of white cloud curling around the mountaintops, birch leaves beginning their change of colour, air redolent with the scent of pine. Nell Maclachlan was convinced that there was no other place on earth more beautiful—in any season. Winter could be long and cold, with its icy grip sometimes lasting until late April. A winter seldom went by without their being snowbound for a week at least once, but on fine days it was a joy to put on her skis or snowshoes and head out into the sparkling white world. On stormy days she would curl up with her favourite book by the fire in the library, or snuggle down under her eiderdown in her bedroom. Spring was a time of melting snow, thick muddy roads, and the river in spate with brown rushing water and tumbling boulders. It was also a time for the inevitable spring cleaning mercilessly overseen by Janet Stevens. There was a promise of summer in the thin green stalks appearing out of the earth, and the heather blooming on the hillsides. Summer sometimes could be rainy and cool, but mostly it was a time for taking the horses on long rides, helping in the vegetable garden, and enjoying the long hours of daylight. She had travelled very little; her aunt Katharine had taken her to Edinburgh once. She had enjoyed the history and the architecture, but not the traffic and jostling tourists. Last year she had visited Oxford with her father to see where he had been to school; she had been fascinated by "the dreaming spires" and liked the peaceful countryside, and on the way back had been glad meet her Yorkshire cousins, but she had been happy to return to her own country with its wild hills and uncertain weather.

This morning she had been up early and had worked with the stable lads mucking out and taking the horses for their daily exercise, had grabbed a quick bite before changing into her running things, and now she was heading out to her own private jogging path. She waved vigorously as her father passed her in the car on his way to his office at the distillery. Her father had been away last week, over to Fort William at a meeting, and had stopped to see his aunt who lived not far from that town. They all had expected him back on Friday, but he'd put a call into the office that day to say he was going to spend the weekend on Mull, and not to expect him home until Monday morning. Nell grumbled to her Aunt Katharine after Kirk on Sunday why on earth hadn't he called the Castle directly instead of sending a message via the office? Her aunt had answered with a smile in her voice, remarking briefly that Mrs. Sims wasn't likely to ask any questions! It was true, thought Nell. Dad's secretary would have taken the call, duly relayed the message to Janet, not even curious as to why her employer was not coming home on the Friday as originally planned. Nell had then telephoned to Aunt Sarah, but there was no answer, so Nell had remained in the dark.

Last night at dinner her father casually mentioned that he had invited a Mrs. Lindsay whom he had met at Aunt Sarah's to be a guest at the Castle for the weekend of his birthday party. He was so off-hand that Nell was immediately suspicious. Her father, to her knowledge, had never had a woman friend, let alone contemplated inviting one to the Castle for an important weekend like this one. She quizzed him about her, but her father would not be drawn; only saying that she was a Canadian and a widow.

"Does Aunt Sarah like her?" she persisted, and her father had laughed and returned her question with another: "Do you suppose Aunt Sarah would have someone to stay whom she didn't like?"

No matter how hard she tried she couldn't get any more information out of him. She considered asking him straight out if he and Mrs. Lindsay had spent the weekend together, but decided not to risk being cheeky; it was all very unsatisfactory. She phoned Aunt Katharine at the Manse and quizzed her; her aunt said, "There's no point in asking me questions—I don't know any more than you do." But Nell thought she probably might—her father was apt to confide in his sister. Janet accepted the news quite calmly; Nell went so far as to think that she wasn't the least bit surprised. She knew Nell's father almost as well as Aunt Katherine did—after all, they had all grown up together back in the olden days when Janet's mother was the Castle housekeeper and her father the head gardener. Now poor Mrs. Stevens was in a nursing home and her daughter had taken over her job. Nell scarcely remembered Mrs. Stevens when she had been at the helm—Janet had come to help out around the time Granny Fee had died, and had stayed. Nell was very fond of Janet.

As she passed the Dower House, she craned her neck to see if she could catch a glimpse of Iain, but he wasn't in the nearby farmyard or in the paddock closest to the barn, so she stepped up her pace, and turned off the road on to the pony track that led down to the glen. She could see her father's car, its tires churning up a brown cloud of dust as it passed the golden barley fields and turn into the wide gated driveway of the distillery. The rainstorm that had hit Aunt Sarah's had missed them—it hadn't rained here for two weeks.

Nell's three mile jogging route led her along the road to the distillery, around the top of the barley fields, down the other side, and back across the footbridge that spanned the river. When she had crossed the bridge the second time, she returned up the road leading back to the castle, a longer, but less steep route than the pony track. At the top of the hill she slowed to a walk, perspiring and breathing heavily. As she walked briskly back toward the castle she swung her arms for the sheer joy of being alive. At the Dower House driveway she stopped and did a few stretches and was rewarded by the sight of Iain on the back porch waving to her.

"I've made coffee," he called. "Have you time for a cup?"

Nell always had time for Iain. He had been her hero since she was small, when she had announced firmly that she was going to marry him when she grew up. At about age twelve or so she had stopped saying this, but had certainly never changed her mind. It was too bad that right now she was red faced and sweating, her hair dragged back and fastened with an elastic band. She hesitated for only a moment, and then pulled on the fleece shirt that had been tied around her waist. As she trotted up the driveway she unfastened her hair and ran her fingers through the red gold curls which now cascaded over her shoulders.

The driveway, which curved around the house, accessed both the front and back doors. These days nobody used the front door; at the back there was a large porch that caught the morning sun most of the year. Iain had made a table and two chairs which, except in winter, furnished the outside area. He sat there now with two large mugs of steaming coffee in front of him.

"Grand morning, isn't it?"

"It's perfect," answered Nell happily, flinging herself down in the opposite chair.

"Do you run every day?"

Nell blew on the coffee and took a cautious sip. "Not every day, but I like to get out two or three times a week when the weather's good."

"We've had a fabulous autumn so far, haven't we?"

Nell smiled at him. Did he know at all how attractive he was? He had rugged good looks, dark hair and eyes, and his skin was deeply tanned as one who worked out of doors constantly. He was lean and muscled—all in all, very good to look at. She sat back, grinned, and threw her bomb.

"Did you hear that Dad has invited a woman friend to his birthday party?"

Iain's eyebrows rose almost into his thick thatch of dark brown hair. His eyes crinkled up in surprise. "You're not serious!"

"I am. They met at Aunt Sarah's. All Dad would say about her is that she's a Canadian and a widow."

"And he's invited her here next week. How interesting."

"Exactly." Nell's eyes were sparkling in delight at surprising him. "I wonder what she's like...."

"What do you remember about your mother, Nell?"

Nell looked at him in surprise. She thought a moment, her wide forehead wrinkled in a perplexed frown. "Actually, nothing! Isn't that weird? Nanny has a photo of her and Dad, and Aunt Eleanor holding me at my baptism, so I sort of know what she looked like..." She put her coffee cup down. "She was very pretty, wasn't she?"

"She was."

Something in his tone of voice caused Nell to look at him sharply. "Did you not like her, Iain?"

"Ah, what does it matter, Nell? It was a long time ago." He regarded her seriously. "I actually was wanting your advice about my kitchen. I'm thinking of some renovations..."

Heart fluttering, Nell followed him into the old fashioned, cavernous kitchen. She didn't think anything had been done for years and years, and said so.

"Your grandmother planned to do some major ones but she died before she could get started."

Nell's grandmother had left the house to Iain, along with two acres around it, and he had been living there for several years now. The big room had once been the dining room, explained Iain. Back in those days when the house had been built the kitchen had been located in the basement, and a dumbwaiter connecting the lower floor with the butler's pantry. He showed her the little door in the wall.

"Katherine and Janet lowered me down on it when I was a wee lad," he said. "Nobody lived in the house for a few years after Uncle Robert's mother died, and we found a way to get in and play. Oh, wasn't Mrs. Stevens mad when she found out what the girls had been up to! They were grounded for a week—had to come home from school straightaway and go to their rooms. I think they also got lectures from Aunt Fee and Uncle Robert as well. They were in everyone's bad books. But I've never forgotten it—it was a wild adventure for me." He chuckled at the memory.

Nell was peering into the fitted mahogany drawers in the little room. Their brass fittings gleamed and the wood shone. Obviously, Mrs. Rose had been cleaning here recently. Nell was not overly fond of their daily cleaning woman, but she knew her job and did it well.

"Look, these drawers were made for keeping silverware," she said. "See the lovely felt lining. You'd think it was brand new."

Iain, apparently not impressed with silverware drawers, led her back into the kitchen.

"If you were to redo this room, what would you do with it, Nell?"

Nell had been in this room only a week or so ago when Iain, having to be away for much of that day, asked her feed the hens, gather the eggs, and bring them into the house. She had wandered around the kitchen, looked into the other rooms on the ground floor, briefly and lovingly touching his possessions and wondering if he were ever going to bring a wife in here to live with him. She remembered wishing fervently that she had been born ten years earlier; perhaps she would have had a chance with him. Now she recalled her thoughts about improving the room and she stated them.

"It's a big dark room, but if you removed those awful drapes from the windows a lot of light would come in." She demonstrated by hauling on the curtains and revealing the wonderful view of the hills beyond the paddocks. That day she had almost ripped the offending material from the curtain rods. "See the beautiful window frames and sills. It's a shame to hide them, and you don't need the draperies for privacy." She circled the room like a cyclone, waving her arms. "The sink shouldn't have been put in this dark wee corner; it should be in front of a window where you can see if you've scraped all the egg off your frying pan. You could divide the room in two with counters and cabinets, and put that big round table in the study here in front of the fireplace and buy bright cushions for the chairs…" She paused, blushing, knowing that she had revealed her snooping.

Iain was staring at her in amazement. "You've been thinking about this," he exclaimed.

"Aye, well, you asked me to bring in the eggs, and I couldn't help looking about a bit." She was pink with embarrassment.

"I think you're wasted in the stables, love," he teased. "Why, you should be consulting the County about interior design. What about paint?"

"Well this room should definitely be painted a light colour—" She broke off, realizing he was pulling her leg. "Hmmph. Why don't you ask her what colours she likes?"

"She? Whoever do you mean?"

"Whoever you're thinking of redoing the house for," retorted Nell.

It was Iain's turn to blush. He didn't say anything, but strode into the next room and regarded the table Nell had mentioned. "That's an excellent idea about dividing up the room and using this table. All I use it for is to pile my correspondence on," he added ruefully.

Nell fairly danced up the road a short time later, Iain's praises singing in her head. She didn't really know if he had a lady seriously in mind, but she had hit a nerve, hadn't she? She hoped it was anyone but that odious Bernice Porter. Nell had to admit grudgingly that she was very good looking, sophisticated, and her father was a rich English peer. They had recently moved to the valley and purchased a big house in Carbridge. Sir Joseph Porter had business connections with Nell's father—she wasn't sure in what way, and he also boarded two horses at the Maclachlan stables.

In the past, Iain had brought home several different girls; the one Nell remembered was at Christmas five or so years ago. Her name was Maggie, and she was actually quite nice, but twelve-year-old Nell was having none of it. She took Maggie out snowshoeing and spun a tale of the castle being infested with ghosts, and the Dower House with rats. Nell even staged a haunting that night. It had also been a very cold Christmas. Whether it was because of ghosts, vermin, or freezing temperatures and impassable roads, Maggie did not reappear. Aunt Katharine was fairly disappointed, for she had tried and failed at matchmaking in the past, and she considered Maggie a suitable candidate. As Iain and Maggie were leaving to take her to the Inverness station, Nell overheard her remark to Iain, "Your little sister's a bit of a horror, isn't she," and Iain replying shortly that Nell wasn't his sister. Nell hadn't been sure whether or not to be comforted by Iain's remark.

She paused as she jogged by the stables. She had over a half hour before her first student of the day would arrive. Plenty of time to shower and change into her riding togs, and grab a snack from Janet's well-stocked pantry. She strode across the yard to the kitchen door and into the back hall. She generally used the back stairs up to the first floor where her bedroom was located; it was easier and more convenient than the front stairs. She had occupied the smallest guest room with the connecting bathroom since she was quite young, after her mother and Granny Fee died, even though Malcolm was still in the "nursery wing" on the floor above. At one point her father suggested that the room next door beyond the little bathroom could be furnished as a sitting room with her books and tape player and chairs to entertain her friends. When she left school last spring and continued her work with the horses and riding lessons, she had refurnished it as an office. She still had her floor to ceiling bookcase, but her tape collection had been put aside and a computer installed on a lovely new computer desk that her father bought her for her birthday. There was still the big old comfortable overstuffed chair in the corner with a reading lamp by it; on the table by the chair was a photograph of Aunt Eleanor and beside it a silver christening mug, lovingly polished and engraved with her name and date of baptism.

Nell jumped into the shower, and warbled "She loves you, yeah, yeah, yeah" as the steaming water poured over her. After dressing she tidied her bedroom and commenced to head out. On the landing she stopped and looked up the flight of stairs leading to the top floor. It was funny how Iain had asked her what she remembered of her mother, and then clammed up when Nell accused him of not liking her. She hadn't remembered Iain ever mentioning her mother's name.

At the top of the stairs were two large walk-in closets; one was cedar lined and was the storage place for woolen winter coats, the family kilts and other formal accessories. Hanging in one corner were two fur coats swathed in muslin which apparently had belonged to her mother. A year or so ago, Nell had unwrapped them and tried them on. They were too small; her mother obviously had been shorter and narrower across the shoulders than she. Nell had put them away with a sigh—it might have been nice to have something that had belonged to her dead mother. The second closet was the main linen closet, and it was one of Nell's household jobs to make sure this was kept orderly. Once or twice a month she would refold towels and sheets and reorganize the shelves. There was something about piles of linens and towels with their folded sides out and matching colours that satisfied her sense of neatness and orderliness. It was the same in the tack room at the stables. There was a place for everything, and Nell made sure that saddles, bridles, and other equipment were kept on their proper hooks.

The stairs continued to the attic, and in the past she had helped Janet clear out rubbish and trunks of old clothes while just ignoring the door leading to the children's old bedrooms. Her father and Aunt Katharine, then in turn Iain, herself and Malcolm had all occupied various bedrooms down the hall from the old nursery, which was now Malcolm's playroom. Even Nanny hadn't been able to persuade her to keep her old room. She just didn't like it up there. Malcolm, on the other hand, was glad to have the whole upper floor to himself, and to occasionally share with Simon when they came home for weekends.

She hesitated a moment, then ran lightly up the stairs and through the doorway into the so-called nursery wing. She strode down the long hallway past the bedrooms used by generations of Maclachlan children to the door leading to the playroom. It was a large room, more like a suite, with a kitchenette and a separate bedroom where Nanny had slept when the children were babies. Next to this room was a smaller bedroom with two cots where she, and then Malcolm had presumably slept when they were toddlers before graduating to a proper bedroom outside the nursery. There was another door in the wall opposite to where she had entered from the hallway. Suddenly Nell, whose stomach had inexplicably begun to churn, was very reluctant to cross the room and open that door.

There's something bad behind the door.

That was crazy; the upper landing of the main staircase was behind the door, and across the landing was another door leading to her parents' flat, now unused. Nell opened the door and stepped out on to the landing. She could hear a vacuum cleaner, its drone rising faintly to her ears from the ground floor. She heard Janet's voice, and then a door closing somewhere two flights below. She looked at the big double doors with their brass fittings, and the churning in her stomach progressed to a sharp pain that almost doubled her up. What was the matter with her? She strode the few feet across the landing and reached for the door handle. A wave of nausea engulfed her; her hand paused, and then turned the knob. It was firmly locked. Another wave of nausea hit her, and she turned and fled back into the nursery, crossed the room and let the door slam behind her. She didn't stop until she reached her bedroom on the floor below. She sat on the edge of her bed, her hands to her mouth, heart racing, until the nausea passed. She went into her bathroom and regarded herself in the mirror. She was pale and perspiring, but otherwise looked quite normal.

"What was that all about?" she asked her reflection.

She washed her face, and then went downstairs where she sat down by the back door and pulled on her riding boots. As she went out she saw Janet coming from the kitchen garden with a large basketful of root vegetables. Janet would be sure to see that something was wrong, so Nell waved at her and trotted across the yard to the stables. Her student, young Charlie White, was waiting for her, his pony already saddled and ready to go.

"I'm sorry I'm late, Charlie."

The freckle-faced youngster grinned. "That's okay, Nell. See, I helped Henry saddle the pony."

The head lad smiled. "He did indeed, and a fine job he did."

Nell smiled down at the freckled ten-year-old. She ruffled his hair affectionately, and said, "Let's go for a ride."

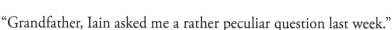

"Grandfather, Iain asked me a rather peculiar question last week."

Nell was driving the ancient station wagon down the hill from the castle. Their destination was the Inverness train station where her grandfather was meeting an old naval crony who was to be a house guest for a week or so.

"And what was that?"

"He asked me what I remembered of my mother. It was funny, his asking me out of the blue like that, don't you think?"

There was a short silence.

"And what do you remember of her, Nell?" the earl asked gently.

"Why, nothing at all! That's odd, too, don't you think?"

"Well, your mother wasn't around a whole lot when you were small, you know. She did a lot of travelling. I think your Grandmother Shaw was not well for a time."

"And what's more," Nell went on, "Iain said something that made me ask him if he liked her, but he just changed the subject!"

Nell changed gears and slowed the car they neared the village. They both spotted her Aunt Katherine in the Manse garden and Nell tooted and waved. Katherine, her arms filled with colourful autumn flowers, waved back enthusiastically. Nell crawled through the village, and then started down the long hill to Nethy Bridge.

"Did Iain not get on with my mother?" she persisted.

Her grandfather considered the question. "Well, there were times when she teased him, and made unkind remarks," he said finally. "He was only a boy, and I think she made him feel an outsider at times."

"Oh, I thought he might have had a boyish crush on her, or something. Nanny has a snapshot of her at my baptism, and she looks as though she was very pretty. Did you like her, Grandad?"

"Hang on, Nell," he said, ignoring the question, "will you stop at the golf club for a moment, and I'll reserve a tee time for tomorrow morning."

Nell obligingly turned just before they entered the small village of Nethy Bridge, and drove up the long graveled road to the golf course. She drew into a parking space, and the earl got out and strode up the paved walkway to the pro shop, He was only a few minutes, and he returned smiling.

"Eight fifty-one tomorrow morning. Cam will be pleased," he remarked, as he got back into the passenger seat.

They were well past the village and nearing the highway before Nell continued the conversation. She repeated the question.

"Did I like her? I did at first. And you are right; she was very pretty indeed, and also extremely charming. But your parents' marriage was not a success—in fact they were very unhappy...and before you ask me whose fault it was, I really cannot say."

He turned and gazed out the window as Nell maneuvered the car on to the motorway. Nell glanced at him and decided not to ask any more questions. She hoped she had not upset him too much. He murmured something which sounded like, "He married the wrong sister," and Nell asked, "What did you say, Grandfather?" The earl merely said, "Nothing, dearie. I was just thinking out loud," and changed the subject. "What has Janet planned for dinner tonight?" he asked.

"Oh, she's entrusted me with getting the salmon for tonight— and oysters, if they're very fresh," she added with a shudder. "Apparently the Commander is fond of oysters."

"I do believe he is, and so am I. Not you, I take it?"

"I suppose I could eat them chopped up and well cooked in a fish chowder," Nell answered with a grin. "The thought of them sliding raw down my throat gives me the shivers."

The rest of the drive into Inverness was made in silence, but as Nell left the highway she said,

"Grandfather, do you still want me to drop you off at the station now? There's probably time for me to do my errands before the Commander's train arrives."

"You can drop me off now, lass; I've got my golfing magazine and my copy of the *Scotsman*. We'll catch a cab to the library car park (is that where you're leaving the car?) and we'll have a pint at the pub nearby if you haven't returned."

Nell bypassed the main part of the city and found a place to stop in front of the Inverness Terminal. She watched her grandfather slowly climb the stairs to the main building, then started the car and threaded her way through the traffic back into the city centre. She thought that he was not moving as quickly these days; but, after all, he had celebrated his eightieth birthday earlier this year, and that wasn't young.

What had he said earlier in the car? It sounded something like "he married the wrong sister." Did he mean that Dad should have married Eleanor? Nell knew that Aunt Eleanor and Dad had known each other long ago before he married her mother, but there was never any indication that they had been more than friends. Maybe she had misheard. She had never before considered these things: what her mother had been like, and how she had died. She had been told her mother had been very ill after Malcolm was born and had passed away. It was all Iain's fault; she thought crossly, as she drew into the library car park and eased into a parking stall. If he hadn't asked that thoughtless question last week she wouldn't have gone upstairs and frightened herself silly. Maybe there really *was* a ghost in the castle! She laughed at herself, and trotted into the library to exchange the books she had brought with her. Both Janet and Mrs. Pepper had given her detailed instructions as to what books to bring back, and she had a couple of her own to return as well. Nell loved books, and just being in these rooms with row upon row of book-filled cases soothed her. She forgot about Iain and her mother's unkindness to him, her grandfather's odd remark, and the possibility that her father had also loved Aunt Eleanor. *That* was something she'd probably never find out about—she wasn't likely to quiz her father about a long ago relationship with her mother's sister, especially not now when a woman friend was coming to visit.

Her book bag agreeably filled with new books, she was on her way back to the car when she heard her name called.

"Nell! Nell Maclachlan!"

She turned to see a girl hurrying after her and recognized one of her former school classmates.

"Betsy! How nice to see you," she exclaimed. "No classes today?"

Her friend Betsy Jones had remained in high school to work on her A-levels—she had always declared her intention of going to university after she finished school. Tall and dark haired, she was wearing a checked mini-skirt, knee high boots, with a lime green scarf casually draped around her neck, and on her forehead sported oversized sunglasses. Nell thought she looked quite elegant.

"It's a half holiday, and I am as usual behind in a project, so I am spending this gorgeous afternoon slaving away in the library," she answered gaily. "How is the riding business going, and are you glad you left school?"

"I'm fine, and I just love running the stables. I have three students."

"Care for another one? Look, do you have time for a coffee or something?"

"I have to buy some fish at the shop up in the High Street," she answered. "Walk with me and we can have a coffee in the little tea shop next to McAllister's Fish and Seafood. It's only about a five minute walk. Here, drop your books in the car and lighten your load."

The two girls stowed their bags in the boot, and started up the street arm in arm.

"What did you mean, did I want another student?" asked Nell, as they crossed the street.

"Dad sent me some money for my birthday, and I'd like to take riding lessons from you."

"Cool! Do you have days in mind, a Saturday or another half holiday? This weekend coming up is very busy—we have house guests arriving and a birthday party for Dad on Saturday." She thought for a moment. "I don't know how long the guests are staying, but how about a week from this Saturday? I'll let you know if it doesn't work. Oh, this will be fun."

When they were settled in the tea shop, and the waitress had brought them their coffees, Betsy took a sip, put down the mug and grinned across the table at Nell.

"How's that handsome Cousin Heathcliffe of yours? Married yet?"

"His name is Iain, and no, he's still single," Nell answered with dignity, and then buried her face in her coffee cup. Changing the subject, she asked Betsy about her parents.

"My Dad's living in Wales with his new wife. They've got two little kids."

"He comes from Wales, doesn't he?"

Betsy nodded. "He got married five years ago in Wales. I didn't go down there, and I've only seen him a couple of times since then when he came up to Inverness. He wants me to visit, but I don't know....anyway, Mum doesn't really want me to go."

"That's a shame. Does she think you'd stay there or something?" Nell couldn't think of anything worse than being separated from her father.

"I think she's worried about being left alone. There's just me, you see."

"But you're going to leave home when you go to university. Where are you thinking of going?"

"I haven't decided yet. I don't even know what I what to do. Unlike you, who wants to work for your father and stay at home forever."

Nell smiled, put some money down on the table, and rose to her feet.

"I must pick up the fish and get back to the car. Grandfather and Commander Lee will be waiting for me."

The salmon was fresh, and so were the oysters. Mr. McAllister wrapped everything up in thick waxed paper and added a plastic bag of crushed ice in her carry bag.

"Wish your father a very happy birthday from me," he said, smiling down at her.

As the girls walked back down the hill to the library, Nell asked, "Do you remember Katie Murchison? She was three years ahead of us. A whiz at gymnastics."

Betsy nodded. "I think so. Was she small and slim and dark haired?"

"That's her. She's from Rannoch Village, and she's getting married on Saturday. Nice guy, a local fellow, and they are settling practically next door to us. She was awfully good to me when I was first going into town on the school bus—in fact, quite the mother hen. I wish I could go to the wedding, but with Dad's birthday party and all, I'll just be too busy."

"What's happening with the birthday?"

Nell briefly described the various activities and guests, though she omitted mentioning Mrs. Lindsay. She still hadn't come to terms with her father having a lady friend. She hoped she wasn't going to disrupt their lives, like taking him away from the Glen. She mentally shook her head. That would never happen. Dad belonged here, just as she did.

Betsy was looking at her sidewise. "Penny for your thoughts."

Nell wasn't about to share her father's news with anyone outside the family, so she fibbed. "Just thinking of all the things we have to do before Friday. It's my brother's school's long weekend, and we always make a big deal of that Friday night. Janet has a list a mile long for the weekend, and she has me doing all kinds of things."

When the girls returned to the car, Betsy retrieved her books. They embraced briefly and said goodbye.

"I'll call at the beginning of the week and confirm next Saturday," Nell said. "Plan to stay for lunch."

"I'll look forward to it," Betsy said. She turned away and Nell watched her stride out to the street, the green scarf floating behind her.

"It'll be fun having Betsy as a student," Nell told her grandfather and the Commander as they drove away from the city. "Betsy is a very nice person. I've known her since primary school, and I've always enjoyed her company. I didn't think I'd miss my school friends, but I am so glad I ran into her."

"You don't get about enough," said her grandfather. "Before you know it you'll be an old lady and stuck in a groove."

Nell snorted. "You sound like Janet."

The salmon had been perfect, and the oysters superb. Commander Lee leaned back in the large easy chair beside the fireplace and sighed with pleasure.

"Miss Stevens, you are a witch. What on earth did you put in the sauce?" he asked Janet as she passed a tray of coffee to the James, his father, and their guest, who were enjoying an after dinner brandy in the library.

"My secret ingredient is Scotch," she replied with a smile. "Oh, don't worry, my Lord, not the twelve-year-old stuff," she reassured the earl, who had looked up with a startled expression. She left them to help themselves to cream and sugar, and hurried out to help Mrs. Pepper and Nell clear away.

Nell was in the little dining room setting the table for breakfast. Usually her father and grandfather made their own meals in the flat upstairs, and quite often she would join them, but with a guest in the house, breakfasts would be served downstairs. The small dining room near the kitchen was also used by the family mostly for lunch and dinner, the formal dining room usually reserved just for parties and other special occasions. Janet had already begun to prepare the dining room for the Boys' Tea on Friday, and she and Mrs. Pepper would be extremely busy all day Saturday getting ready for James' birthday dinner.

"Nell, can I have a word?" Nell looked up to see Iain standing in the doorway. She finished wiping the table, put four place mats down, and handed him four goblets while she found salt and pepper, and the sugar bowl. Iain obediently set the glasses at each place. "I need a huge favour from you on Friday," he said.

Nell smiled at him. "If I can do it, I will," she answered.

"Bernice Porter has asked me to show her around the estate. She wants to come and ride her horse. Now I'm completely tied up on Friday——"

Nell could not hide her dismay. "Iain! Have you completely forgotten the boys are coming home for their long weekend? Can't you see her around another day?"

"She's going off with her parents on a holiday on Saturday, and she won't be back until after Christmas. D'ye think you could fill in for me? Besides, she said she'd love to meet you and get to know you."

Nell turned away so that Iain wouldn't see her thundering frown. *Yeah, sure, she wants to get to know me. What a crock of cow dung.* "But I have Jemmie Burden coming for his lesson at three—that hardly gets me finished in time for tea."

"She said she could come at one pm; oh, come on, Nell, you're so much better on horseback than I am—I'm only good for a walk around the paddock, not a tour of the whole property. Oh, please...."

She had the time, and Iain knew it. He must have checked her schedule. She was suddenly very annoyed—at Iain, and at herself as well, because she knew she wasn't going to turn him down. *Oh, Hell, why can't I say no to him?*

"Well. Okay, but I have to be finished before three..."

"Nell, you're a darling!" He brushed her cheek with a kiss and hurried away. Nell stood still for a moment, her face tingling. Then she slowly finished setting the table, retrieved the toaster from the cupboard, and stacked plates and bowl on the sideboard. As she left the room she saw Janet standing in the hallway.

"Why didn't you just say 'no'?" she asked.

"Oh, Janet....."

"I know, I know..."

"I guess I won't be able to manufacture ghosts and rats this time," she said wryly. She heard Janet's chuckle follow her down the hall all the way to the library.

Chapter 10

ROBIN AND KATHARINE

The Friday afternoon sun painted long shadows across the village square as Robin carefully edged the car through the narrow street and up the hill toward the church. The little valley was bathed in sunshine, and the leaves on the trees were turning to gold and scarlet. The heather on the hillside was a mass of purple, and the long rays of the sun gave it texture, so it looked as though a purple and gray mantle had been flung down by some careless giant. She had found the way from Nairn with no trouble at all, and now glancing at her watch, realized that it was much too early to arrive at the castle.

"I'll stop at the church and have a look round," she said to herself. She got out of the car, and stood for a few minutes, admiring the setting. Whoever had built the church had chosen his site well. It overlooked the village and beyond it the valley. Trees had been planted around it, and behind was the kirkyard. The manse was close by, and there was a beautiful flower garden next to it. A gate led out of the garden into the main road from where she had turned. The church itself was made of stone, square, plain, with a Norman tower. There were stained glass windows, however, and the wooden door was curved at the top, with huge iron hinges. She went up the stairs, opened the massive doors, went in, and sat down on one of the pews. It was cool and inviting, the decor plain. The polished wood communion table, plain and undraped, stood in the chancel, a large Bible carefully centered upon it.

She was feeling better about herself. She had stayed for two nights in a small bed and breakfast just outside of Nairn, and as the only guest she was made to feel a part of the family. Mr. Dunne, a very genial man, operated a dry cleaning establishment in the town, while his wife ran the bed and breakfast. Mrs. Dunne invited her to join them for dinner, and didn't charge her a penny more. When Robin protested, she merely said that she had been missing her own daughter since she had moved to Canada, and it was a pleasure to have Mrs. Lindsay to dine. Yesterday morning after her husband had gone to work Mrs. Dunne had asked her if there wasn't something worrying her. Robin replied cautiously that she had had a very unpleasant experience in St. Andrew's, and she couldn't get it out of her mind. Mrs. Dunne did not ask any questions, but said sympathetically,

"You know, my dear, you can deliberately put things out of your mind if you want to. Every time you find yourself dwelling on what happened, just firmly and gently put it away, and think of something else. However, sometimes it helps to talk it out, and a comparative stranger is often a good person to confide in. Like a minister or doctor."

Robin found herself telling Mrs. Dunne the whole sordid story. The only thing she left out was the insinuations about Tim. "What I can't believe is that I didn't have any idea that he was like that. He had never made a 'pass' at me before, and my husband seemed to like him all right."

"I've been told by widows that their brother-in-law or their husband's best friend have made propositions like that," she said. "And there you were, alone in a strange city, nobody knowing either of you, his friend out of the way—I'm sure it seemed to him an ideal opportunity to try to get you into his bed. What a poor excuse for a man! It's a pity you got back into the car with him, but you would have had no idea he'd be violent. What a frightful experience! You just keep putting it out of your mind, and I'll say a prayer of thanks tonight that you escaped."

Robin regarded her with sudden affection. What a dear lady! And she had escaped, and she could take satisfaction in that vicious kick in the shins she had given him.

She sat quietly now and gave thanks for Mrs. Dunne's advice. Yes, Charlie Morrison was a 'poor excuse for a man,' and she was glad she hadn't stayed in St. Andrew's. Nairn was a charming town, and she had done some shopping, and bought a 'house' present to bring to Rannoch Castle, some fine French red wine that she found in a wine shop. In an antique shop she had found an old book on the history of Iona, and thought that she'd give that to James for his birthday. She had so enjoyed her visit there. She had peeped into the book, and it looked fascinating.

Outside in the garden Katharine Perry was weeding her flower beds while she waited for Mrs. Murchison to arrive. Katie Murchison was being married tomorrow in the Kirk, and Katharine had promised her mother flowers from the manse garden to decorate the sanctuary. She had noticed the car stop beside the church, and had seen a woman go in. She wondered if she could be Jamie's friend who was coming to stay the weekend. She was pleasantly surprised when James announced last week that he had met a woman at Aunt Sarah's and had asked her to come to his birthday dinner. She had never heard of his seeing anybody special, let alone inviting her home for the weekend. The children had never lacked a mother figure, for she had nursed Malcolm from the time he was a few weeks old when his mother died, and he had grown up between the Manse and the Castle with her own Simon as his best friend; Nanny and Mrs. Stevens and her daughter Janet had been there to fill in the gaps with both the children, and working on the estate, James was always nearby. Nell had grown into a quiet, self-possessed girl, who never discussed her mother, and Malcolm, who of course had never known her, looked upon his Aunt Katharine as mother, and was now an active, bright nine-year old, with many interests. Simon had to scramble to stay with him. Not for the first time she gave thanks that Roger had been called to this congregation. Roger always said that the Lord led him first to her, and then to Glen Rannoch Church.

Katharine's musings were interrupted by the creaking of the garden gate. Mrs. Murchison, a small, wiry, dark haired woman with a perpetually worried expression on her face, came into the garden, flushed from riding her bicycle up the hill. She was very fit, with a trim athletic body, for she rode her bicycle everywhere. She was even known for cycling all the way into Nairn for errands or shopping, and cycling back! She lived in the new development below the village with her husband, who was the banker in Glen Rannoch, and her two daughters. She now was looking even more worried, if that were possible.

"Oh, Mrs. Perry, I'm *so* sorry to keep you waiting. Katie wanted me there for her final fitting. Miss Hemlock had to do an alteration on the dress. Katie has put on a bit of weight lately." Her voice dropped to a whisper. "I'm so afraid she might be, well.......*expecting*. She hasn't *said* anything, if course and I haven't asked her. She just looks *that way*. Whatever should we do?"

Katharine had gotten up, taken off her gardening gloves, and pushed the hair out of her eyes.

"Do? Why pick flowers, of course, and decorate the church."

"But doesn't it *matter*? I mean, won't the Reverend *mind*?"

"Mrs. Murchison, Katie and Josef love each other, and are being married tomorrow. If your first grandchild happens to arrive a little early, what's the problem? I assure you Roger will marry them happily, and baptize any arrival early or late with the same enthusiasm. And if anyone has the bad taste to make a remark, just consider the source and ignore him or her. Now," she added serenely, "what flowers do you want?"

Mrs. Murchison sat down on the bench by the gate and mopped her face. "Too kind. Thank you, Mrs. Perry; you *do* have a way of putting things in *perspective*." She took her garden shears out of her carryall bag, and briskly got to her feet. "You are *so right*. We have work to do, don't we. And I haven't even *thanked* you for giving this time to me."

Katharine turned away, hiding a smile at Mrs. Murchison's dramatic accents. She knew Katie quite well, and thought her a sensible girl who would be amused by her mother's suspicions. They then both fell to work selecting and cutting Katharine's beautiful autumn blooms.

A half hour later, they entered the sanctuary, arms filled with flowers. As they went through to the kitchen area at the back, Katharine notice the woman, who had been sitting a pew, get up and go out the side door to the graveyard.

"I'll get vases for you, and then leave you to do your artistry," she said. "I love growing flowers, but I'm no good at arranging them." Mrs. Murchison belonged to the flower committee and quite often made the flower arrangement for the Sunday services.

"I'll do two arrangements in the brass vases we use for Sundays, and one big one in the pottery vase you said I could borrow. I thought we could leave the two for Sunday, and *would* it be an imposition to take one to the reception?"

Katharine brought the two brass vases, gleaming from a recent polishing, and the large brown and blue pottery jug she used in the manse. "Heavens, no," she said gaily. "Just make sure whosoever job it is to do them for this week's service know that her job's already done."

"Oh, *thank you* for that reminder. It's Martha Davidson; I'll phone her today."

Katharine smiled, and said that she would see her tomorrow at ten am, and to hang in there. *Mother would hate to hear me using slang,* she thought. But 'hang in there' was a good metaphor. She always had a mental picture of someone dangling, and clinging to a bough, white-knuckled from the exertion.

Out in the graveyard, Robin had found the Maclachlan burial plot, and was busy trying to identify who was who. She looked up to see a dark-haired woman approaching. She had a youthful face, beautifully molded with high cheekbones, widely-spaced, dark, smiling eyes, and a head of thick, wavy black hair brushing her shoulders. It was expertly cut, and shone in the sunlight.

"Would you be Mrs. Lindsay?"

"Yes, I am. You must be Mrs. Perry?"

"Katharine. Please call me Katharine."

"And I'm Robin."

The two women shook hands, each assessing the other. Katharine saw a woman, perhaps her age or a little older, medium height, her slim body dressed in tailored slacks and a linen shirt under a red blazer. She had curly brown hair with glints of gold, and a fair amount of grey as well. Katharine sensed some shyness as well, but her smile was cordial, and her handshake firm.

"I gave myself too much time, and got here early. What a lovely setting your church has."

Katharine smiled and looked around. "It is that. One of my ancestors had it built about 200 years ago. If mother were alive, she could tell you all about it. She was very knowledgeable about the family history." She paused and looked at her watch. "Roger has gone to pick up the boys, and they should be back by four or so. Why don't I come with you up to the castle now? I'll change—(I was gardening and helping Mrs. Murchison pick flowers for the church. Her daughter is being married tomorrow)—and leave a note for Roger for him to come straight up. Come on into my kitchen; I made some coffee just before Mrs. M arrived." She grinned ruefully. "I completely forgot to offer her some. Ah well, it should be fresh still. I'll be about fifteen minutes."

Katharine led the way into the kitchen, got out a mug from the cupboard, and filled it, placing it in front of Robin.

"Milk and sugar?"

"Just milk, please."

She produced from the refrigerator a charmingly squat cream jug of robin's egg blue, and put it on the table, and indicated the spoons, stacked in a silver caddie on the table. She went away without a word, and Robin sat down and sipped the steaming beverage.

It was less that fifteen minutes later when her hostess appeared, dressed in a corduroy skirt of a soft purple, with a matching pullover. She wore over her shoulder a white Friable sweater, and sensible brown moccasin shoes on her feet. She tacked a large sheet of paper on the refrigerator ("Our message board.") and led the way out the kitchen door to Robin's car parked by the church.

"Let me tell Mrs. Murchison I'm leaving," she suggested. She went into the church and reappeared in less than a minute. Robin was in the driver's seat and had the passenger door open for her.

"Turn left up the road here, and just keep driving. It's only a few miles. We walked to school every day when we were children. Sometimes old Finlay, mother's head groom, would bring the ponies down at three o'clock, and we would ride home. Always the long way round, too. He died last year, bless his heart."

Robin drove the car up the road to where it flattened out. They passed a farm, with several acres of vegetable gardens gold and green in the late afternoon sun. Two greenhouses stood behind the house, and there were pickers in the field, harvesting the autumn produce.

"The Ranapurs own this farm. They are East Indians and produce the most wonderful vegetables."

The road turned, and wound up into the hills and after about a mile another valley came into view. They crossed a bridge over a sparkling burn and Katharine pointed to the golden fields.

"This is what we call the Upper Glen. That was the River Rannoch we just crossed. We are on our land now, and that is the barley we harvest to make the whisky. You can see the distillery in the distance. All the ingredients of Glen Rannoch Whisky are found right here. The river flows through peat beds and gives it a distinctive flavor. But you probably know all about it. James is sure to give you a tour of the distillery sometime this weekend. My eyes glaze over when it comes to explaining how the whisky is made. Chemistry was never my favorite subject, and don't tell a soul, but I prefer wine to spirits!"

The road had forked there, the left hand road leading to the distillery, so they turned right onto the road which snaked up the hill. Robin geared down as it curved around two or three sharp turns, with a steep drop to the valley below.

"My mother's car went off the road on one of these curves," Katharine said suddenly. "They say she was killed instantly."

Sarah Donaldson had told Robin that James' mother had been killed in a car crash, but she had envisaged a collision on the highway somewhere, not an accident on their own property.

"Mrs. Donaldson mentioned it briefly. It must have been a dreadful shock to you all."

"Daddy will never get over it," Katharine said quietly. "James took it so very hard, too, and then of course Claire died about three weeks later. Yes, it was a terrible time for the family."

They were silent for a moment, and Robin concentrated on negotiating the car around the last curve and up into a grove of pines and birch. The road came out onto an area of rolling meadows, through a large gate, and by barns and fields. Cows were munching placidly, tails swishing.

"The dairy farm, which my cousin Iain runs now," said Katharine. "Did Jamie explain about Iain? He's like a young brother to us. He grew up here after his parents were killed in a plane crash. They were coming home from a medical conference in Paris and the airplane went into the sea." She glanced at Robin apologetically. "Jamie told me your husband died that way, too. I'm sorry I brought it up."

Robin shook her head. "Don't apologize. You don't expect people never to mention car accidents, do you? What a lovely cottage that is. Well, more than just a cottage."

She slowed down and was admiring the slate roofed house tucked in amongst trees. It was surrounded by a stone wall, trees and garden.

"That's the Dower House. It was built for my great-great grandmother, I believe, who refused to live in the same house as her daughter-in-law. Iain lives in it because he prefers to be independent. He's doing a fine job with the farm. He took over from James about the time we moved back to Glen Rannoch, and it's making a good profit. Rannoch Fields milk and butter are sold in Inverness, as well as many towns and villages around here. Nell and I help in his flower garden when we have the time."

Robin continued on, and the road came close to the cliff, and around a curve, through another grove, and she braked, and exclaimed, "Oh, Katharine, how beautiful!"

Rannoch Castle was, as James had said, not a traditional castle with towers, turrets and battlements. It was, instead, a large manor house with a wide front entrance flanked by a double set of stairs. There was a graveled drive which encircled a garden consisting of a lawn, trees and a fountain. Tall trees stood at the far side of the house, and there was a wall and gate leading away through the trees. To the right of these trees were a high stone wall and an arched entrance to a cobbled yard. The house itself had been built of a lovely reddish colored stone, which had, over the years, faded to a muted pink. The windows on the ground floor were wide and shining in the last rays of the westering sun. The front door reminded Robin of the church door, massive, wooden, with a curved top and huge hinges.

"Mother always stopped here with her guests who were seeing it for the first time. She always liked to see their reaction. It is lovely, and you can't even see the view from here. The castle overlooks the upper glen and the barley fields and distillery. Why don't you park the car by the front door, and let's go in and get you settled. Daddy could be around, but Jamie is likely to be down in the fields or the distillery."

As they got out of the car the front door opened and a middle aged woman came out with a welcoming smile on her face.

"Miss Katharine, how nice to see you. You didn't wait for Reverend Perry and the boys, then."

"Robin, this is Janet Stevens, who looks after everybody and runs the house. Janet, this is Mrs. Lindsay from Canada."

Robin shook hands with the housekeeper, liking her immediately. She was small and dark, with a brown homely face, brown eyes and a brilliant smile.

"Welcome to Rannoch Castle, Mrs. Lindsay," she said formally.

"It is good to be here," answered Robin simply.

"How is your mother these days, Janet? I plan to go into Nairn next week and visit her."

"Och, she loves visitors, even though sometimes she's not so sure who they are," replied Janet. "Some days she's no' so grand, though....."

"We can take Mrs. Lindsay's bag upstairs, Janet. Where have you put her?"

"Mr. James ordered the Gold and Silver Room. It's all ready."

"The Boys' Tea is at five as usual? We won't be late." And Katharine picked up Robins' large bag and led the way upstairs. As they ascended she explained the layout of Rannoch Castle, pointing out her father's suite of rooms. "He has shared them with Jamie practically ever since Claire died. He was lonely, of course, with mother gone, and it has worked out well. It takes up the whole wing—lots of room for two old bachelors. Nobody sleeps upstairs on the second floor now, except Malcolm on weekends and holidays, and half the time Simon is with him. Jamie and I had rooms up there while we were growing up; there's a big nursery area with a kitchenette and bedroom where Nanny slept when we were small, and another bedroom we had as toddlers under Nanny's sharp eyes. I remember when I graduated to my own room. I had started school in the village, and I felt so grown up. Our parents had a suite of rooms next to the nursery, and then moved down to the first floor here after Grandfather died. James and Claire moved into the suite upstairs when they got married. I believe it's closed up now, everything covered in dust sheets. I think Janet goes in there a couple times a year, airs everything, and vacuums like a dynamo. Nell has a room on this floor. She didn't like being up there all by herself. The guest rooms are through the gallery here."

She led the way through a long room whose walls were lined with portraits. Some fine antique furniture was placed at intervals, and double bow windows overlooked the upper glen.

"We call this the gallery. In the old days it was a ballroom. We had dances as teenagers up here, but it hasn't been used for parties for years now."

They went through double doors at the end of the room and into a wide corridor, with doors on each side.

"Here we are," she said, pushing open double doors and leading the way into a spacious room with a huge four poster bed. It was also furnished with an enormous wardrobe, sofa, chair, and small table. There was a fireplace, laid with kindling, ready to be lit. A door led into an *en suite* bathroom, paneled in mahogany with brass and porcelain fittings. "This was a dressing room in the old days, and daddy had it converted into a bathroom years ago."

"It's a magnificent room," Robin said, gazing at the gold and silver draperies and wall coverings. There were some fine old pictures on the walls, too, one of which looked like a Sargent.

"It is the finest of the guest rooms," said Katharine. "Princess Anne has slept here."

"Really! James never said you had entertained royalty."

"I knew the Princess fairly well through equestrian events. We've competed with and against each other in the past. Now, I'll let you unpack and refresh yourself. It's nearly four o'clock and Roger and the boys will be home soon. Come down when you're ready and I'll show you the gardens. I'll meet you in the library. If you turn right at the bottom of the main staircase, it's the first door on your left. I'll see you in a short while then." And she went out and closed the door quietly.

Robin unpacked her suitcase, hanging things up neatly in the wardrobe, and folding others and putting them in the drawers. She had a quick shower, and put on her pleated white wool skirt and blue sweater. Retracing her steps through the gallery, into the wide landing and down the stairs, she found the library as Katharine had described. It was empty, but she took the opportunity to look at the bookcases and their floor to ceiling contents, the comfortable looking sofa, the gracious reading chairs and the unique bar. It was like a tall china cabinet, crystal drinking glasses of all shapes and sizes stored behind glass doors, a marble shelf with a double cabinet below, and several interesting bottles displayed on a silver tray. There was a silver soda siphon, something she had read about in books but never seen, and on another silver tray an exquisite crystal whisky decanter with matching glasses grouped around it. Corner windows overlooked the front entrance and the circular lawn. A newspaper had been left on the sofa. It was the Thursday edition of the Inverness daily and as she picked it up a small headline caught her eye. 'Mystery Death in St. Andrew's.' She read, 'The body of a man, approximately fifty years old, was found early Wednesday in Murray Park by two local citizens out for a morning walk. Neither the victim's identity nor the cause of death has been disclosed. Police are treating it as a suspicious death and are investigating.' Robin dropped the paper, then picked it up again and looked at the date. Wednesday. While she had been creeping out of Aslar House, feeling like a thief in the night, someone was finding a body nearby. She shivered. Murray Park. That was where....She heard Mrs. Dunne's advice again: *Put it out of your mind, dearie.* She dropped the paper again and crossed the room to gaze out the window. She was standing there, still looking out the window when Katharine came in, who remarked on how quick she had been, and wasn't this a lovely room?

"Wait until you see the drawing room, though, it was mother's pride and joy. James is sure to give you the full tour sometime before you go. Janet tells me that Daddy and the Commander are playing golf at Nethy Bridge and should be home momentarily. Come on; let me show you the garden."

The two women went out and down the corridor to the left and out a set of french doors. Two steps led down to a small formal garden laid out with evergreen hedges, and hardy shrubs. A path curved away and through the trees was a glimpse of the view across the valley. Fall flowers bloomed along the path. In the center of the garden were a pond and two rustic benches.

"It's very attractive."

"Claire designed it and had workers come in and lay it out for her. There wasn't much here before. At the other end of the house is a walled kitchen garden with some apple trees and a herb garden. Janet is clever with fruits and vegetables and herbs. What they don't grow ourselves they get from the Ranapurs."

There was a crunch of wheels on gravel at the front of the house, and presently two boys appeared on the path that led from the driveway. The smaller of the two was dark and thin and wiry. He had his mother's smiling eyes, a generous mouth and was tanned from playing out of doors. His cousin Malcolm Robin recognized from the photograph at Sarah Donaldson's house. He was taller, with his father's reddish brown hair, and very dark blue eyes. He saw the newcomer and stopped running.

"Mummy!" yelled Simon. "I beat Malcolm at the marathon!"

"Simon, you ass," said Malcolm gruffly, "we've got company."

"Yes. Robin, these are my two ruffians, Simon Perry, and Malcolm Maclachlan. Boys, this is Mrs. Lindsay."

Simon gave his mother a hug, and then shook hands politely with Robin. Malcolm came over, and shook hands and said gravely, "Welcome to Rannoch Castle, Mrs. Lindsay." Then he gave Katharine a hug, saying, "Hi Auntie Kath. Simon did splendidly in the marathon. It wasn't a real marathon, of course, just ten kilometers."

"Is tea almost ready?" queried Simon.

"Not until Grandfather and Uncle James and Iain and Nell arrive. Why don't you go in and wash your hands and put your bag upstairs?" Simon turned and headed for the side door as his father appeared. Robin saw a man of medium height, softly bearded, and wearing rimless glasses.

"Their energy astounds me," he remarked. Katharine introduced Robin to her husband and the three turned to go in. Malcolm had jogged down the path through the trees to the lookout, and had now returned.

"I saw Dad's car leave the 'Still'," he announced. "He'll be here in five minutes. Where's Nell?"

"We've only been here less than an hour," Katharine said. "I haven't seen her."

Robin's pulse had quickened at Malcolm's words, but she said to him, "Is Simon the runner, then? What is your specialty?"

Malcolm turned his extraordinary violet blue eyes to her and considered this. "I'm fairly good at cricket, but I'd rather read about animals and birds. I'd like to be a vet when I grow up, like James Herriot. Have you read his books, Mrs. Lindsay?"

"I have. They're excellent reading."

"Grandfather reads to me sometimes before bed. Simon says that's babyish. Do you think it is?"

"Heavens, no! Probably your grandfather enjoys it as much as you do."

"Did somebody read to you when you were young?"

"My mother did sometimes. All sorts of neat books like Tales of Narnia and Doctor Doolittle and the Anne books. In fact, I still like reading the books I read as a child."

And they followed Roger and Katharine, deep in bookish conversation.

As they came down the corridor to the front hall, a deep voice was heard and Katharine said, "Dad's home." The earl was putting his golf clubs away in the closet under the stairs, and as he heard their approach, turned to greet them with a warm smile.

"Hello, Dad, how was the game?" said Katharine, giving him a kiss. "Dad, this is Mrs. Lindsay."

The Earl of Rannoch was dressed in tartan plus fours and a navy sweater. He removed his tam, flung it on the hall table, and came forward.

"Robin, this is my obstreperous parent, Robert, Earl of Rannoch."

Robin found her hand being taken and kissed in a very gallant manner. A pair of eyes as blue as the sea twinkled down at her. His hair was thick and grey and he smelt of Old Spice.

"My Lord, it's a pleasure to meet you," she said and blushed deeply.

The earl observed the blush and was enchanted that a woman of her age could accomplish this. He smiled down at her, still holding her hand and asked if she had had any trouble finding them. Robin shook her head wordlessly, and finding her voice went on to say how good James' instructions were, and how she had stopped at the church and by chance met Katharine, and her kindness in accompanying her up to the castle.

I'm babbling.

"Jamie told me about meeting your cousin on Iona. He seemed to be very impressed by her."

"Celine is quite a marvelous person. She was such a rock to me when I was growing up in Montreal after my mother died. She has a Presence, you know. There was a teacher I had once. She wasn't tall and stately like Celine, rather she was short and stocky, but she could walk into a classroom full of chattering teenagers, and she wouldn't have to say a word. She would just stand and look around. The class would be quiet—like that! It always amazed me. She was a good teacher, too. Celine is something like that."

Am I babbling again?

"She sounds like a remarkable woman." He replied. "Normally we have drinks in the library before dinner, but on the Fridays that the boys come home we have an enormous tea at five o'clock, and sherry is served in the hall here. Ah, here's Iain. His father, who was my first cousin, was killed along with his wife when Iain was very small. He's grown up here, and now runs the dairy farm and loves it. Did Katharine point out the Dower House on your way in? Iain lives there now. Iain, come and meet Mrs. Lindsay who blushes prettily when her hand is kissed."

Robin blushed again, of course, but she couldn't take offense at the earl's remark, which was said with a smile and a wink and a squeeze of the hand. He was flirting with her mildly, and she was enjoying it. Contrast his gentle attentions with those of Charlie——

Put him out of your mind, Mrs. Lindsay, dear, she could hear Mrs. Dunne say.

Iain was dark haired, dark eyed, and his skin had the permanent tan of a person who spends a lot of time outdoors. There were fine lines around his eyes, and his handclasp was firm. He wasn't handsome; his features were too irregular, but he had a mobile mouth and a cleft in his firm chin.

"Hello, Mrs. Lindsay, welcome to Rannoch. Uncle Rob, Nell says for me to pass on her apologies. She will be late, as she is having a wee bit of trouble with young Jemmie Burden, and the lesson is taking longer than usual."

"My granddaughter gives riding lessons and supervises the stables. We board horses, and breed the occasional one. Nell is like her grandmother—a natural with the animals. Do you ride, Mrs. Lindsay?"

"Actually, I have just recently taken it up seriously. I do wish you would call me Robin."

"Robin it is, then. That was my nickname when I was growing up. My wife always called me that."

The earl paused, remembering when she had last called him by that name. His face must have taken on the sadness of his thoughts, for Robin squeezed his arm in sympathy, and he felt the waves of concern and yes, love, emanating from her. He looked at her face turned up to his, filled with sympathy, and knew why Jamie had fallen for her. She wasn't beautiful, but her eyes were lovely, and he knew she was kind and honest. He recalled vividly what James had said about her. "Dad, she's all gold clear through. It's not like it was with Claire. That was a kind of madness, I think. Robin makes me want to be a better person."

Chapter 11

JAMES AND ROBIN

James had spent the day busy at work, but at the back of his mind there was a delicious anticipation. Today he would see Robin, and know for sure if what he was feeling for her was real. He had replayed the three days they had spent together over and over in his mind like a video program. He was sure that she was attracted to him, but she had been widowed for only three years. It might be that it was far too soon for her to get seriously involved. He didn't care. He'd wait forever, if necessary.

What if she changes her mind? Banish the thought. She would have telephoned. Only he hadn't given her his telephone number. She would have written. Only he hadn't given her his address. Fool! And he didn't have her address either! He had picked up the telephone several times last week to call her in Edinburgh, for she had mentioned that she was staying at the Balmoral Hotel. The third time he had telephoned, only to be told that she was out, and he didn't leave a message. What an idiot he was, to invite her to his home, and then just walk away, and not get in touch with her. She wouldn't get lost; he had marked her map well. What if she had changed her mind? He glanced at the clock and flung down his pen. It was a quarter to five. His secretary put her head in the door, and reminded him that it was four forty-five, and wasn't Malcolm coming home today for the weekend?

He left the building, and paused to look about him. His home stood on the hillside, looking as though it was anchored to the rock, as in actual fact it was. The birches were turning yellow, and the barley fields were at their golden best. He climbed the steps to the car park and got into his station wagon. He drove quickly down the glen to the fork in the road, and up toward the dairy farm and the castle beyond. Everyone was gathered in the hall as he came in, but he saw only Robin standing there with his father, her face turned up to his, listening seriously to what he was saying. She turned as he came in, and smiled at him. He stood for a moment, relief flooding through him. What a fool he was to have doubted her. He strode across the room and took both of her hands in his.

"You came. I was afraid that you might change your mind."

"I almost came early, but I didn't want to inconvenience anyone."

"You've met everyone?"

His father remarked, "Nell will be late, we're to start without her. If you are going to change, Jamie, I thought I'd change out of my golf clothes."

Jamie nodded, still gazing at Robin, then turned and raced up the stairs, the earl following at a slower pace. At that moment Janet appeared with a tray of sherry glasses and two glasses of lemonade for the boys.

"Tea will be served in fifteen minutes," she said.

"It's late, Janet. I'm starved!" Simon complained.

"Och, you're always hungry," she said with an indulgent smile, ruffling Simon's hair as she passed.

Malcolm hissed at him, "Mind your manners, you ass."

Tea consisted of a hearty supper of steaming vegetable soup, fresh bread with cheese, meat, tomatoes, and pickles. There was an apple upside-down cake for dessert, and a pot of tea for the adults. Nell came flying in as the soup was being served from the sideboard by Katharine. The family always served themselves unless there was company, explained Malcolm seriously to Robin, and then paused and considered what his words sounded like.

"Mind your manners, you ass," hissed Simon, triumphantly getting even with his cousin.

Robin smiled at Malcolm. "I consider that a compliment," she said quietly.

The earl's friend, Commander Lee, turned out to be an interesting, genial man with a flair for telling humorous stories. It usually bored Robin to hear stories of people she didn't know, but the Commander was so amusing, and his tales so interesting, and the details so vivid, that she couldn't help but be entertained. He was a short man, with a florid complexion and thin white hair, and twinkling eyes behind glasses. His only claim to fame, he told her, was that he had a photographic memory, and that is how he could remember the stories so accurately. The earl said dryly that the great memory didn't always work perfectly, as he had heard that particular story before. Ah, but Mrs. Lindsay hadn't, was the retort, and Robin knew she would hear a few more before the weekend was over.

Nell had nodded a conservative welcome to her as she sat down, and at once tucked into her tea, with the appetite and enthusiasm of an active young person. Robin had been anxious to meet James' daughter, and she watched her eating her meal hungrily, the golden red hair that was her chief beauty hanging down and covering half her face.

"Is Jemmie Burden a problem, Nell?" asked her father.

Nell shook her head as she finished her soup, tucking her hair behind one ear. She buttered her bread and said, "He's not so much of a problem, he just doesn't take riding seriously. I shall have to speak with his parents and see if they want him to continue."

"Is he getting to be a 'burden', Nell?"

Nell glanced scathingly at her grinning brother and continued to eat. James smiled and told Malcolm that the pun was the lowest form of wit, and Malcolm replied that Shakespeare used it a lot, didn't he? James agreed, but continued,

"I'm tied up at the 'Still' tomorrow, Nell; will you be able take Mrs. Lindsay out riding?"

"I have to go and see the Smiths at Crickletop tomorrow morning. If she'd like to come along, that's okay with me," Nell answered.

James frowned at his daughter, but merely said, "That's a good ride, Robin, and pleasant scenery. You should be all right. Nell will look after you."

Once tea was over, the boys excused themselves, and the adults took their tea cups to the library. The Commander accepted a whisky and soda from the earl, and sat down heavily on the sofa. Robin had expected to be captured for another tale, but he sat and sipped his drink in silence.

"Are you tired, sir?" asked Iain.

"I've suddenly begun to fade a bit," he confessed. "I must be getting old if I can't play eighteen holes of golf without feeling played out. Will you excuse me; I think I shall retire early with a warm bath and my book."

James said goodnight to him as he made his exit, then came over to Robin and said, "Let me show you the garden. There is still a little light left."

Robin put down her teacup and followed him out. They went out the door at the end of the corridor into the garden that Katharine had shown her earlier that day.

"Your sister took me out here this afternoon. She mentioned that your wife had designed it."

James took her arm, saying, "Yes. It was a project that she took on when Nell was a baby. She had workers come and do the planting, but she supervised everything. I had this path put in to the edge of the cliff, though, and this wall built. The children always called it 'the lookout' because they could see their grandfather or me leave the 'Still', and time our arrival."

They had walked to that particular spot, and they leaned on the wall looking over the Upper Glen. The light in the western sky was rapidly fading, and the hills were purple and grey. Streaks of red stained the sky, and the first stars were coming out.

"How was your time in Edinburgh?" he asked.

"I enjoyed it very much. Edinburgh Castle is fascinating, isn't it? The war memorial is quite remarkable. You know, James, the atmosphere actually moved me to tears. The concerts were good. It would have been even more enjoyable had I a companion to share it."

"You know, I've been feeling the most almighty fool ever since I left you in Oban. I hadn't given you my address or phone number, so there was no way you could get in touch if you couldn't make it. You told me your hotel in Edinburgh—I telephoned once, but you were out, and I didn't leave a message. I've been nervous as a schoolboy on his first date."

Robin smiled. "Now I feel better. I've been nervous as well."

They stood in companionable silence for a few minutes, the James said, "You mentioned something about coming early, did your plans change in St. Andrew's?"

Robin took a deep breath. *Shall I tell him?*

"Yes they did. I left Wednesday morning and decided to stay in Nairn for a couple of nights. I found a wonderful B and B; Mrs. Dunne treated me like family, and I visited Culloden Fields, and found Nairn itself to be very pleasant indeed." She paused. "I enjoyed the drive to St. Andrew's from Edinburgh. I just took my time, and spent the day exploring the countryside. Tuesday I walked around the town and it was a beautiful day...."

They had been standing fairly close to each other, and James had felt Robin stiffen when he inquired about St. Andrew's. Now her voice trailed away, and her legs sagged. He glanced at her and was alarmed to see that she was very pale, so that the golden freckles that dusted the bridge of her nose stood out like blotches against her skin. He put his arm around her waist, and walked her to the nearby bench.

"Robin!" he exclaimed. "Put your head down."

She caught her breath and said, "I'm all right now."

"What happened, Robin?" When she didn't answer, he said quietly, "If you'd rather not say any more, that's all right with me."

She shook her head. "I want to tell you, James. I'll warn you, it's not very nice." His arm tightened around her as, in a low tone, she related the events of Tuesday evening. James suspected it was a watered down version, but he didn't press her for details. He was so angry he couldn't speak for a few minutes.

"I suppose you think I'm a fool. Mrs. Dunne knew that something was on my mind, and I told her a little bit. She said he was 'a poor excuse for a man' and that I was to put him out of my mind."

He put both arms around her and drew her to him. There were other words he could have used to describe Charlie Morrison, but he didn't say them. He took a deep breath and said, "Robin, I'm so angry and appalled that I could murder the man." He paused. "You're safe here with me. Do you understand?"

"Yes." He went on holding her gently, thinking that there were once two halves, now a whole.

She gave a long sigh, and said with a catch in her voice, "James, I didn't think it was possible to feel this way about someone, so soon after Tim died."

James closed his eyes and drew her even closer, and said carefully, "Robin, I want to tell you just a little about myself. I haven't been a very nice person since my wife died. Even before that. You said at Sarah's how difficult it must have been to raise two children on my own. Well. I didn't do much of the raising, I'm afraid. Nanny and Katharine did most of it, and my father as well. I've spent most of the time immersed in running this estate. I was through with women. Oh there've been one or two that I've encountered. I traveled to France a few years ago and met a woman on the train. I'm not very proud of how I used her. We all make choices we regret. You are not a fool, Robin. When I met you at Sarah's it was different. Oh I know that sounds like rubbish, but it's true. Remember in Oban I said I didn't know where this was going to lead us, but I wanted you to see my home and meet my family. Now I think I'm falling in love with you." He stroked her hair gently. She had had a nasty experience, and he wasn't going to take advantage of it. That might finish it forever for them! So he said quietly, "Here I am, warts and all, if you can stand me. I'm not asking for any commitments, we'll 'just take it nice and easy', as the song says. How does that sound?" And there was warmth and affection in his voice.

Robin looked at him with eyes brimming, and nodded wordlessly. He looked at her and his resolve to go slowly began to fade. "May I kiss you, Robin?" he asked urgently.

"That's the best offer I've had today," she answered with a half laugh, and lifted her mouth to his.

Katharine and Roger were saying their goodnights to her father and Nell and Iain. As they come out of the library, Katharine turned and saw James and Robin come in through the door from the garden. They were walking side by side, not touching, but it was as if there was stream of electricity connecting them. Both their faces were glowing. Katharine held her breath for a moment, and then let it out in a sigh. *Oh God please let this work out for them.*

"There you are, you two. We're going home. Thanks for the tea as usual, James."

Robin came back to earth slowly. "You have the wedding tomorrow morning, don't you. Thank you so much for introducing yourself to me at the church, Katharine, and coming up here with me. You made me feel so welcome."

Katharine impulsively bent and kissed her on the cheek. "Bless you, Robin, it was a pleasure." She grinned at her brother. "Can you get that scamp of mine home by at least five o'clock tomorrow? Simon always takes forever to get kilted up and I want him to look smashing for your birthday party. We have the wedding breakfast at the pub after the ceremony; we probably won't be home until threeish. See you at seven, then."

Roger smiled at both of them and followed his wife out into the hall and out the front door.

They got into their small car, and Katharine said fiercely, "I'm going to pray so hard for those two. Oh Roger, he deserves some happiness!"

Roger regarded his wife with pleasure. She still had the capacity after nearly seventeen years of marriage to make his heart turn over within him. "My darling Kath, if they are as half as happy as we are, they'll be blessed. I'll pray, too."

Katharine reached over and her kiss fell on his ear as he started the car and engaged the gears. "I love you, Roger."

Chapter 12

ROBIN AND NELL

Robin woke up in the big four poster bed, stretched and considered the events of the previous evening. She was glad that she had been able to tell James about Tuesday evening. If he hadn't asked she wondered whether she would have just bypassed the whole thing and have tried to forget. He had been so angry at Charlie ('I could murder the man,' he had said), and had been so kind to her. He had told that story about himself to make her realize that she wasn't the only one to make an unfortunate choice. How bitter he must have been about losing his mother and his wife in the space of a few weeks. He hadn't said how she had died. Someone so young, it could have been cancer, or perhaps a complication following Malcolm's birth. Sarah Donaldson had hinted that it had been very tragic. Robin had visions of the beautiful woman who was his wife dying in great pain, her family at her bedside. Nell not quite taking it in, James struggling to keep back his tears, taking the tiny baby that was Malcolm from her dying arms. She wondered when he would tell her about Claire. ('She was the most beautiful girl I had ever seen. I was completely bowled over.') She shook herself mentally. It didn't matter. Today was today, and James had said he loved her. ('We'll go "nice and easy", as the song says.') She swung out of bed, tidied it expertly, and went into the bathroom, humming the song to herself.

Breakfast was always held in the small dining room next to the kitchen and pantries which they also called the morning room. It faced east over a pleasant green space with the herb and vegetable gardens beyond with french doors leading out. Chairs with gaily colored cushions, and a large oval table set with matching serviettes for the morning meal. There was a sideboard where juice, cereal, coffee, cream and fruit were laid out, and as Robin entered on the heels of the boys, Janet Stevens was there, inquiring if anybody wanted a cooked breakfast. "There is oatmeal porridge and muesli," she said. "And I'll bring some fresh bread for toasting."

Robin said that would be plenty for her. "I had huge breakfasts at the B and B in Nairn," she confessed, "so it is time I cut down." The boys were happy to tuck into fresh fruit and muesli, and be out of the door in five minutes flat. Nell was there before her, and was spreading marmalade lavishly on her toast, and politely wished her good morning.

"Dad said to tell you good morning, and that he'd be tied up until lunch time. Do you still want to go riding?"

"Yes, I would, if it's convenient, Nell. I don't have any riding boots, though."

"Hmm. My grandmother had small feet, they might just fit... Janet, are those riding boots of my grandmother's still in the glory hole? That's what we call the closet under the stairs," she added as an aside to Robin. "What about a saddle? Would be more comfortable in a western saddle? We have both."

Robin poured herself a cup of coffee and warmed up Nell's as she considered this. "I think the western, though I've ridden with both."

Nell got up and went down the corridor to the stairs. A few minutes later she was back with a pair of brown leather boots, worn, but in good condition. Robin tried them on. "This is amazing! They fit as though they were made for me!"

Nell smiled. "I thought they might. Don't you want any more breakfast than toast? Mrs. Pepper would be happy to cook you eggs and bacon."

Robin smiled. "Is Mrs. Pepper your cook? What an appropriate name."

Nell smiled her small polite smile, and sipped her coffee.

Have I been snubbed? Or are jokes at breakfast not done?

After breakfast Nell led the way across to the stables where two lads were busy unsaddling the horses in from their morning exercises, and rubbing them down. She led a grey mare out into the yard, and said to Robin, "This is Morag, and she's a dear, and knows the way to Crickletop with her eyes closed. My chestnut is called Flame. Daddy gave him to me for my fifteenth birthday. He's a clever boy, aren't you, Flame."

She looked up and saw Iain walking across the yard toward them.

"Oh good, you've got Morag for Robin. She's gentle and sure footed. Have you ridden much, Robin?" he asked, as Robin was stroking Morag's forehead and getting acquainted with her.

"I've been taking riding lessons for nearly a year now," she replied.

Nell frowned slightly, two lines forming themselves between her eyes. "Did you think I'd give her Sir Joseph's stallion or something?"

Robin smiled brilliantly at Iain. "You're very kind to worry about me, but I am sure Nell will take good care of me."

Nell looked from one to the other, another line appearing. She lifted her chin slightly, turned on her heel, and strode back into the stables, calling for Henry to come and help Mrs. Lindsay saddle up Morag.

"Have we offended her, Iain?" Robin inquired in a low voice.

"Nell? She never takes offense. She's a good kid."

Nell, reappearing with Henry, overheard Iain's remarks, and in icy silence, saddled Flame.

A half hour later found them astride the horses and walking them down the drive to a trail that snaked down the hillside to the floor of the Upper Glen. It was a frosty October morning, with mist lying on the fields. Robin's mount was sure-footed and evidently knew the way. For a time they rode in silence, Nell's back uncompromisingly straight. Finally Robin hesitantly asked about their destination. Thawing slightly, Nell explained that it was about a forty-five minute ride to Crickletop where Mhoira and Fraser Smith lived. They had leased the land from Rannoch ten years ago and had been raising sheep ever since.

"Mhoira is an expert quilter too, and sometimes is in the village Saturdays selling her craft. She paints as well, and plays the Celtic harp." She paused, and then said, "You were saying that you've been riding only a year? You're doing very well."

Robin smiled. "Thanks. I've never ridden seriously up until last year. I fell off a horse once, though, years ago. Tim and I went to Puerto Vallarta, Mexico, on our honeymoon, and on one occasion we were having happy hour martinis with some people on the beach. A couple came by on horseback and we all were chatting and one of them asked if any of us wanted to take a ride. Well, I had ridden a few times before this, but never bareback! I thought that I could do it—you know, nice docile horses for the tourists, and a gentle walk on the sand. I didn't reckon with one of the horses taking off into a gallop. My mount did the same, and I just got shaken off! Tim told me later that he had never seen anything so funny in all his life. He said I just went 'bumpity bumpity' backwards, and fell off the end! The sand was soft, and I had a large bruise, though, on my back, but the biggest bruise was on my ego. People came running over to ask if I was all right, and I remember jumping up, and saying I was fine. Tim was laughing so hard he couldn't move. I guess I was squeezing my knees to keep astride, which made the horse move faster. I must say it was awhile before I ventured into riding again. Or martinis."

Nell smiled politely.

Here I am, babbling again. She'll think I'm a lush, or something, as well as an idiot.

"The trail is a little steep here," was all Nell said.

The trail led down the side of the hill to the valley floor. Glen Rannoch was not a large valley, perhaps less than a mile wide, and three or four miles in length. Robin found it hard to judge. The distillery could be seen more than a mile up the valley, across the fields of barley, and about another mile from where the River Rannoch came tumbling down from the mountainside. The river flowed through peat bogs, around the fields, and eventually down to the upper glen, past the village, through the lower glen, and eventually into the River Spey. Presently the trail led up the hillside and through groves of pine and birch, now turning gold. The trail was steep and narrow, and Nell led the way on Blaze, with Morag eagerly behind.

"There's a scenic view just up through the trees there," Nell said, stopping and dismounting. "We usually leave the horses here and hike up on our own. It won't take long, and it's worth the climb."

She led the way, and Robin had to scramble to keep up. They came out on a sort of ledge, and Robin found herself about two hundred feet above the valley floor. The mist had dispersed, and the sun was shining brightly. Across the valley was Rannoch Castle, shining in the morning sun, and looking like a picture in a fairy story. The golden fields, the trees in their autumn colors, and the sparkling steam winding through the valley all added to the beautiful scene.

"What a wonderful view! The Castle looks as though it has grown out of the rock itself!"

"In actual fact, the foundations on the cliff side are built out of the living rock. The cellars are always cool. Granddad has an extensive wine cellar; it's one of his hobbies..." She paused as Robin made a rueful face. "What's the matter?"

"It's only that I brought him some wine as a 'house gift'. I hope it measures up."

"Grandfather isn't a wine snob, far from it."

"I didn't mean that..." *Have I put my foot in my mouth again? Why is she so prickly?*

Nell was turning and trotting down the path to where they had left the horses, saying that Mhoira was expecting her. Robin decided to ignore Nell's prickles, and just talk naturally.

"Nell, thank you for showing me the view. It's very special."

Nell had already mounted, and she gazed down at Robin and gave her a little smile. "It's nicest this time of day, too. I always stop here."

Mhoira Smith stood at the door of the cottage in which she and her husband Fraser lived, and watched Nell emerge from the trees on Flame. There was a stranger with her, riding old Morag, and Mhoira wondered who it was. The cottage was built practically into the hillside; there was a large outbuilding nearby which was her studio, and further away were the barn and various other sheep farm buildings. She loved her mountain home. They were isolated, it was true, but managed most of the amenities of life. A nearby well brought clear, clean drinking water to her kitchen and bathroom taps, the lavatory was modern and connected to a septic field, and a generator installed by her clever husband made electricity most of the time. There were paraffin lamps and candles when the generator failed, and many was the time that she was grateful for her big, old-fashioned coal burning kitchen stove, especially in the winter. There was a huge fireplace in the sitting room, and in their bedroom a pot-bellied heater kept them warm at night during the cold months. Her studio was well insulated and heated by another stove that Fraser had installed when he built it for her. There was plenty of room for her quilting equipment and painting materials, and he had also installed a small toilet for her convenience. They were connected to Glen Rannoch by only the footpath and trail that Nell had ridden; the narrow metaled road fit only for a four-wheel drive led down to the highway by way of Glenmore, so it was a long way round to Glen Rannoch Village. A modern mobile phone kept them in touch with the outside world.

"Welcome!" she called, as the riders stopped and dismounted.

Introductions were made and Robin shook hands with her hostess. Robin saw a big, tall woman perhaps ten years her senior, long graying hair braided into one fat plait that hung down her back. She had rosy cheeks, snapping brown eyes, and a warm, engaging smile. She wore a loose tunic over faded and patched blue jeans, well-worn boots, and a headband of a blue material. Her voice was a deep as a man's, and her laugh matched her size.

"Fraser is expecting you; he'll be in from the byre soon for his cup o' tea. I know you'll want to discuss the *ceilidh* after dinner tonight. D'ye ken what a *ceilidh* is, lass?" she asked, turning to Robin.

Robin nodded. "A talent concert?"

COME FILL UP MY CUP

Mhoira's laughter boomed out. "You might say so, indeed you might. Nell has been planning this for a wee while and she says she expects everyone to contribute. What is your talent, Mistress Lindsay?"

Robin was quite taken aback. She looked at Nell a little reproachfully saying that this was the first she had heard of it.

"It's to be a surprise for Dad," she said. "I didn't think to ask you if you wanted to participate. Would you like to? I didn't mean to sound inhospitable."

Robin smiled, accepting the apology. "I love to sing, but my talent is small," she admitted. "I can play the piano a little, but what I can do is recite, and I know 'The Cremation of Sam McGee' by Robert Service. Have you ever heard of Robert Service? He was a Scot, and went to the Yukon during the gold rush and wrote some fantastic verse. We think it is uniquely Canadian, and I'd love to share it with you."

Mhoira clapped her hands appreciatively. "The very thing!" she exclaimed.

"It occurred to me on the way up that you ought to be in the village this morning at the market. I had completely forgotten that it was Autumn Fete today." Nell said to Robin by way of an explanation, "We have a market in the village every Saturday during the summer and on the first Saturday of the month all the artists and artisans join in and sell their creations. On the first Saturday in October it's the Autumn Fete, with games for the children, food kiosks, the fortuneteller, and all sorts of fun things. People come from all over to the Glen Rannoch Village Autumn Fete. Mhoira makes the most wonderful quilts, and she paints, too."

"I knew I'd be missing it today, because I hadn't finished framing your father's birthday present. Would you like a preview?"

Nell and Robin both eagerly nodded, so the three women got up and went out the door. Mhoira led the way across the yard to her studio. "Molly was happy to carry on and cope with any sales." She turned to Robin. "Molly Boone and I share a kiosk at these affairs, and we share the profits. She is a potter, and lives right in the village."

159

They entered Mhoira's studio, and she led them to her worktable, where she had almost completed the job of framing a large picture. She turned it over and held it up. "What do you think?"

Robin clapped her hands and exclaimed, "It's the view from the ledge! Robin took me there on our way here this morning. You have caught the light beautifully, Mrs. Smith."

Nell added her approval. "Dad will love it, Mhoira."

Mhoira looked pleased. "I just have to finish the backing and attach the wire for hanging. Oh, here's Fraser," she said as they emerged from the studio. "You have your conference, and I'll make the tea. A wee moment, Mistress Lindsay, I'd like to show you something." So saying, she turned back into her studio as Nell waved at Mhoira's husband and strode briskly across the yard to meet him. Robin followed Mhoira back inside and watched as she removed a cover from a large frame. She was in the midst of making a large quilt of a pattern Robin had never seen before, its colors mainly blue, white, and aubergine.

"I'm not nearly finished, but quilting by hand takes a long time. It will be reversible, and the sides quilted individually. Here is the reverse side." She held up another large piece of material, a gigantic white diagonal cross on a blue background.

"It's the Cross of St. Andrew!" exclaimed Robin. "And what a beautiful pattern for the other side. I have never seen it before."

"That's because I designed it myself," Mhoira said modestly. "It is to be Nell's Christmas present. Do you think she will like it?"

"You know her better than I, Mrs. Smith, but if she doesn't, she's crazy, and you know who you can give it to. It would look very well on my bed at home."

Mhoira smiled, re-covered the quilts, and turned off the light as she went out.

"Won't you please call me Mhoira?" she asked as they crossed the yard together. "Everyone does, even young Malcolm and Simon. Mrs. Smith sounds like a stranger."

"Only if you call me Robin. Mistress Lindsay sounds so formal."

"Tis done! You're a Canadian, Robin. A friend of Jamie's?"

Robin related the circumstances of their meeting, the trip to Iona to visit Celine, and James' invitation to stay. "Everyone has been enormously kind, especially Katharine and Mrs. Donaldson. What a grand lady *she* is."

"Has Nell been difficult?"

Robin considered this. "Not really. She probably is wondering just what James' and my relationship is. It would be normal for her to be uneasy and maybe jealous."

"I don't think Nell would be jealous of you and her father. She is always saying he needs a wife."

Robin blushed. "We're just friends."

Mhoira smiled, and opened the kitchen door and into a large sunny room redolent with the smell of freshly baked bread. She went to the stove, removed the kettle which had been boiling merrily and got out mugs and an enormous brown teapot. She made the tea, set it aside, and took oatcakes and the freshly made bread out of the pantry and arranged a plateful. Butter and cheese and jam were already on the large, well-scrubbed kitchen table.

Shortly thereafter Nell and Fraser came in, the latter going to the sink and washing his large, capable hands. He was a big man, lean and strong, and probably stood over six foot five. He had a big round face with the widest smile that Robin had ever seen, twinkling brown eyes, and was completely bald. Only the barest wisp of grey hair was present at the back of his head. His voice boomed even more loudly than Mhoira's, and when he laughed he threw his head backward and hooted. Conversation was not easy with the two of them together. Jokes flew back and forth, and gentle teasing and clever rejoinders. It was entertaining just to sit and listen. The love and affection between them was obvious. Robin thought that her Aunt Julia and Uncle Jean had a similar relationship—they also loved to tease each other in an affectionate way. Though it was usually done in French, and, in the early days, not as easy for Robin to follow.

It was nearly twelve o'clock before Nell and Robin tore themselves away. "Lunch is at one, and I've got a riding lesson at two. You'll be staying the night, tonight, Mhoira?"

"Only if we can sneak away before breakfast. We've got a lot to do this weekend. Don't let me forget to stock up on your eggs, butter and cheese."

"Aren't they a marvelous couple? I just love them all to bits," Nell remarked, as they guided their horses down the trail. She paused and then said, "I'm sorry if we put you on the spot about the *ceilidh*. You don't have to give a performance unless you really want to."

Robin laughed. "You had better let this 'wannabe' actor do her stuff," she replied firmly.

They reached the Castle at a quarter to the hour, and saw another car in the drive.

"It must be Aunt Sarah! Oh frabjous day, halloo hallay," Nell exclaimed. "The party is growing. Dad said that he'd been trying to get her to come. It's been ages since she's visited us."

Chapter 13

SARAH AND ROBIN

Sarah Donaldson had driven slowly and carefully through the village around noon. Glen Rannoch was thronged with people, the village square was filled with booths, tents and tables, and music was playing from loudspeakers. A bridal party was entering the Raven and Gate Pub, and she caught a glimpse of her niece Katharine amongst the wedding guests. Sarah had also forgotten that this was Autumn Fete day, and she wished that she had left a bit earlier to give herself some time to stop and wander about. There was always excellent art work to look at and perhaps buy, homemade jams and jellies and pickles, home baking, pottery and other fascinating goods for sale. Perhaps there would be some time after lunch to return and have tea and a good look around.

She left the village, geared down, and purred up the hill past the Kirk and Manse, past the Ranapurs' farm and up the winding road to the Upper Glen. At one of the sharp curves above the valley, she stopped the car, got out, and gazed down the hillside. She never failed to stop and think about her beloved sister-in-law who had met her death here over nine years ago. She loved her brother very much, but she had adored Fee, and the gap Fee had left had been enormous. She could only dimly imagine her brother's grief. The villagers and folk who lived in the neighboring countryside had expressed their sorrow by depositing flowers at the crash site. Robert had protested, and after the investigation was complete had all the debris removed, including the flowers. Still more had appeared, and someone erected a small white cross there as well. Sarah had tried to explain to Robert that this was their way of showing their grief and respect.

"Don't think you were the only one who loved Fee," she had said sharply. His face looked so bleak that she could have bitten her tongue. She gave him a long, wordless hug.

"Ah, Sarah, you are right," he murmured. It was not long after their conversation that Claire died so tragically, and the family was plunged once more into mourning.

Now she stood there and sighed. She hoped that Jamie had at last found someone to love. Perhaps it would be good for all of them. Presently she got back into her little car and continued her way up to her old home.

She was sitting in the garden enjoying the autumn sunshine and admiring the riot of flowers growing there, when she heard the sound of horses as they clattered into the cobbled stable yard, and it was a short time later that Robin and Nell came through the trees following the path from the front driveway. She was greeted affectionately and enthusiastically by her great-niece, and after they exchanged hugs and kisses, she took Robin's outstretched hand, and then dropped an affectionate kiss on her cheek.

"How nice to see you both. Jamie told me about the jaunt to Iona, and that you'd be here after your stay in Edinburgh. Nell, I forgot all about its being Autumn Fete in the village. Will there be time to go down after lunch?"

"I think so. I have a riding lesson, but I'll bet the boys would enjoy it, and maybe even Daddy too. Robin, you should go and see some of Mhoira's quilts and Molly's pottery. They are both fabulously talented. Did she show you some of her quilts when I was talking with Fraser about the *ceilidh* this morning?"

Robin grinned. "Yes," she answered.

Nell regarded her quizzically. "Hmm. It sounds mysterious. By the by, I should tell Janet that the Smiths will be staying the night, but no breakfast." She turned to go. "See you at lunch shortly."

Lunch was being served in the little dining room, as Janet and her staff were preparing the dining room for that evening's dinner party. It was a buffet meal, with hot soup, sliced meats for sandwiches, pickles and other condiments. Shortly after one o'clock James came in and with pleasure observed Robin, Sarah and Nell chattering away like old friends. Malcolm and Simon were waiting impatiently for their elders to arrive.

"I'm sorry to be late, but our meeting has gone on longer than I had thought, and we still have more business to cover, so I brought Mr. Macquarie in for lunch. I've warned him that it's an informal meal, but he said he didn't mind. He'll be here shortly with Father. Has Iain returned from Nairn?" Not waiting for an answer he stooped and kissed his aunt's proffered cheek, then casually touched Robin's shoulders. "How was the ride?" he asked.

"Which question do you want answered first?" asked Nell. "No, I haven't seen Iain since we returned, and the ride was fine."

"Nell showed me the marvelous view from the ledge across the valley, and I met the Smiths, who are perhaps the most extraordinary couple I've ever had the pleasure of meeting. She gave us this wonderful morning tea, and we toured her studio, and I was so impressed with her artistic talent."

At that moment the earl came in with a stranger; introductions were made, and they all sat down to lunch.

"We were hoping that you would have time to come down to the village with us to the Fete," said Sarah presently.

"We shouldn't be more than an hour or so," explained Mr. Macquarie. "I must apologize for keeping James so long on a Saturday, with guests, and I believe it's your birthday, too?"

James smiled and admitted that it was. "What if I should meet you at three or so down in the village. Don't forget that your mother wants you home by five at the latest," he reminded Simon. "Why don't you all go down and I'll see you later."

"I'll drop you in the village on my way out," offered Mr. Macquarie.

"I have a riding lesson in about half an hour; will you all please excuse me?" And Nell slipped away with an apologetic smile.

There were still many people thronging the village square when Sarah, Robin and the two boys arrived after lunch. Music was still blaring from loudspeakers; children were running about playing and enjoying the games. Sarah gave to the boys 2£ each, and they were off like rockets to the games of chance. The two women strolled about, looking the stalls over.

"Let's have our fortune told," suggested Sarah as they came upon a small tent with the sign reading, "Madame Zuleika—Fortunes Told". She went in first while Robin admired the pottery in a nearby stall. Sarah emerged a short while later, smiling ruefully. "A fool and her money are soon parted. What a load of rubbish. Your turn, Robin. You might as well spend 50p as badly as I have."

Robin grinned at her, ducked, and went into the tent. 'Madame Zuleika' sat at a round table, a crystal ball in the center, and a pack of cards at hand. She silently held out her hand, and Robin gave her the 50p and sat down opposite her. She dealt out the cards and said, "Ah! You have come from a long distance across the water." Robin was silent. It was an easy guess, if she had been listening to her speaking outside. She rattled on a lot of nonsense, and then she said suddenly, "The Jack of Spades signifies death." She looked up and her eyes, strangely unfocussed, seem to gaze over Robin's shoulder. "The man is dead." Robin was taken aback. How did she know about Tim? "You are in danger..."

"Oh come, now," began Robin.

The woman blinked and said, "What was I saying?"

"You said that I was in danger."

The fortune teller shivered. "Did I? I can't see any more. Here's your money back." She stood up suddenly, knocking over her chair. "Be careful or you will be hurt."

Robin stood and backed away, then turned and went out of the tent. Sarah was waiting for her, and said, "That was quick. Robin! Is something wrong?"

Robin shivered. "Only someone is walking over my grave. She spouted a lot of nonsense, then spoke of a man dying, and that I was in danger, then she gave me my money back. Extraordinary!"

Sarah looked up and said, "Here's Jamie! I shall go and find the boys."

James strode over to her, smiling, took her arm and tucked it into his. "Well, we haven't had much time together, have we? This has turned out to be a rather chaotic day. Are you all right, Robin?"

"Oh yes, now that you are here," she smiled at him, making his heart turn over. "The fortune teller was rather odd, and gave me the shivers."

He drew her closer to him and they walked in between the stalls and tables, absorbed in each other. He explained to her a little about what his meetings had been for, and she related in more detail her ride to Crickletop, and her delight in the view from the ledge. She had to bite her tongue not to mention the *ceilidh*, or the painting that he would receive later for his birthday, but she did mention the beautiful quilt that Mhoira was making for Nell.

"You must be pleased that Sarah could come. I think that she's glad you persuaded her."

"Good. It's about time that she came for a visit."

"Here's Sarah and the boys, should we be on our way? Oh, James, look at that picture! I simply must see how much..." She detached herself from him and went over to the booth. "It is one of Mhoira's." And she chatted with Molly Boone (for it was she) and presently came away with a small water color of the church on the hill. "I know exactly where I will hang it at home," she declared, as flushed and smiling, she bore her package away. James caught up with her, took the parcel from her and carried it, like a schoolboy carrying his sweetheart's books. Sarah and the boys followed, and she saw him take her hand.

"I think Daddy's sweet on her."

"Do you mind?"

"Gosh, no, Aunt Sarah. I think she's really cool. Simon likes her too, don't you Simon?"

"Brilliant. Uncle Jamie with a girlfriend. I think she's a super lady."

The rest of the afternoon and evening were magic. The day had started off uneasily, with Robin not sure of Nell's mood, but the girl had thawed, and Robin had enjoyed the ride up to Crickletop, and meeting the Smiths had been the first highlight. She was pleased to become better acquainted with Sarah, and when James came into the morning room and gently and lovingly touched her shoulder it had felt like a kiss, and warmth had suffused her whole body. She pushed away the memory of her curious encounter with the 'fortune teller' and thought only their walk at the fair. Later in the afternoon he gave her a tour of the house. He showed her the drawing room, and she was enchanted with the magnificent portrait of his mother over the mantelpiece, the elegant furnishings, and the carved moldings.

"We'll have our drinks in here at seven," he told her. "Now let's go upstairs and I'll show you my father's suite of rooms, which he shares with me. My mother decorated the rooms, and she was always very proud of the results." Robin had brought the earl the wine she had bought for him, and he was sincerely appreciative, and put them aside to add to his cellar.

Later Malcolm showed her the playroom and his bedroom. "Don't you mind being upstairs all on your own?" she asked him.

"Och, no, it's like having my own castle. At school there are four of us in the dorm, so it's super being all by myself. That's where my parents used to have their rooms," he added, indicating the closed double doors across the hall in the other wing. "Nobody goes there now. My mother died when I was a baby, so Daddy moved in with Grandfather downstairs. Nell never comes up here either. Her room was next to mine." He led her through the playroom, opened the door to Nell's old room and Robin peeked inside. It was decorated with equestrian wallpaper, a white comforter on the bed, bedside lamps in the shape of horses, rag rugs on the faded hardwood floor. She closed the door, feeling that she was intruding, but then realized that there was nothing of Nell there now. It had been many years since she had slept in that room.

At six o'clock everybody was busy getting dressed. Robin didn't have to choose her outfit, as she had only one, a long black skirt and top, gold jewelry, and low heeled black shoes. She looked at herself in the mirror as she put on her earrings, and saw a glowing face smiling back at her.

You'd think I was sixteen, and getting ready for my first date. Oh Tim, am I being disloyal?

The guests arrived all around seven o'clock. Besides the Perrys and the Smiths, there was a youngish couple who was the local doctor and his wife, Hugh and Margaret Rennie. Margaret gravely presented James with a gift, which joined the others on a table in the drawing room. He would open them after dinner with liqueurs and coffee. Everyone was in the drawing room sipping drinks of their choice when the last people to arrive were announced. James and his father, resplendent in their highland regalia, were still in the hall greeting. Robin was chatting with Mrs. Rennie, when voices were heard from the hall.

"Oh, it must be the Porters," said Margaret, cocking an ear.

"Who are they?"

"Sir Joseph and Lady Porter. They're Sassanachs, but have come to live near Carbridge. They bought a beautiful manor house there a few years ago. They board horses here, I believe. They have a daughter, Bernice. I think I hear her voice, too."

Robin happened to be watching Nell's face when the newcomers arrived, and she saw her eyes widen, and her face grow pale. Bernice Porter was a tall, slim, sophisticated young woman in her late twenties, perfectly groomed and coiffed. When she entered the drawing room, she made a beeline for Iain. Her accent was very upper class English and she sipped a martini, completely monopolizing the young man. Nell straightened up, her lips in a firm line, and went from group to group inquiring if their drinks needed replenishment. She busied herself going to and fro from the library until dinner was announced.

The party was a great success. Janet and Mrs. Pepper outdid themselves. The soup, a sherry consommé, was delicious. The earl carved the lamb expertly, and the vegetables, fresh from the garden, were mouthwatering. Dessert was a homemade lemon ice, with a magnificent birthday cake complete with forty-five candles. "Happy Birthday" was sung as James blew out the candles, and later cheese and biscuits were passed. During coffee and liqueurs in the drawing room James opened his presents. He smiled broadly and exclaimed with pleasure when he opened Mhoira's painting, and sent a smile of thanks to Robin when he saw the book she had given him. Then Fraser Smith appeared out in the hall playing the bagpipes, and piped everyone up the stairs to the Gallery, where chairs had been arranged for the *ceilidh*. It was a merry evening, indeed, and Robin found herself the center of attention after her recital of 'The Cremation of Sam McGee'. Nell and Malcolm sang a duet, with Katharine at the piano, Mhoira played the harp, and Robin joined in with singing 'Will Ye No' Come Back Again?' and 'Auld Lang Syne' to wind up the evening. It was midnight before the last guests left, and the family and house guests could creep off to bed, thoroughly tired out.

Robin lay in bed going over all the events of the evening in her mind. She thought about Iain and Bernice, who had flirted with him all the evening, and of Nell's tight face. If Nell was in love with her cousin Iain, it explained some of her behavior. *I was in love when I was seventeen,* she thought. And if Iain thought of her only as a younger sister, or worse, a niece, no wonder she was prickly at times. Robin decided to try and draw her out, and see if she could be of any help. She then lingered on the memory of James taking her by the hand, and leading her into the darkened library, and there kissing her lovingly. She had gasped with delight as her body responded to his loving caresses. If he had asked then and there to share her bed she would have gladly agreed. But he only held her, and then silently looked into her face, brushing her hair gently back. In the dim light from the corridor she could see his face searching hers. She then reached up and kissed him gently on the lips. Later she realized that not a word had passed between them. It had not been necessary.

True to their word, Mhoira and Fraser slipped away quietly before breakfast, so there was just Robin, Commander Lee, Sarah and the family for the morning meal. Mhoira's picture was a complete success, of course, and James had it hanging in the hall before breakfast. Afterwards everyone trooped down to the village to church, and Robin, her heart full to the brim with happiness, joined in the singing and the prayers.

After the service Iain said that he'd go down to the pub and get the Sunday paper, while the Commander made noises about packing his things and being on his way. "I've been here for over a week," he remarked as they piled into the various cars to return to the Castle. "It's time I went home." When Robin inquired where home was, the Commander stated that he lived just outside Edinburgh. "Near a golf course," he added with a smile.

Robin sat in front with James' father, and he asked her where she had bought the book on Iona. "Did you know that it's a first edition?" he asked. Robin told him that she had found it in a second hand shop in Nairn, tucked away with a group of reference books in an old bookcase. She had paid twenty pounds for it, because it was leather bound. The earl sighed and said that she had got a bargain, and that he'd get an expert in to appraise it, but he expected it was worth twenty times that. Robin gasped and asked if she should go back to the shop.

"No, lassie; you bought it in good faith, and he sold it in ignorance. If you planned to resell it, that might be a different story, but I think that Jamie intends to keep it." This he said with a sideways glance and a twinkle in his eye. Robin blushed and thought to herself, *I love this man, too. He's the father I never had.*

Chapter 14

ROBIN AND NELL

During lunch, James announced that he was taking Robin for a drive that afternoon, but they'd be back in plenty of time to drive Malcolm and Simon back to school.

"Sarah, you'll be staying a few days more?"

"Just tonight, Jamie, lad, and then I must be off. I've enjoyed being back at Rannoch. It's still my old home. Nell and I will do something together this afternoon. I don't see her as often as I would like," she said, smiling at her great-niece.

Nell wandered into the library to read the paper, and at that moment the telephone rang, and James was called to take it in his father's study. Robin followed Nell, and said to her as they sat down, "I thought you did a marvelous hosting job last night. It was a wonderful party—everything went smoothly, and the *ceilidh* was entertaining and fun."

Nell nodded politely and thanked her. Robin persisted. "Margaret Rennie told me that the Porters are fairly new here." Nell looked up sharply. "You know," Robin said, laughing, "after meeting him a song went round and round in my brain all evening. 'Sir Joseph Porter' is a character in *HMS Pinafore*, do you know it?" Nell shook her head, frowning. "It's a comic opera by Gilbert and Sullivan, quite a satire on late Victorian politics and the Navy."

"Oh yes, I've heard of them." She murmured, turning over the pages of the newspaper idly.

"There's one song, 'When I was a Lad', when he sings about becoming 'ruler of the Queen's Navee', but the one that I kept hearing is sung near the beginning when he's coming aboard the ship. Offstage the chorus sings, 'tump de tump de tump over the sea, (I forget the words) Comes Sir Joseph Porter KCB,' All the ladies' chorus are his 'sisters and his cousins and his aunts, His sisters and his cousins that he reckons by the dozens, and his aunts!' I had the greatest difficulty not to ask him about them." She smiled ruefully at Nell. "You probably haven't the least idea of what I'm talking about. It just amused me, that's all. Is his daughter a friend of Iain's?" she asked carelessly.

If Nell felt like jumping up and running out of the room, she was too well brought up to do so. She merely gazed at Robin, and to her dismay her eyes filled with tears. Robin said sympathetically, "She did monopolize him, didn't she."

"Do you think she's pretty?" Nell asked, struggling not to let her eyes overflow.

"In a hard, plastic way, I guess she is."

"They're very rich."

"Do you think Iain's interested in her?"

Nell didn't answer, but it was clear that she was afraid of that very situation.

"Nell, Iain has known you since you were a baby. I'm sure he remembers when you were born. He probably thinks of you as a dearly loved younger sister."

Nell nodded, and plunged into confession. "Oh Mrs. Lindsay, I've loved him ever since I can remember. He's never seemed to have a serious girlfriend, and I hoped.....It's not just a crush, you know."

"I wasn't about to suggest that. Actually, I think you'd suit each other very well. But you can't make it happen. All you can do is be yourself, and hope that he hasn't fallen for Miss Porter."

"I wish I was ten years older, and sophisticated. He might notice me then," she said bitterly.

"You wouldn't be you, would you? Maybe what you need is a new hairdo and a terribly feminine outfit." Robin sat back and regarded Nell in a friendly way. "The dress you wore last night is very pretty, but it's definitely a teenager's dress. Would you like to go shopping one day?"

Nell hesitated, and Robin hoped that she hadn't said too much. "Think about it. And Nell," she added, as she picked up the paper, "What you've said to me will go no further, you can be sure of that." She glanced at her watch. "Your father's telephone call is certainly a long one."

She opened the paper and the headline immediately caught her eye: MURRAY PARK BODY IDENTIFIED. MYSTERY WOMAN SOUGHT. There was a sudden tightening in her chest as she began to read the story. And then, with mounting horror, said, "Oh my God. Oh my God."

Nell looked up in surprise and saw Mrs. Lindsay, her face white as a sheet and round-eyed with horror, struggle to her feet, drop the paper, then as her legs buckled, collapse into the cushions.

"Mrs. Lindsay, Mrs. Lindsay! What's the matter? Aunt Sarah, Aunt Sarah! Help me with Mrs. Lindsay!"

Sarah had just entered the library in search of her niece, to find her bending over Robin, holding her head down between her knees.

To Robin, Nell's voice seemed to come from a long way off, and there was a buzzing sound in her ears. *Good grief, I think I'm going to faint!* Then she felt Nell's hands on her shoulders firmly putting her head down. Her vision cleared and a moment later Sarah was there with an arm around her. She struggled to sit up.

"I'm all right..."

"I'll get Jamie," said Sarah firmly, and hurried out of the room.

"Mrs. Lindsay, it was something in the paper."

Robin nodded. "So stupid of me...the man killed in St. Andrew's...I knew him."

"Dear God!" Nell picked up the paper and found the article as her father strode in with Sarah at his heels. "Daddy, this story in the paper—Mrs. Lindsay knows him."

174

James sat down next to Robin and put his arms around her. "It's all right, Robin. Let me see the paper, Nell."

James read in consternation: "St. Andrew's. Police have released the name of the man found dead in Murray Park Wednesday morning. He has been identified as Charles Morrison; age fifty-two, of Vancouver, Canada, by Mr. John Eden, of the same city. Mr. Morrison and Mr. Eden were on a golfing holiday, and their wives were to join them yesterday. He was last seen by Mr. Eden Tuesday afternoon, who said that Mr. Morrison had met a woman, and was taking her out to dinner. When asked why he hadn't reported him missing until Thursday, Mr. Eden said he hadn't wanted to 'spoil Charlie's fun.' Death was caused by blows from a blunt instrument, and police think that his face was battered after death, perhaps to hide his identity. Nothing was found in his pockets except a Visa receipt from the Peat Inn, an upscale restaurant outside of the city, and the hired car he was driving was found abandoned several miles away. Police are looking for the woman to aid them in their inquiries. She is described by the restaurant's staff as about forty-five, medium height, with curly brown hair. The waiter remembered the couple because Mr. Morrison had evidently been drinking heavily, and was very rude. They left the restaurant about nine o'clock, and she has not been seen since. Mrs. Georgia Morrison is, of course, devastated, and is waiting for police to release the body of her husband."

James got up, went over to the bar, and poured a stiff brandy. "Drink this, Robin," he said gently, "you've had a nasty shock."

Robin swallowed the brandy, coughed, but her color was returning. "James, he's dead! Who would do a thing like that?"

Sarah and Nell were looking at her in distress, obviously trying not to ask awkward questions. Robin felt an explanation was needed, and said slowly, "Charlie Morrison was a fellow pilot of my husband's, and I ran into him, quite unexpectedly, in St. Andrew's on Tuesday. Goodness, it seems like years ago. I agreed to go out to dinner with him. As the article says, he was drinking heavily, and he was very rude. In fact, he was horrible to me. I finally had to get out of the car and go back to my hotel on my own. It was rather upsetting, so I decided to cut short my visit to St. Andrew's, and I left the next morning. This is the first I've heard about it........No, actually there was an article in the paper here, Thursday or Friday's, I think, very short, about a body found in Murray Park. I remember thinking that was where...." She stopped. "That was where I last saw him." she finished.

"How horrible for you!" said Nell sympathetically. Sarah glanced at James and wondered if he had heard the story before now. He had asked no questions, and Robin obviously had omitted many details. Sarah could guess what had happened, watching Robin tell her story. Her voice was still shaky, and her eyes, always expressive, mirrored her feelings as she remembered Tuesday evening.

James said firmly, "I think we had better call St. Andrew's police. If they want you to go down there, I will take you, Robin." He bent down and took her hand. "Do you understand? I will be with you. I won't leave you. Everything will be all right."

She looked up at him, and nodded. Her face, so pale a few minutes before, now was flooded with color. "Thank you, James," she whispered.

James went out, and Sarah followed him. "I'll get someone to make us some tea. Robin will be tipsy if she has another brandy. Nell, will you stay here with Robin?"

Nell folded up the paper and put it on the table. She sat down beside Robin again and took her hand. Robin was leaning back against the cushions with her eyes closed, her face pale again. "Mrs. Lindsay, I'm so sorry," she began.

Robin opened her eyes and regarded the girl with affection. "You had better start calling me Robin. You should be on a first name basis with someone whose head you have just shoved down between her knees, don't you think?"

Nell squeezed her hand. "I'm sorry I was so horrid to you yesterday."

Robin opened her eyes again, sat up and smiled at her. "You weren't horrid, Nell. You were just....terribly correct."

"I was very upset with Iain, and I took it out on you. The other day he persuaded me to spend some time with Bernice Porter. She wanted to see around the estate, and Friday was the only day she was available—Iain thought she was going away with her parents on Saturday, but I guess he was mistaken, as they all turned up at the party. I didn't even know that they were invited! Bernice didn't let on at all.....we rode around the property, and all she could think about was why Iain wasn't in line for the title—'after all, he's older than Malcolm'", imitating Bernice's posh English accent. "I had to explain that Iain's a distant cousin, and Malcolm is the grandson of the earl. I couldn't believe anyone could be so ignorant. If she's only interested in a title, she'll be sadly disappointed," Nell finished, face flushed with indignation. Robin heard the hurt in the voice of the usually so reserved girl.

"I thought you were very dignified at the party—nobody noticed that you were upset."

Nell covered her face with her hands. "I'd be so embarrassed if he knew..."

"I don't know what advice to give you except to repeat: be yourself."

"Does Deborah have a boyfriend?"

"She tells me she isn't ready for a commitment. She has lots of friends, one or two of them boys."

"It's hard, when you've known forever where your heart is," declared Nell, "and he thinks of you as a 'good kid'. Oh, I heard that remark he made Saturday morning." She was flushed again.

"Well, at least he didn't call you an ugly brat," teased Robin.

Nell smiled her little smile. "Maybe I'd prefer that."

Robin risked giving the girl a small squeeze. Nell smiled again, and said, "Can I ask you a personal question?" When Robin nodded, Nell said slowly, "Are you in love with Dad?"

"Oh Nell, I think so! It's difficult, because it's only been three years since Tim died, and I loved my husband very much, and I guess I feel as though I shouldn't be feeling this way..."

"Daddy is *very* fond of you," she stated firmly. "I've never seen him so, so, so....lighthearted, I guess is the word I want."

"Do you remember your mother?"

"Funnily enough, Iain asked me that very question last week. I don't remember anything at all about her! I wasn't even eight years old when she died. Daddy never talks about her."

"Do you have a picture of her?"

"No, I don't. That's weird, isn't it? I've never thought about it before. I never go upstairs to the second floor anymore. I slept up there when I was a kid, but that was years ago. There's a painting of her somewhere, I remember Janet telling me a long time ago, but I've never asked Dad about it. It is probably in the upstairs flat, but Janet keeps it locked. I think she goes in and cleans it sometimes, but I haven't been in there since...Actually I went up there last week after Iain asked me what I remembered of my mother, but the door was locked..." Nell went on to describe the curious reaction she had had when she approached the flat. Robin wondered if there weren't some suppressed memories here. She started to ask her about her mother's death, but stopped when she saw Nell's expression.

"What is it, Nell?"

"I just had a flash of memory. You know how sometimes a song or a smell will bring back a memory? It's gone, now."

"What was it?"

"I'm not sure. Something to do with the picture, I think."

At that moment, Sarah came in with a tray of tea and four cups. "Jamie is coming; I think he has talked to St. Andrew's."

She poured out the tea, hot and strong, and passed it to Nell and Robin as James came in. He sat down and said to Robin, "They're going to send the investigating officer up tomorrow, Chief Detective Inspector something. I didn't catch his name. He thanked us for letting them know, and said he'd be here after lunch, about half past one. I also put in a call to my solicitor in Inverness, and he asked if you would like him to be present tomorrow."

Robin looked startled. "Oh, James, I don't know...do you think it's necessary?"

"It might be a good idea. I wouldn't let the officer browbeat you or anything, but George thought it might be helpful if he were there. I could invite him for lunch, and you could tell him your story, and he would advise you how to tell the officer."

Robin nodded. "Yes, I agree with you. Thank you, James."

Sarah was looking troubled. "I've been planning on going home tomorrow, James; I feel a bit of a brute, though, abandoning you. Probably fewer people hanging about would make Robin more comfortable."

"Sarah, you've been so kind, I wish you would stay, you're so sensible. But I understand if you feel you must get home. We'll let you know what happens, won't we, James."

James nodded. "I'll go and phone George back, and then I suppose we must think of returning those two rascals to school. We'll get that drive in after all, Robin. They're both down at the Manse, I guess. I'll call Katharine, too. About the boys, I mean," he added.

"I don't mind Katharine knowing about this. It's bound to be in the papers, too. Oh James, I'm so sorry to be causing you all this trouble."

Right in front of a delighted Sarah and Nell, he gathered her into his arms and said into her hair, "Don't apologize, darling. I'm proud to be your white knight."

Robin blushed to the roots of that hair, but she didn't pull away. Presently James released her, and went out to the telephone. She glanced at the two others, who were beaming at her happily. Together, they both went to her and put their arms about her, enfolding her in a warm embrace.

Robin was very grateful the next day for the advice of James' solicitor, George Sinclair. He was a man of middle age, balding, with a dry twinkle behind his horn-rimmed glasses. There was just the five of them for lunch, as Sarah had departed soon after breakfast. She had hugged Robin and wished her well, and Robin had promised to telephone as soon as there was news. To Nell she gave a fierce embrace and whispered that Robin needed lots of female support as well, and she knew that Nell would give it. Nell nodded and whispered back, "Oh yes, Aunt Sarah! I do like her, don't you?" Sarah smiled and nodded her agreement, and had got into her little car and had driven away.

Nothing but pleasantries was exchanged over lunch, and when coffee was served, Mr. Sinclair suggested that he and Robin should take their cups into the library and there they would talk. Robin was a little nervous, but soon she was put at her ease by the solicitor's pleasant manner. He asked her first to tell him about herself, and Robin, at first feeling she was on the witness stand, gave him a rough sketch of her life. He inserted a question here and there, and it wasn't long before Robin was telling him about her marriage and her children. ("Twins," he remarked. "How wonderful for you.") She went on to tell him what they were doing, Deborah studying massage and physiotherapy, and Denis in pre-med. "Deborah has been talking about eventually setting up a joint practice together," she added. She then went on to tell him about her husband's death, her move to the smaller city, and her trip to Scotland. She paused, and then took a deep breath.

"Now I suppose we come to St. Andrew's."

"First tell me how you and James met," he suggested.

Robin smiled at the memory. "It's quite simple. I got lost in a raging thunderstorm, and my car got stuck at the bottom of Sarah Donaldson's steps. James was visiting his aunt, and they took pity on me and let me in."

"Sanctuary. Marvelous Highland hospitality."

"Yes. It was sanctuary indeed."

There was a silence, but it was a comfortable one. "Now tell me about your meeting with Mr. Morrison. You knew him from home?"

"Yes. He flew for Canadian Pacific Airlines, too. He and Tim played golf together sometimes, and I know his wife fairly well."

"Were you close friends, then, the four of you?"

"Well, not really. Tim knew him well as they worked together, and flew the same routes at times, so they would be away at the same time. We would meet them at parties and such, but I don't think we ever were at each other's home for dinner or anything like that."

"More a business relationship, as far as you were concerned."

"They were very kind to me after Tim died."

"Did you like Mr. Morrison?"

Robin considered this. "I guess I didn't like or dislike him," she confessed. "He was a bit conceited, I thought. He was very good looking, and he knew it. He had never made advances at me before, if that's what you mean."

"Now tell me what happened."

Robin drew in a deep breath. Her heart was beating a bit faster, and her color ebbed, leaving her cheeks pale, and then rushed back. She could feel her cheeks burning as she remembered Monday evening. She began with the unexpected meeting in the woolen mill, and related the events in a low voice which shook at times. She described his boorish behavior in the restaurant, and then the drive back, culminating in his appalling behavior in the park.

"I hadn't been frightened up to then," she said. "I was only angry and disgusted that he wouldn't take no for an answer. Then when he grabbed me in the car park, I was terrified. I thought he was going to rape me."

"So you grabbed one of his golf clubs and hit him over the head," Mr. Sinclair said.

"Whaat! Good grief, no!" She stared at him in consternation. "Do you think that?"

"I'm sure the police are going to ask you that. To answer your question," he said, taking off his spectacles and polishing them furiously, "No. I don't know what the murder weapon was, and I don't believe you killed him." He put his glasses back on and regarded her owlishly. "Have you told me everything?"

Robin hesitated. "I only left out some of the appalling things he said about me and Tim. I haven't told anybody—he made me feel so...soiled." She went on and repeated Charlie's insinuations about Tim and herself. "When I got back to my hotel, ("Which was?" "Aslar House",) I decided I didn't want to stay another day, so I checked out that night and left early the next morning. I thought maybe he'd be coming round to hassle me some more, and I couldn't bear the thought of even laying eyes on him, let alone hearing more abuse or even a soppy apology. I just ran away, I guess."

"The police will want to know what time you left the restaurant, and when you saw him last, and what time you got back to the hotel."

"There wasn't anybody at reception when I got in. I was glad at the time, because I was so upset. It must have been about a half hour later that I came down and settled my bill. Maybe longer. I'm not sure."

"How did you get away from him, Mrs. Lindsay?"

She shuddered at the memory. "I kicked him in the shins and, er, bit his tongue."

Mr. Sinclair blinked. "Most resourceful, Mrs. Lindsay."

And Robin burst out into rather hysterical laughter. Then she sobered. "I looked back as I was running up the street, and he was getting to his feet. He had tripped, you see, as he came after me, and had fallen. Do you think someone was nearby and took advantage of the situation?"

"I think that's what had to have occurred. He was robbed, and the car stolen. Of course, the police might say that you killed him, and made it look as if it were a robbery."

"But I wouldn't have had time to drive the car out of town and get back to the hotel."

"I know that, and I am sure that when they interview the hotel staff, you will be vindicated. You see, you likely are their only suspect at the moment."

Robin shook her head in wonder. "I can't believe it. I still can't believe it. I think I shall have to go to St. Andrew's and see Georgia—Mrs. Morrison. She must still be in shock."

Mr. Sinclair rose to his feet said, "You don't have to make that decision yet. They may want you to go and testify at an inquiry, and you can be sure that James and I will be by your side if that occurs."

There was a tap on the door, and Nell put her head in. "The policeman's come!" she said in a low voice. "Dad has taken him into Grandfather's study."

"Now come along and answer the man's questions. You needn't volunteer those dreadful insults, unless he specifically asks you for chapter and verse," he added.

Chapter 15

NELL 1996

Robin and Mr. Sinclair had been in the library for about fifteen minutes when a black car came into the drive and stopped on the other side of the circular lawn and garden. A tall man in a dark overcoat got out and came across the drive toward the front door. His driver, dressed in similar fashion, followed him. Nell was standing in the dining room looking out the window. She had helped Janet clear the table, and had put the placemats away in the built in linen drawers, and had carefully dusted the table's shining surface, then replaced the fresh flower arrangement in the center. She searched a small drawer in the pantry, found scissors and cut off several dead blooms, then added a little water. She then went to the telephone and called Mrs. Burden, whose son Jemmie was due to have another riding lesson after school, and canceled it. Something had come up, she told Jemmie's mother in a steady voice, and she would not be available today. She rescheduled it for the same time tomorrow. She also asked Mrs. Burden to discuss with her son as to whether he really wanted these lessons. Jemmie didn't seem to take the lessons very seriously, she added, and perhaps they were wasting his time and her money. She hung up quietly on a startled Mrs. Burden, and went to the window to await the policeman.

When the doorbell sounded, Janet answered the door, and she could hear their voices in the hall. Her father, she knew, had gone upstairs to explain the situation more fully to Grandfather, so she went out of the dining room and into the big front hall. The two men were taking off their hats and overcoats, and Janet was taking them to the cloakroom.

"How do you do," she said. "I'm Nell Maclachlan. My father will be down directly."

The tall policeman came over and shook her hand. "I'm Chief Detective-Inspector Marshall, and this is Sergeant Coverly. He smiled down at her. You don't remember me, do you, Miss Nell. I was here nine or so years ago. Twice. You were quite small."

Nell inexplicably felt a chill. ('*I do not like you, Dr Fell, The reason why I cannot tell.*')

"I was just plain Detective then. You could have knocked me down with a feather when the call came through from here. I used to be in Inverness, you see."

Nell said hurriedly, "I'll go up and tell Daddy that you're here," and she turned and trotted up the wide staircase to the first floor. There was an unexplained tightness in her chest. Her breath came in little gasps, and her mouth was dry as she turned and pushed open the double doors leading to her Grandfather's suite of rooms. Her father and grandfather were seated by the sitting room fire, and were having a drink.

"Daddy, they're here," she said. "It's a Detective Inspector Marshall. He says he knows us, that he's been here before." Her eyes were wide and distressed.

James jumped to his feet. "Does he, by God," he exclaimed. Her grandfather's face had turned a pasty white and in a second looked years older. Her father's face was grim. "Did he say why he had been here?"

"No," said a bewildered Nell. "Dad! Was it when my mother and Granny Fee died?"

James put his arm around her. "Yes, my dear. You don't remember your Grandmother's accident, do you? The police always come when there's an accident."

"I just remember her funeral, I think. Or maybe it was my mother's. I remember Aunt Eleanor coming, because of all the letters she had written me, even when I was a baby."

"That would have been your mother's," James said gently. "Now let's go downstairs. I'll take the gentlemen into your grandfather's study, is that all right, Dad? Nell, will you please go to the library and tell Mr. Sinclair and Robin that, and then come back up and keep your grandfather company."

She followed her father slowly down the stairs, a little calmer and deep in thought. After the three men had disappeared down the corridor, she went and tapped on the library door. Robin emerged from her conference with Mr. Sinclair looking more like her old self.

"Dad has taken them to Grandfather's study," Nell said, and watched them go down to the end of the corridor by the garden door. She turned, and instead of going back upstairs, she went quietly down the opposite corridor towards the kitchen. The only sound that emerged was that of the dishwasher. Janet was probably busy in her rooms and Monday was Mrs. Pepper's day off. She went into the utility room where there was a row of keys hanging, and selected one. Then she hurried up two flights up the back stairs, and breath coming quickly again, went into the wing where her old bedroom was.

She wasn't sure when she'd been there before she came up last week, but she had refused to sleep up there after her mother had died. Nanny had tried to persuade her, and assured her that she would be there, but Nell had been adamant. After a while it was just accepted that Nell would have the small guest room on the floor below. The room next door had been converted into a place where she could bring her friends, as neither the library nor the drawing room was appropriate for schoolchildren. Now this small room was her office, where she kept her files and notes on the horses and her students.

She paused in front of her old room, where Robin had stood and peeked in a few days ago. As Robin had noticed, it could have belonged to anyone, there was nothing remaining of the small girl that had been Nell. She opened the door to the old nursery, the room that Malcolm called the playroom. It was filled with his personality;

his posters were on the walls, his Lionel train laid out on its tracks, his books in the bookcase. She paused and studied a few of the titles. Here was Nell's old set of 'Swallows and Amazons' and her row of Enid Blyton adventure stories. There was the set of 'The Tales of Narnia' that she had given him for Christmas last year. Aunt Eleanor had sent him some of the Thornton W. Burgess animal books from America. Nell thought that they were funny and old-fashioned, but Malcolm was enchanted with them. The fireplace still seemed to be the center of the room, and the shabby rocking chair was still nearby. She remembered Nanny cuddling a very small Malcolm in it; he couldn't have been more than a year old. Well, she obviously had come upstairs once or twice.

She went out of the playroom and onto the landing of the main stairs. She stood for a moment and listened. The house was completely silent. The tightness in her chest returned. Was she going to have another attack of nausea? The double doors, similar to those that led to her grandfather's suite of rooms on the floor below were tightly closed. She tried the knob. It was locked. She took a deep breath and put the key in the lock, and turned it. It moved smoothly and silently. She hesitated for a moment, and then pushed open the door.

The air that met her was stale. She knew that Janet cleaned here regularly, and probably aired out the rooms, but still the atmosphere was fusty. She went to the windows and raised the Roman shades. Sunshine streamed in, and she looked around. Her mother had redecorated these rooms. She remembered the workmen coming and putting up the drapes, and her mother hovering anxiously to make sure they did it right.

"I remember that!" she said aloud. Her mother's room had been the first room on the right of the wide corridor that led from the sitting room. There was a small kitchen opposite, and a large bathroom between her mother's room, and the room that was her father's study. Funny! If anyone had asked her before this to describe her parents' suite of rooms, she couldn't have told them anything. Now, just standing here, she knew which room was which.

She shivered and a memory flashed back to her.

"Nell, isn't Mummy up yet?"

"No, Daddy. Malcolm won't stop crying, and Mummy was cross with Nanny last night, and Nanny's in a high dungeon."

"Dudgeon, Nell. I'll get Nanny to wake her."

"I'll do it, Daddy!"

"All right, Pumpkin."

Running up the stairs, past Grandma and Grandfather's double doors and the doors to the Gallery with its rows of fascinating portraits and curious furniture, up the second flight to the nursery floor, through the polished doors into her parents' sitting room...What was that smell? Mummy!

Nell opened her eyes and found herself standing in the open doorway of her mother's bedroom. She was staring into the past and her mouth was wide open in a silent scream.

Chapter 16

NELL 1986-87

The world that was seven-year old Nell Maclachlan's was filled with all sorts of people who were absolutely essential to her.

There was comfortable Nanny, who had been making noises about retiring. "Now that Nell is in school, nobody needs me."

"Nanny, that's not so! Why, we couldn't get along without you!" Nanny was flattered at her words, for hadn't the Good Book had said something about truth and the mouths of babes, though Nell certainly wasn't a babe anymore. She had been in school for a whole year now, and was growing like a weed.

Nanny was very old, of course. She had been Daddy and Aunt Katharine's Nanny when they were wee bairns. She had rosy cheeks that were soft as velvet, and eyes that were black and sparkling. Her hair was getting grey. Nell told her seriously that she could get a bottle and make her hair dark again. Nanny was quite amused and told her that God had made her that way, and who was she to question Him? Besides, it wasn't right to try and be something you weren't.

"Mummy says it gives her hair a body. How can hair have a body, Nanny?"

"Now, you just run along and forget about hair and bottles, young miss. *I'm* quite satisfied with my hair the way it is. Though there are some that aren't but should be," she muttered darkly as Nell "ran along."

Mary Rose was Mummy's maid, and sometimes she sat with Nell when Mummy and Daddy went out, and Nanny wasn't there. Nanny visited her sister in Lossiemouth occasionally, especially when the sister was "no' so grand", and she would stay the night with her. She was even older than Nanny, and Nell had heard Daddy say that Mrs. Ross (that was Nanny's sister) had been enjoying poor health for years. Lossiemouth was away over at the seaside. Nell loved the name 'Lossiemouth'. To her it was a huge dragon with an even bigger mouth. Sometimes she thought it would swallow up Nanny, and Nell would never see her again. Daddy had explained that the Lossie was a river, and the mouth was where the river flowed into the sea, hence the village's name. It made sense when Daddy explained things, and now that she was seven, she knew that her dragon was only a fancy. But sometimes at night she would still imagine the dragon and its gigantic mouth open, ready for the unaware. Nell would shiver with delight and pull the bedclothes around her. That old dragon would never get her!

Mary Rose was very pretty, and she confided to Nell that she wasn't going to work here forever. "I've been here since before you were born. My, you were a tiny wee thing. Came early, you did."

"What will you do if you leave us, Mary Rose?" asked Nell in a worried tone. She didn't like change at all. (She had cried all night when they had to cut down a dead tree in the paddock. "It's got every right to be there," she had sobbed. "And what will the owl do without his house?")

Mary Rose said, "One day I'm going to run a hotel." Nell knew that Rose was her surname, because Mrs. Rose down in the village was her mother. But she could never say 'Mary' without tacking on the 'Rose'.

Granny Fee was Daddy's mother, and she had taught Nell to ride a pony when she was small. In fact Nell couldn't remember not being able to ride her pony. Nell knew that Mummy didn't like her riding, but Daddy had said it was all right, and Nell just loved the feeling when her pony galloped, and the wind sang in her ears and whipped her hair back. Her pony's name was Delbert. When Granny asked her where on earth she had heard that name, Nell shrugged and said she didn't know. It was simply Delbert's name. Her pony couldn't be anything but Delbert. Granny, who must be old because all grandmothers were old, didn't look old at all. Nell thought that she was very pretty for an old lady, and told her so one day. Granny threw back her head and laughed long and merrily. Nell hadn't meant to be funny. Sometimes grownups were—well, weird.

Grandfather was Daddy's father, and was Granny's husband. Nell had worked that out all by herself once when she was five. He told her stories at bedtime, or else he would read to her. Sometimes he read from the set of Beatrix Potter books. Grandfather told her that her Aunt Eleanor had brought it for her when she was baptized. There was also a silver mug that Nanny kept polished, and from which Nell drank her milk every day. (She remembered Granny Fee showing her how to polish it, but somehow Nanny always wound up doing it.) Aunt Eleanor was Mummy's sister and lived in far away America. She wrote to Nell at Christmas and on her birthday, every year. In fact, Nell had a wooden box filled with letters from her aunt that had come before she had even learned to read. Sometimes Grandfather read Aunt Eleanor's letters. She had learned a lot about America and music and church and Aunt Effie. She hadn't quite worked out where Aunt Effie fit in. Daddy said that she was Nell's great-great aunt, but Nell wasn't clear on what that exactly was.

Grandfather had also given her books, "Treasure Island" and "Kidnapped", and was presently reading to her from "The Hobbit." Mummy said that it was too old for her, but Nell could hardly wait to see how Bilbo Baggins and his friends were getting on. Grandfather said that there were three more books that carried on with the adventures of the Hobbits and Elves and Dwarves. They were called "The Lord of the Rings", but they might be a little old for her. He promised her a set of hard cover books when she was twelve or thirteen, and then she could read them herself.

Grandfather had a Title, but he hardly ever used it. Granny was a Countess because she was married to Grandfather. Mummy would be a countess, too, someday, but not until Grandfather died. That wouldn't bear even considering. Life without Grandfather was unthinkable. He had bright blue eyes that twinkled when he smiled at her over his reading glasses, and he smelt of pipe tobacco sometimes. It was spicy and pleasant, and Nell didn't mind it a bit. Granny only let him smoke in his study on the main floor, or outside. Sometimes, when Granny called him 'Lord Rannoch' in cool tones instead of 'Robin' in her normal voice, Nell knew he was in for a scolding. Likewise, when Granny called her 'Katharine Eleanor' she knew she was in trouble. Her parents had named her after her two aunts, and they also were important in Nell's life.

Aunt Katharine was Daddy's sister and she lived in the manse in the village. Uncle Roger was the minister, and they had moved to Glen Rannoch just over a year ago. Aunt Katharine was quite tall and dark and very pretty indeed. She always smelled of roses, and she had a comfortable lap to climb on to. Nell was pretty big to be sitting on laps, but occasionally she allowed her aunt to give her a cuddle in the manse rocking chair. After all, she had no bairns of her own. Uncle Roger had warm twinkling eyes, a beard, and hair that was quite long for a man. When he removed his spectacles Nell thought that he looked exactly like the picture of Jesus in her Children's Bible.

Aunt Eleanor in America had visited once, when Nell was baptized. That's when she had brought the set of Beatrix Potter and the silver mug. On the dresser in the nursery there was a framed picture of the whole family outside the church the day of Nell's baptism. Nell could pick out everybody. Daddy was holding her. She was dressed in a long white gown, which Nanny told her was a very special dress to be worn only when you were baptized. It was family heirloom, very old, and Aunt Eleanor had also brought it with her. Nell knew that Aunt Eleanor was the lady standing next to Mummy. They didn't look a bit alike, as Mummy was small and dark and slim, while Aunt Eleanor was tall and fair. There was another picture taken the same day that Nanny treasured. Framed in silver, it stood in a place of honor on Nanny's bedside table. It was a photograph of Nanny holding Nell, still in her christening dress. Aunt Eleanor had snapped it after they came home from the church, and had mailed it to her later, along with the group picture. Nanny said there had been a wonderful reception after church, with champagne and tiny sandwiches and cakes and a delicious trifle swimming in sherry and cream. Nell thought it a shame that she had been too young to remember this lovely party. Nanny smiled indulgently and told her that very likely she could have a party like this when she was sixteen. But that was eons away, and she would be more than twice the age that she was now. Nell felt she couldn't wait *that* long.

Nanny had shown her the box of letters from Aunt Eleanor when she had been very small. She said that her aunt had asked her to keep them for Nell until she was old enough to read them herself. The letters still came, twice a year on her birthday and at Christmas, and Nell put each one carefully away in the box, neatly lined up, and in order. Sometimes the letters weren't written all at once, but over several weeks and even months, and then mailed at the proper time. Nell loved reading her letters. It was as though Aunt Eleanor was talking to her. Nanny thought the world of her, Nell knew, and wished with a sigh, not for the first time, that her darling aunt would come for a visit. She wrote to her aunt too, printed carefully, under Nanny's supervision. She was learning to write now, and hugged herself at the thought of how surprised Aunt Eleanor would be when she received Nell's letter, not printed, but written like a grown up!

Daddy's pet name for Nell was 'Pumpkin', and Nell wouldn't let anyone else call her that, even Mummy, though Mummy wasn't prone to calling people by pet names. Everyone in the family called Daddy Jamie, but sometimes Mummy called him 'Jimmy' just to annoy him. Daddy also read to Nell sometimes, when Grandfather wasn't available. Daddy was usually busy, either at the farm, or at the Still. Nell couldn't get 'distillery' around her tongue, and Aunt Katherine laughingly called it the Still, much to Granny's disapproval, so Nell followed suit. She knew that the Still was where the whisky was made, and it was important. Grandfather had taken her there once, and Nell was impressed by all the huge equipment that was there. Queer names like mash tun, wort, pot stills, wash and draff were bandied about and the all pervasive smell made Nell wrinkle her nose.

Nell preferred the stables and the horses, and the farm with all the cows. She gave all the new calves their names, and usually named them after flowers. Clover, Sunflower, Milkweed (wasn't that

COME FILL UP MY CUP

a good name for a cow?) Zinnia and Rose were her friends, though the big cows that gave milk were *very* large, and sometimes Nell was slightly nervous of them. Daddy explained that the cows gave them milk (when they weren't feeding their calves) and from that butter was made and the milk and cream bottled and sold to the stores. Nell loved the buttermilk. It was cool and creamy and slid down her throat like a dream. Mummy wouldn't drink 'that horrid stuff', as she called buttermilk. She didn't care for whisky, either, and said it smelt horrible, and even smelt worse on someone's breath. Nell couldn't wait to have a 'wee dram' with Daddy when she was older. Dad said she had to be eighteen, and then she could also try the sherry that had been laid down for her at the time of her baptism. Aunt Katharine had brought it, and it now reposed in Grandfather's wine cellar. Life was full of waiting, Nell thought, but on the other hand, it was fun to look forward to things: Aunt Eleanor's letters, the Christmas Pageant, Santa Claus arriving (though Nell knew that Santa Claus was just a fancy, like her Lossiemouth dragon.) Mummy and Daddy filled her stocking every year, but it was fun to pretend; and they knew she was pretending, but they pretended that she still really believed.

If the Lossiemouth dragon existed she would prefer Iain to rescue her from it. Iain was her white knight, and she adored him absolutely. In the family picture outside the church he was only fourteen, and he was wearing his kilt, which was blowing in the breeze. Iain was grown up now, not as old as Daddy, of course, but a pretty ancient twenty-one. When she was very young she followed him around, and he would pick her up and carry her on his shoulders. She kept a picture of Iain under her pillow. He was still away at university reading agriculture and farming, and when he came home for good he was going to manage the dairy farm. When Nell grew up she would marry Iain, and they'd run the family farm together. She didn't ever want to leave Glen Rannoch or the Castle or the village. She belonged here.

Mummy left the Castle quite often on little holidays. She would go to London and shop, and see the shows, and visit with her friends. Sometimes, when she was away, Nell and Daddy would have breakfast with Granny Fee and Grandfather in their suite on the first floor. It was fun, just the four of them. Granny was always interested in what Nell was doing and thinking and she never told Nell to sit up straight and eat with her mouth closed. Nell's manners were usually very good. When Mummy was home they never went down to Granny's rooms. Nell would have breakfast with Daddy early before he went to work, and usually Mummy didn't get up until after she had gone to school.

At times, and especially after she had been away, Mummy and Daddy would have Words. They never shouted at each other, but Nell always knew when they disagreed about something and Words were said. Once the door to their suite wasn't entirely closed, and Nell was about to go in for breakfast when she heard them quarreling in Mummy's room. She didn't hear what they were saying, but she heard her name once (Mummy usually called her 'the child' and Daddy would say quietly that her name was Nell). Mary Rose's name was mentioned, too, on one occasion. Daddy would have a grim expression on his face, and Mummy would look pained and long suffering. (Nell had heard these words from Nanny.)

Her friend Laura Lee had parents that had rows. Laura Lee said they hurled bitter accusations at each other, and once her mum had thrown something at her dad. But it cleared the air, said Laura Lee, and neither of them held a grudge. Maybe if Mummy and Daddy had a real row, it would clear the air. Nell felt that whatever Mummy was mad at Daddy for (or vice versa) it never got resolved.

Mary Rose said they fought about sex, whatever that was. As Mummy's maid, she would hear things said. Mrs. Stevens overheard Mary Rose's comments to Nell, and gave her a good talking to.

"If I ever hear of you talking like that again, my girl, it will be out the door without a reference! I'm ashamed of you." She had taken Mary Rose into her rooms, but Nell still overheard what she said. Nell had keen hearing, and Mrs. Stevens' voice was penetrating. Nell didn't ask Nanny what the mysterious 'sex' was; usually she was full of questions about things she heard. Mrs. Stevens had been very upset over Mary Rose's remarks, so Nanny would probably wash Nell's mouth out with soap.

This time Mummy had been away for all of August and September. Her mother, Nell's Grandmother Shaw, was not well, and she had felt it was her duty to go and be with her. She was put out that she'd be away during the best weather in Scotland, and that it would be very hot and humid in Washington, but in her mind she was already planning her winter holiday. She missed Nell's seventh birthday, much to Daddy's displeasure. She booked her flight to America as soon as she heard of her mother's illness, and it slipped her mind that the 10th was her daughter's birthday.

"Really, Claire. Could you not have put your trip off for a week or so?"

"James, she's my mother, and she's ill! I couldn't possibly delay that long."

"Don't worry, Mummy, I have lots of birthdays left to celebrate," Nell said hurriedly. She didn't want them to have Words. She slipped away and made a get-well card for Grandma Shaw. Mummy admired it in a distracted manner, and put it aside and forgot to take it. Nell was heartbroken. Daddy comforted her and said, "See here, Pumpkin, lassie, I'll make a special trip into Inverness and send it special delivery. Perhaps it will arrive even before Mummy does."

Nell was more than satisfied by this solution. Her birthday dinner was held at the Manse, with Granny and Grandfather and Daddy, Uncle Roger and Aunt Katharine. Aunt Katharine brought out her best china and made a scrumptious cake with 'Happy Birthday Nell' written in icing on the top. There were seven pink candles. The highlight of her day was a telegram from Iain, wishing his best girl the happiest of birthdays. A long letter from Aunt Eleanor had arrived the day before, and Nell had read it over twice. ("Letter are so satisfying, Nanny. You can really digest them properly.") Nell was in heaven. She didn't even think of Mummy sweltering in the Washington heat and looking after Grandma Shaw.

Now September was coming to an end, and the evenings and the mornings were cool and misty. Daddy drove to Edinburgh to meet Mummy's plane, and they were going to spend the night at a hotel because the airplane wasn't to arrive until six o'clock. Nell and Granny Fee rode as far as the gates the next morning to welcome the travelers back. Daddy had taken Mummy's elegant sport car to meet her. It was still in first-class condition because Mummy took excellent care of it. She knew how cars worked, and sometimes even supervised maintenance on it. Nell, sitting on Delbert beside Granny Fee on her gelding Kinsale, could hear the car as the driver changed gears before starting up the long curving road from the Upper Glen. They waved furiously, and Mummy (for it was she driving her car), looking neither right nor left, swept by in a cloud of dust.

"I thought she would slow down and wave, didn't you, Granny?" Nell commented, as they trotted back down the road.

"Yes, I did, child, but she must be in a hurry. We'll see them in a few minutes."

Nell was having tea at the Manse like a grown up. Mercer, who worked in the garden and looked after the family cars, had driven her down, and would pick her up at five o'clock.

"Auntie Katharine, does having babies make you ill?"

Katharine looked at her niece in surprise.

"Sometimes, dear. What makes you ask?"

"I heard Mummy say to Daddy, 'If I'm pregnant, I'm not going through that misery again and be sick for the next eight months.' I found the word in the dictionary and it says 'being with child'."

Katharine's eyebrows had almost disappeared into her hair. Nell watched her gathering her thoughts together and she then cautioned her niece not to say anything to anybody. She explained that her mother had not meant her remarks to be overheard. Having babies is a private affair, she went on, and if there was one on the way, she was sure that there would be an announcement soon.

"Don't you and Uncle Roger want a baby?"

"More than anything in the world, dear, but they don't seem to arrive when you want them to."

"Betsy and Honey have calves every spring; maybe Daddy and Iain could give you some advice," said Nell the farmer's daughter seriously.

Katharine's lips twitched. "Well, maybe we could do with some help. But I don't think I'll consult the vet. Thank you for your concern, dear. Why don't you remember us in your prayers? Make them silent, though," she added. Nanny always heard Nell's nightly petitions, and perhaps she might be surprised by a prayer for a baby for Aunt Katharine and Uncle Roger.

"I wonder why Mummy is so unhappy," Nell went on. "I asked Nanny, and she said it was my 'magination, but it's not, Auntie Katharine. I heard her say to Daddy, 'You haven't even tried to make me happy.' And Daddy said, 'Claire, self-centered people are never happy.' I couldn't find that in the dictionary. What does that mean, exactly?"

"Oh, Nell, darling, you've been listening to private conversations again. You shouldn't be telling me this." Katharine was very distressed. "Please don't repeat them to anyone else. Promise me?"

Nell, her eyes wide, nodded. She couldn't have helped overhearing. She had been curled up in one of the big chairs in the library when her parents had come in, talking in low, urgent tones. Nell knew they were having Words again. She tried not to listen, but they were just a few feet away. She didn't move, and presently Daddy went out and Mummy said to herself, "I refuse to have it. I refuse to have it." Nell wondered what she wouldn't have, but thought better of revealing herself. After Mummy had left she went to the dictionary and looked up the words.

A few weeks later Nell unexpectedly entered her parents' suite and to her surprise heard Granny Fee's voice in Mummy's bedroom.

"Claire, you will have this child because it is the right thing to do." Nell had never heard her grandmother speak in such tones before. Her voice was like a knife, and it made her shiver. She stopped dead, remembering Aunt Katharine's admonition about listening to private conversations, and then turned and fled.

There was an official announcement soon after that Mummy was going to have a baby toward the end of June. She was ill for weeks and weeks, and Nell crept around like a lost soul, wondering if she was going to die. Nanny, who had abandoned her plans for retirement at this point, reassured her that the doctors were looking after her very well and that Mummy would be fine. However, there would be no winter holiday for Mummy this year. Nell was so miserable that she could scarcely get excited about the news from the manse. Auntie Katharine was also going to have a baby, about four weeks later than Mummy! This was a good thing, thought Nell, when she saw that Mummy was feeling better and in no danger of dying. The babies would be cousins, and they would be almost the same age. She hugged her aunt when next she saw her.

"I guess God does listen to prayers," she said.

Katharine agreed whole-heartedly.

The babies were born three weeks apart, Malcolm James Maclachlan on June 25th, and then Simon Roger Perry on July 16th, two days after Granny Fee was killed in that car crash. Nell, dazed with disbelief and grief, slept for days. Nanny was at her wit's end, caring for a crying Malcolm, who it seemed, was allergic to cow's milk, and his mother was having the greatest difficulty feeding him. Nell overheard Nanny grumbling to Mrs. Stevens that Mrs. James was not trying hard enough. Mrs. Stevens was giving Nanny a hand in the evenings, and Nell was thought to be asleep. Nell heard Nanny say that Mrs. James was even queerer than she was after Nell was born. "She doesn't seem to want to nurse the baby," she said to Mrs. Stevens.

"You could get mother's milk at the hospital," Mrs. Stevens said.

"Perhaps it will come to that, sighed Nanny," rocking a screaming Malcolm in despair.

Mummy queerer than when she was born? Mummy having words with Nanny. Nanny saying that she would have left long before now if it hadn't been for Nell and Mr. James needing her, and now the puir wee Malcolm.

Mummy outside in her nightgown. Daddy bringing her in and settling her in bed. 'For God's sake Claire, take a hold of yourself! Don't worry, I'll not bother you. I'll be downstairs. Can't you see that Father is beside himself with grief?"

The next morning at Sunday breakfast in the dining room . . . .

Nell, isn't Mummy up yet?

No, Daddy. Malcolm won't stop crying, and Mummy was cross with Nanny last night, and Nanny's in a high dungeon.

Dudgeon, Nell. I'll get Nanny to wake her.

I'll do it, Daddy!

All right, Pumpkin.

Nell, standing in the doorway of her mother's room. Mummy! Mummy! Daddy! Daddy!

Who was that screaming? Nanny, what's the matter with Mummy? Oh dear Lord! Oh Mr. James, come quick! Call the doctor . . . .

Chapter 17

NELL 1996

Robert, Earl of Rannoch sat in his sitting room and thought about the policeman downstairs now interviewing Robin. What a coincidence that it was the same man who had been here investigating Fee's car crash, and then Claire's death. He hadn't liked him then, asking question after question, insinuating that Fee had been drinking, and that Jamie and Claire were not happy. Claire had been in a worse state than she had been after Nell's birth: outside the house in her nightgown, refusing to try and nurse Malcolm. Finally, Katharine took him to the Manse and was feeding both the boys herself. It was, at length, ruled an accident, and Claire's death had been called "Suicide, whist in an unbalanced state of mind due to post partum psychosis." He could still hear the jury's words.

Suicide. It had been a nine days' wonder. But Fee's death had been well and truly mourned by the villagers and the folk living in the area. He had hated seeing those flowers appear, day after day. His sister had been quite sharp with him, reminding him that there were others who also had loved Fee. She was right, course, and after that he closed his eyes to the flowers, and even the small white cross that someone had erected.

He remembered speaking to a shocked and grieving Eleanor over the telephone, and telling her that it was unnecessary for her to come all that way to the funeral. He knew her thoughts were with them all. And then three weeks later James had to call her with the news of her sister's death. Eleanor came to Glen Rannoch for Claire's service. He remembered her pale and sorrowful face as she came to him and put her arms around him.

"I am so sorry," she whispered. And he added his condolences for her loss. She held the baby to her as if it were her own. When she gave him back to Katharine, she said, "I know you'll be a wonderful mother to him." And as soon as she could, she went away.

Robert knew that his daughter dealt with her loss by caring for the two babies. She kept herself very busy and was happy, her father knew. One day a few months later, when one of the babies did something clever, she had laughed out loud. He had been down at the manse with Nell visiting. He had been reproachful, but Katharine had said, "I think Mother would have wanted us to get on with our lives, Dad. I love her and I'll never stop missing her, but she of all people would want us to be happy. Remember how she could laugh, Dad? She found joy in many things. She would have loved our boys here. Roger has been so good to me, too. I am so blessed. Please, Dad, let me be happy."

He kissed her and told her that she was right, of course, and that she should be happy. That would be the best tribute to Fee.

———◦◦◦◦———

The door opened and Nell come in, interrupted his reverie. Her face was pale and drawn.

"Grandfather, I've been upstairs and I've been remembering things. I can't understand how I could forget. Will you tell me the truth about my mother? Did she take poison?"

His face was grey with his remembered grief and anger. He took a deep breath and answered, "Yes, my darling child, she did. And you found her like that. I had hoped that those memories would never come back. Your father never forgave himself for letting you go up to her room."

"How could he have known? They were very unhappy, weren't they? Do you think that's why she did it? Did she leave a note?"

"No, there was no note, and that's why the police took so long investigating. But the jury at the inquest ruled it suicide, and there was no reason to think anything else."

Nell went to the older man and put her arms around him. "It must have been dreadful for everyone. And did Granny's accident come before or after? I don't remember that clearly."

Her grandfather sighed and explained that she had been killed three weeks before. "It should have been me," he said sadly.

"What do you mean?"

"I always took the car into the village on Tuesdays. I would pick up anything we needed, and play darts in the pub with a couple of my old cronies. And smoke my pipe. Tuesday was darts day. It was a habit I had. That day I had a touch of the 'flu, and there was Malcolm's milk to pick up at the hospital in Inverness, so Fee said she'd go...."

I'll go, Robin, it's no problem.

Fee looking over her shoulder at him as she left his bedroom. Be back soon, darling.

James and Mrs. Stevens coming to him half an hour later...

He shivered. Nell held him closer. "Grandfather, I love you."

"I know, my darling. And I love you."

Chapter 18

THE INQUIRY

Thursday afternoon James drove Robin and George Sinclair to St. Andrew's. The interview with Detective-Inspector Marshall in the earl's study had gone smoothly. James had been rather proud of how Robin handled herself. She had only hesitated once and asked for advice from George, and the only thing she wasn't sure of was the exact time she had left Morrison. She was firm in her statement: "I looked over my shoulder, and saw him getting to his feet. No, I didn't see anybody at all. Not in the park, or on the street. I didn't look at the time when I got in. There was no one in reception, and I was very upset. All I wanted to do was get to my room." Marshall then told her that the waiter thought they'd left the restaurant shortly after nine-thirty. "Say fifteen minutes to get to Murray Park," he suggested. "Did Mr. Morrison drive straight there?" Robin replied in the affirmative, and went on to describe the events that took place then: her getting away, Charlie falling, and her run back to the hotel. He also asked her about his golf clubs, and Robin said she hadn't seen them, and she supposed they were in the trunk. She signed a statement finally, and it was then he asked her to testify at the inquiry on Friday morning.

On Thursday afternoon they took the A9 to Pitlochrie and Perth, changed to the motorway, and then east on A91. James had booked rooms at the Temple Hotel on the Scores, overlooking the bay, and the three of them had their dinner there. George said he would make an early night, while James and Robin decided to go for a walk. The evening had turned quite cool, so they bundled up in warm sweaters and sallied forth.

"Don't worry about tomorrow," George told Robin as they said their good nights. "It probably won't be as onerous as the interview with Marshall."

They strolled along the street arm and arm, the wind off the North Sea whipping about them. They walked in silence for a while, until James asked anxiously,

"You're not worrying about tomorrow, are you?"

"I actually wasn't even thinking about it," she told him. "I was thinking about Nell, and the shock of her recovering those buried memories. Did she talk to you about it very much yesterday?"

"She told me what she remembered. I've never forgiven myself for letting her go up to her mother's room." He paused, and steered her aside along a path to a series of park benches that overlooked the sea. There was no one in sight. He drew her down beside him and for a few minutes looked across the harbour to the grey sky where gulls were wheeling and calling. He took a deep breath, and took both her hands in his.

"Robin, I hope you will forgive me for not telling you the circumstances surrounding Claire's death before now. A couple of times I started to tell you—the first time on the ferry to Mull, and later that day when we were with Celine. The words literally stuck in my throat. And the next two days were so much fun—I hadn't laughed like that in years—I just couldn't spoil the mood. I don't expect you to understand how I could keep it all from you. Your story of your childhood made me appreciate how fortunate I had been, growing up. You spoke of your mother's death with so much passion, but I couldn't even discuss Claire's death!"

"It wouldn't have mattered if we'd gone our separate ways, would it? I understand, James, because I don't often talk about my parents to anyone—I believe in getting on with life! So there's really nothing to forgive." She gazed at him, and wanted to reach up and smooth away the lines of worry and distress between his eyes. "I also didn't want to upset people by asking awkward questions...."

"I know. I don't think it was a 'conspiracy of silence' or anything like that. It's just that we never discuss it. You know, I can't even remember a lot of details about Claire's death myself. I must tell you that they suspected that I had killed her."

"Oh Jamie! Because she didn't leave a note?"

"Yes. And that has always puzzled me," he said, as they stood up and continued their walk.

"She, of all people, would have done so. I can't imagine her doing such a thing without a long tale of woe."

Robin, hearing the bitter tone to his voice, tightened her hold on his arm. She didn't voice what she had been thinking, that perhaps Claire had deliberately not left a note, but merely said, "You really don't know what is in people's minds, do you."

He didn't answer, but bent and kissed her lightly on the cheek. "Tomorrow, when this is all over with, we have a lot to talk about," he said.

"But will it?"

"Will it what?"

"Be all over with."

James felt a small chill at her words. He stopped, and turned and put his arms around her.

"My darling dearie, everything will be all right."

Robin hoped so.

The inquiry took place at ten the next morning, and was over by noon. There were only a few witnesses who gave evidence: the forensic doctor, who stated that the cause of death had been a single blow to the head by a blunt instrument. Subsequent blows had been administered after death. When asked if a woman could have done this, he replied cautiously that it was possible, depending on her strength and the weapon used.

"I think it could have been a golf club," he said. "The wound was consistent with that of an iron. If that was the case, a small woman with little strength could have killed him." And he demonstrated the action. James, sitting next to Robin, felt her shiver.

John Eden was the next to testify, as he had reported Morrison missing, and subsequently identified the body. He stated that his friend had told him that he had met a woman he knew from Canada quite by chance in the woolen mill, and had asked her to dinner. He had hinted that he knew her very well, Eden said. He had not reported him missing until Thursday morning when he failed to turn up for their golf game. When asked whether he thought it was odd not to see his friend all day Wednesday, he admitted that he thought probably Charlie was with the woman. James squeezed Robin's hand sympathetically, and watched Eden go and sit down beside two women, presumably his wife and Mrs. Morrison.

Robin was called next, and told her story in a clear voice. Her color ebbed and flowed, and she was evidently distressed. She said firmly that she had seen Morrison getting to his feet as she ran away. She had looked over her shoulder. She had been frightened. It took her probably four or five minutes to get to her hotel and upstairs. There was no one in reception when she got there, but approximately a half-hour later went downstairs to pay her bill, and to say she was leaving first thing in the morning.

"Had you not been planning to stay longer?"

"Oh, yes."

"Why the early departure then?"

Robin looked at him with the slight frown of one who has been asked a silly question. "I didn't care to see him again," she said simply.

The waiter at the Peat Inn confirmed that Morrison had been drinking heavily and was rude and boorish. He said they had left about nine-thirty.

The clerk at the Aslar House stated that Mrs. Lindsay had paid her bill at ten-thirty. He noticed that she was in her night clothes, with her coat on over top them. He also stated that they locked their door at midnight, and guests coming in late had to ring the bell.

James thought how fortunate it was that Robin decided to settle her bill before going to bed.

The policeman testified that the hired car had been found five miles out of town past Boarhills. It had been driven into a ravine.

The jury went out and returned about fifteen minutes later with the verdict of "Murder by person or persons unknown." They added, surprisingly, to a disapproving presiding magistrate, that in their opinion, Mrs. Lindsay was a blameless victim of circumstance.

James felt Robin relax beside her. He hadn't realized just how tense she really had been. She got up then, and made her way over to where Georgia Morrison was still sitting with her friends. When she saw Robin, she got up and the two women stood face to face.

"I am so sorry for all this," Robin began.

"Please don't be sorry, Robin. It is I who should be apologizing to you." The buzz of the crowd around her hid her words from all except Robin as she whispered in her ear: "Don't you see? I'm glad to be free of him! Glad!" She drew back, and smiled grimly at her. "Come and see me when you get back home."

Chapter 19

NELL AND ROBIN

They left St. Andrew's as soon as they were able. Detective-Inspector Marshall stopped them on their way out, and actually shook hands with Robin, apologizing for her ordeal and thanking her for coming to the inquiry.

"Your evidence was very important. I'm sorry if you felt as though you were a suspect," he said with a smile. Now that he was in a sense, off-duty, he seemed quite human. "I appreciate your getting in touch with us as soon as you saw the article in the paper."

"I was brought up to believe that it was a duty to assist the police," Robin replied stiffly. She shook hands with him, and said good-bye very firmly.

James was smiling to himself as the three of them walked to the car park to James' car.

"The police have a job to do, but I really don't want to see them again," she said, as they got in. Mr. Sinclair got into the back seat, and Robin slid in beside James.

"What did Mrs. Morrison say to you?" asked Mr. Sinclair curiously.

Robin hesitated, and then said, "Actually, it was most extraordinary. I started to say how sorry I was, and she interrupted me and apologized to *me*, and then hissed in my ear that she was glad her husband was dead! She asked me to go and see her when I was back home."

"It sounds as though she had a thoroughly miserable marriage," James remarked.

"You never know, do you? I thought I knew them fairly well, and I never guessed that she hated him. She must have, you know, the way she said it."

"She is fortunate that she was still in London last Tuesday, then, wasn't it?"

"I wonder if anyone checked that out," mused Mr. Sinclair.

"Stop it, you two. Let's have a peaceful drive home. I really don't want to think of Charlie Morrison again."

James smiled at her, gave her hand a quick squeeze, put the car in gear, and drove out into the street. Robin looked out the window and sighed. St. Andrew's was really a lovely place, and she hoped that she could return someday and not let all this business haunt her. It would be a shame to let the memory of Charlie Morrison spoil it for her.

When they passed the turnoff for Inverdruie two or so hours later Mr. Sinclair remarked that it was a pity they had to go all the way into Inverness because of him.

"Och, Geordie, it's no trouble at all."

"I certainly appreciated your presence, Mr. Sinclair. Thank you for coming."

"Mrs. Lindsay, I also think it would be prudent, when you return home, to apprise your own solicitor about what has taken place. It's something he should know, just as your doctor might want to know about an illness when you are away."

"Yes. I shall do that. Thank you for your advice."

After dropping Mr. Sinclair at his Inverness home, they turned and headed back to Glen Rannoch Village. James got out his mobile phone, and put in a call to his office at the distillery.

"We'll be back by four, Mrs. Sims," he said. "Is there anything new? All right...will you telephone Janet up at the house and tell her we're on our way? Yes. We're just leaving Inverness now. Thanks. Good-bye."

He put the phone away, and smiled at Robin. "Penny for your thoughts."

"I think that I should be going back to Victoria soon, James. I've got a lot of things to sort out. I was also thinking that Nell might need to get away for a bit, and I wondered how you'd feel about her going back to Canada with me for a while. I know she'd like to meet her aunt, and that's not far from Victoria."

James drove a while before responding. "Have you talked to her about it?"

"No. It's just been on my mind. She's got stuff to sort out, too, and this may not be the right time for her to leave either. But I thought, if you didn't object, I would ask her."

"When will you go?"

"What I was thinking, Jamie, is that we could fly to Calgary and hire a car and drive to Victoria. There's some wonderful scenery through the Rockies, wine festivals in the Okanagan Valley, but soon it will be winter in the mountains, and I'm not comfortable driving in those conditions. So I thought as soon as we can arrange things. If Nell decides not to go, it's not as urgent, but soon, Jamie."

James slowed down, and turned off the highway on to an unpaved road, and stopped the car.

"Robin, you know I want to marry you."

"Jamie, we must both be sure. Just loving each other isn't always enough."

"I won't ask for a commitment now. Will you promise to give me an answer one day? I can wait for as long as you need to be sure."

"Jamie, I promise not to leave you hanging. Can we be friends in the meantime?"

He laughed, and started the car. "So it's still 'nice and easy' for us? I know, I know, it was me who suggested that." He reached over with his hand and took hers. "I think it would be a great opportunity for Nell to go to Canada with you. And for you both to become better acquainted."

Nell, on Flame, was waiting at the top of the hill, just outside the gates that led to Rannoch Castle. Her newly cut hair blew about her face. She shook her head, and her red gold curls bounced. She wasn't yet used to the light feeling. She had mulled over what Robin had said about a new hairstyle and a more grown up outfit, and had gone into Inverness to Uncle Roger's hair stylist. She had gone down to the Manse yesterday and had a long talk with her aunt and uncle, and almost as an afterthought, asked Roger who cut his hair. It was always expertly cut and styled, and the only luxury in which he indulged. Roger thought that it was such a splendid idea that he telephoned to his stylist and they were able to fit Nell in that very afternoon. He and Katharine actually drove her into the city, and while they did a little shopping, her curls were dropping to the floor. She liked her new look. Iain came to the Castle for dinner last night, took one look and asked what on earth had she done with her hair? Nell replied casually that she had had it cut, wasn't it obvious? Iain frowned and said he liked it better long, but he kept stealing looks all the way through dinner. Grandfather had made an effort and had come down to eat dinner with them, and had said at least three times how different she looked. Janet took her aside and admired her hair, and remarked that she looked older, somehow. Nell was fairly satisfied with all these reactions.

She had gone for a ride on Flame a short while ago, and had stopped by the distillery to see if Mrs. Sims had heard from her father, and this is how she knew that they had left Inverness a half hour ago, and would be home soon. Mrs. Sims had no idea how things had gone in St. Andrew's. She had not asked. Her employer would tell her if and when he chose to do so. His private life he kept quite separate from business and that is how Mrs. Sims liked it. She was a very efficient secretary, and the office was well organized. She never asked personal questions, nor was she curious as to what had happened in St. Andrew's to require Mr. James to take a day and a half off. When he had rung off she telephoned up to the Castle to tell Janet Stevens to expect Mr. James and Mrs. Lindsay within the hour. She repeated this to Nell who put her head into the office a short while later and had asked if she had heard from her father. She heard Nell ride away, and she turned back to her desk to continue what she had been doing before the interruption.

Nell was remembering that other time when she and her grandmother had waited for her parents in this very spot. He mother had been away and her father had picked her up at the airport and was driving her home. Only it had been her mother driving her car, and Dad the passenger, and they had swept by in a cloud of dust without so much as a look at the two waiting at the top of the hill. She remembered that her grandmother hadn't said much, only looked grim, and turned to go back to the stables.

She now heard the sound of the big sedan her father drove coming up the hill, not pausing at the junction that led to the Upper Glen and the distillery. Usually he stopped by the office on his way home, but not today. The dusty maroon car appeared around the final bend and slowed down as it approached her. She waved, a big smile on her face, and was rewarded with answering smiles. Robin fluffed her hair, raised her eyebrows, smiled, and gave her the thumbs up signal. She had noticed Nell's change of hair style, and she obviously approved. Nell waved them on, turned Flame and gave him a kick in the ribs. He broke into a gallop, and they were clattering into the stable yard as her father and Robin were getting out of the car in front of the house. Henry, the lad on duty, signaled for her to go, that he would unsaddle and look after Flame. She smiled her appreciation, turned and trotted out of the stable and back to the house.

James and Robin were in the library, where he was pouring large whiskies for two. Nell came in cautiously, saw them relaxing on the sofa, and asked,

"Was it too awful, Robin?"

Nell smiled and shook her head. "It wasn't as bad as I thought it would be. I'm just glad that it's all over. The Detective-Inspector was quite pleasant afterwards."

"You've cut your hair, Nell!" exclaimed James. He looked at his daughter and thought that she had grown up in the last few days, a fact which was not necessarily caused by a new haircut. He went over to her, and uncharacteristically gave her a long hug. "I think I like it. How are you, Pumpkin?"

Nell returned the embrace, and sighed, "Dad, I'm okay. I've been doing what Robin said her B and B lady told her to do: firmly put it out of my mind whenever it appears." She moved over to the sofa and sat down beside the older woman. "I went down to the Manse and talked to Aunt Katharine and Uncle Roger," she told them. "We talked for several hours, then they took me into town to his hair stylist and I had my hair cut and styled."

"It suits you very well. Was your talk with them satisfactory?"

"Yes, Dad. I realize that none of what happened was my fault, though I wish that you had talked to me about my mother long before now."

James sighed. "Yes, I was wrong not to have discussed things with you. At first I didn't, because it was so painful, and you were so upset, and then, as I put it off, it got harder and harder. I guess I didn't want to face the fact that my marriage had failed, and I felt that somehow I was to blame for your mother's taking her own life."

"Uncle Roger said that we all make choices, and ultimately it was my mother's choice and hers alone to end her life. I can't imagine being so desperately unhappy as not to want to face tomorrow. Oh, Dad, by shutting me out you didn't give me the chance to help you!"

James looked stricken. "I must have seen dreadfully selfish to you."

Nell smiled. "No, Dad, I guess I felt that you didn't need me."

"You know I don't wear my heart on my sleeve."

Nell smiled again and said slyly, "Until now. What are your plans, now?"

"Robin feels she would like to go home soon."

"Soon? Oh, Robin, I had such plans for us all!"

"She's got plans for you," said James. "Listen Nell, and think about this." And he went on to outline Robin's suggestion of Nell's taking a holiday with her.

Nell sat back and considered Robin's idea. "I think it is meant to be," she said presently. "Mrs. Burden phoned to tell me that she was canceling Jemmie's lessons, and the Coulter twins are going away to school and won't be taking any more lessons until the spring. It's just my friend Betsy. She wants to take riding lessons, and I would really like to stay in touch with her. Perhaps we can get one lesson in before we go, and then if the weather is still good, another as soon as

I get home. I'll phone her tonight." She paused. Henry and Carlton will be able to manage to look after everything, don't you think? How long could I be away, Dad?"

James glanced questioningly at Robin. "I thought a week or a bit more, to drive from Calgary to the Coast, including a few days in Vancouver before going over to the Island," she answered. "Then we would have to get in touch with your aunt, and arrange for you to visit her for however long it's convenient. Perhaps a one way ticket would be best, and then we could make a booking when you feel you want to go home."

Nell clasped her hands in delight. "Oh, Dad, may I? It sounds absolutely wonderful. That reminds me, I got a letter from Aunt Eleanor the other day, but with all this upheaval, I completely forgot to tell you about it. Let me go and get it." And she flew out of the room.

James smiled at Robin. "Your offer, is, I think, being accepted."

"I'd be happy to upgrade her ticket to business class the same as mine, if that's a problem."

James shook his head, smiling. "I wouldn't think of your going to that extra expense. No, it's a long trip, and probably worth it. She has money of her own from her Grandmother Shaw that she can use. It would be an excellent way to spend it."

Nell returned with her letter. She read, "'*I'm writing this short note to you (you will be surprised, since this is neither Christmas nor your birthday) to let you know my change of address. You know that Aunt Effie died last spring, and in her Will she left me everything. I was very touched, but at the same time felt a little guilty. My brother is newly married, and could have used a legacy, too. So I have sold the house in Kirkland, given Billy and Kera a nice fat check, and have decided to settle on Salt Spring Island. I'm sure I have told you that Aunt Effie bought a summer cottage there quite a few years ago. I really love it there. It is slower paced than the city, and the piece of property is beautiful. With a bit of renovation, which I won't begin until next spring, it will make a wonderful home. I am even thinking of becoming a Landed Immigrant. Salt Spring Island is in Canada, you know. I got an excellent price for the house in Kirkland—right at the top of the market. My timing was perfect. (Completely by chance, I'll have to admit, though of course, there will be taxes to Uncle Sam.) I plan to move soon, and my new address will be……'* and she gives me her address, but no telephone number. Might be a bit awkward timing to visit her, maybe?"

"She can always come to us," said Robin. "Salt Spring Island is just spitting distance on the ferry from Schwartz Bay. I also think it's a lovely spot. Is her address Ganges? That's the main village there."

"Yes. But just a box number."

"We can find her new telephone number by telephoning Directory Assistance, no problem unless it's unlisted. In that case we would have to drop her a note. Perhaps you should write her a letter before we leave, giving her an approximate time when we would be getting in touch. Shall we say the last week in October? I take it that you think this is a good idea?"

"Oh yes, thank you, Robin! I can hardly take it all in. What clothes do I take?"

Robin smiled happily and took her arm. "We can look at your things, and what you need we can buy in Inverness or Edinburgh. Always a lovely excuse to go shopping," she added to James, who was sitting back and gazing at them. "First things first, then. Your father's travel agent to make our bookings, and thence to the shops!"

Chapter 20

ETTERS FROM CANADA

E xcerpts from letters to Iain from Nell, and to James from Robin

Oct 8, 1996

Dear Iain,

We are comfortably ensconced in our seats in Business Class, and I am so excited about traveling to Canada. (Isn't 'ensconced' a lovely word?) Robin says I shall be completely spoiled for traveling regular class, but she says she wasn't going to sit at the 'back of the bus', even for me, so I'm glad we spent the extra cash. Two air hostesses to do our every whim, lovely snacks and drinks. What a pity I'm underage. Robin says in First Class the seats go absolutely flat and the crew does everything for you except "give you jammies and tuck you in".

We spent two days in London, because we couldn't make the connections, but let me tell you it was spent profitably! Robin took me to see "Cats" which I loved absolutely, we went to Buckingham Palace for the Changing of the Guard (The song, 'They're changing guards at Buckingham Palace, Christopher Robin went down with Alice' kept

*going round and round in my brain.) It rained,
but we didn't care, and we spent practically the
whole second day in the British Museum until my
head was spinning. What a place! AND we went to
Harrods and shopped. Robin insisted on buying me
a beautiful winter coat, very dressy, which she says
I will wear for years. It's navy blue with fur trim, a
furry lining that zips out, and it has a detachable
hood. I love it!*

*The funniest thing happened when we got
to Heathrow from Edinburgh. This little fart of a
Sassanach tried to wrestle a luggage cart from Robin.
You should have seen them playing 'tug o' war'. It
was too funny for words. "My daughter needs it,"
he sputtered. "She's pregnant." "Are you going to put
her in it," Robin wanted to know, and finally gave
in. He was short and round and bounced along in
his horrible shiny shoes. He went off, quite huffy and
triumphant. Robin and I killed ourselves laughing.*

*I'll mail this as soon as we get to Calgary.
Our itinerary, Robin says, will probably be Banff,
Lake Louise, and then over to Drumheller to the
paleontology museum, then down to Waterton Lakes,
Head Smashed In Buffalo Jump (whatever that is)
and to bc along the southern route. I'm copying this
from her notes, and when we get to Calgary we plan
to get some tourist info for me. Robin is delighted
to be a 'tourist in her own country' and can hardly
wait to show it all to me.*

*Give Flame a pat, and please remember to
exercise him every day, Iain.*

Love, Nell the World Traveler

Lake Louise, Oct 10, 1996

Dear James,

Nell has written a long letter to Iain, so I thought I should pen a few lines to you. Once again, I enjoyed my time at the Castle (I remember how startled I was when you casually mentioned it in Oban.) and many thanks to you and your father for the hospitality. You were a rock over the inquiry; I shall never forget your support.

I wrote a long letter to Celine from London, apologizing for not returning to Iona before I went home, and telling her everything. Don't be surprised if you hear from her. I gave her your telephone number, and her address is simply 'Celine laRoche, Iona Community, Baile Mor, Iona'.

We drove to Banff yesterday, and stayed at the Banff Springs Hotel, which is a marvelous old hotel in the mountains up above the Bow River Valley. There are hot springs a short walk from the hotel, and we spent over an hour there last night before going to bed. Banff town itself is crowded and touristic, even now, and will be full in a month or so when the skiing starts in earnest.

Lake Louise is higher in the mountains and it was snowing when we arrived! It is melting now, but it was a pretty sight. You may have seen pictures of the lake, but nothing compares to seeing it at first hand. I remember the first time I was here with Tim. It was June, 'and the golden poppies were blooming 'round the banks' just as the song says. The sky was blue, and the lake such an extraordinary color that I felt if you could drain the lake there would be this turquoise scum left like blue buttermilk in a glass. We're not staying at the Chateau, but at a lodge about a half mile away. They're doing all sorts of renovations and additions to the Chateau, and not for the better, either, I'm afraid. Today we plan to lace on our hiking boots and do a good walk. There are trails for miles with splendid views. You can even hike to the glacier, though I haven't been there for years. It has retreated somewhat in the twenty years since first I was here.

I think we'll stay another night, then off to Drumheller first thing Wednesday morning.

Nell appears to be enjoying herself hugely.

I bought her a winter coat at Harrods. "Shall we tell Dad how much this cost?" she asked as we watched the saleslady wrap it up. "No," I answered, "there are some things you keep from your menfolk." So don't ask, because we won't tell you.

The weather has cooperated so far. Keep your fingers crossed.

Yours ever, Robin

PS Give my dearest love to your father, and also to Celine if you happen to be in contact with her.

Waterton Lakes, Alberta, October 14, 1996

Dear Iain,

We are having a fabulous time. Yesterday we drove from Drumheller to this picturesque hotel by the lake. I've enclosed a postcard so you can see where we are staying. (I also sent one to Betsy.) The Prince Edward Hotel sits on this headland as you can see and there is a magnificent view from the lounge. There is a creaking old lift that huffs and puffs its way up and down, so most of the time we take the stairs. The building is old and creaky and the walls are very thin. The couple next door was making love this morning and we could hear everything. Robin and I stuffed our wash flannels in our mouths to keep from laughing out loud. Robin is such a pet. She didn't make me feel embarrassed at all, but merely whispered that she was glad they were enjoying themselves, and should we have a bet on to guess which couple it is?

The Tyrell Museum in Drumheller was absolutely fascinating, and Iain, the Badlands are indescribable! We were driving along a flat prairie with cows grazing on either side, and there was a sign saying 'Drumheller 15k' and not a building in sight. Suddenly the road just disappears into the prairie, and you are in the Badlands. Fantastic cliffs of different shapes, dry gulches, you expect Red Indians and Cowboys to appear any minute. We spent all afternoon in the museum, and then stayed at a motel on the way south. Apparently in prehistoric times all this area was a shallow inland sea, very warm and tropical, and the dinosaurs abounded. This is the richest fossil treasure trove in the world. There is a park south of Drumheller where there are digs and a good interpretive center, but the season is over, and Robin wanted to push on to the mountains. Next time, she said.

It is such a scenic drive to this part of the Rockies. The mountains just rise right out of the prairie floor, not like further north around Banff where there are foothills. (They call Calgary the Foothill City.) We went for a boat ride on the lake and saw eagles, and there were deer and elk near the village. Tomorrow we drive up to Head Smashed In Buffalo Jump (where the Indians drove the buffalo off the edge of the cliff to kill them). Robin says it is a worthwhile stop, then we will head back down to the Crow's Nest Highway and drive west into British Columbia. Aren't the names colorful?

Robin wants to go for a hike. I hope I can keep up to her. I thought I was in good shape, but she really had me hustling up at Lake Louise.

How is Flame? I hope you all are missing us. I know we miss all of you. (At least I am sure Robin misses Dad anyway.) We are well and having a wonderful time.

Love from your world traveler, Nell

Penticton, BC October 18, 1996

Dear James,

How does the postcard message go? 'Having a wonderful time, wish you were here.' True on both counts. Nell enjoyed the paleontology museum (it's absolutely fascinating and a must see for any tourist who comes to Alberta.) We hiked at Waterton Lakes Parks, saw Head Smashed In Buffalo Jump, (Nell bought T-shirts for you and Iain there), the Frank Slide, which has a very good interpretive center and is 'open every day of the year except Christmas Day and Good Friday.' We took most of the day to get to Osoyoos, as it snowed yesterday, and I was a little nervous. I was extremely glad to get down the road into the Okanagan Valley before dark. We stayed at a B&B winery. It is harvest time and also a pretty time in this valley, though nothing can compare to the spring when the orchards are in blossom. Though many of the orchards have been removed, and vines have been planted. The wine industry is thriving here these days. Tomorrow we are signed up for a winery tour, and I shall drop in on an old friend in Peachland on our way to the Coquihalla Highway. She's the one I mentioned who retired a few years ago with her husband, and they raise horses. He has even learned to ride at the advanced age of sixty! Nell will be interested in meeting her and the horses, of course!

Love to your father, and to yourself, of course.

Yours always, Robin

Whistler, B.C. October 20, 1996

Dear Iain,

We are now in Whistler, which is a gorgeous skiing village in the Coast Mountains. Somehow I used to think that the Rocky Mountains were the only mountains out here, but, bc is range after range of mountains. We had a great time in the Okanagan, tasting wine and touring wineries. We visited a friend of Robin's who raises horses, and we spent the night there after a ride in the hills and dinner with her and her husband. Today we drove to Whistler, and it was a very interesting drive. We stopped at the Hat Creek Ranch, a heritage farm, and that was quite worthwhile. Robin says she's embarrassed that her country is so young; historical things are merely a hundred or so years old out here in the west. It's so different to home, but I really like it.

Tomorrow we are taking the chairlift up the mountain and taking another hike. The ski season doesn't start for a few weeks, sometimes it's early, but there has been no serious snowfall on the slopes yet. The weather is still clear, and we are keeping our fingers crossed that it will remain so.

We are staying with another friend, a classmate of Robin's who came out here after university and never left. She's an avid skier and golfer, and so thinks she has died and gone to heaven. They are talking about the winter Olympics, I am not sure when, but it would be a wonderful venue for the downhill and cross-country skiing. I could watch on the telly and casually say, yes, I stayed there when I went to Canada.

We will be in Vancouver in a couple of days; I shall probably wait and mail this letter then. Maybe I'll add a few lines.

October 23, Vancouver

Just a note before I mail this to you. We had a lovely time at Whistler, and the drive down to Vancouver is SPECTACULAR! The sun shone, and the colors were splendid, and the sea was as blue as could be. We stopped at a waterfall, and walked up to it, but didn't walk the trails at all.

Next time, as Robin would say.

We are staying at a charming hotel right on the edge of the bay, which is called English Bay, (but I have dubbed it Sassanach Bay of course!) It is called the Sylvia Hotel, and Robin says it was once the tallest building in the West End, as this part of the city is called. It is hard to believe, looking at all the skyscrapers.

We are a short walk from Stanley Park, and the sea wall walk and the Aquarium, which we visited yesterday. Today we are going to visit some more parks and gardens, though Robin admits they can't compare to Buchard Gardens, near Victoria. I think she is anxious to get home. She phoned her daughter Deborah last night, and she said that there was a mountain of mail and phone messages waiting for her, but she would try and organize them for her mother before she got home. Deborah has been checking her house every two days or so. She has a flat near the university.

By the way, you can tell Dad that Robin is an excellent driver. The only time she was nervous was last week through the Crow's Nest Highway when it was snowing. There is this long road down the mountain into the Okanagan Valley with several hairpin turns, and it was quite slippery. We were fine, though. She went slowly, in low gear, and had no trouble at all!

Tonight we see 'Showboat' at the new theater, and I think we'll be going to the Island tomorrow or the next day. You will probably hear from me long before you get this letter!

Lots of love from your world traveler, Nell

Chapter 21

VICTORIA

The weather was cool the next morning, and a fine rain was falling, which caused Robin to change her plans for ascending Grouse Mountain, the local ski hill. The views could be spectacular on clear days, but, "Not worth it today," Robin said briskly, getting out her suitcase. "Besides, I've been away from home long enough. Let's catch the eleven o'clock ferry."

They arrived at Robin's home in the early afternoon to clearing skies, and watery sunshine. The house was a three bedroom cottage on Ten Mile Point, hidden away in the trees, with the back garden leading down to the rocky shore. They looked south across Cadboro Bay toward the downtown part of Victoria. On clear days you could see the Olympic Mountains across the straits. Robin showed Nell the guest room, a small room at the back, with its own even tinier bathroom. She opened the windows and the sound of waves pounding on the rocks was heard mixed with the sounds of birds.

"Why don't you unpack and bring the clothes you want washed into the laundry room. I'm going to do the same first, or it doesn't get done. Then I'll tackle the mail and phone messages."

In a short time the washing machine was churning away, and Robin put the kettle on, and sat down at her kitchen table. She was surprised to see her mail all neatly stacked, no fliers or junk mail to be seen, and a long note sitting beside it.

"Deb's been here, bless her heart, what a secretary I've got!" She picked up the note and read her daughter's large scrawl: *Dear Mum, Welcome home to the weary wanderers. After we talked last night, I came over today, bringing milk, eggs, bread and butter, so you won't have to rush off to the grocery store. I looked at the mountain of mail and felt sorry for you, so I've thrown out the junk mail and adverts, put bills in one pile, personal stuff in the other, and all others in the third. I listened to your messages, I hope you don't mind, and made a couple of phone calls, and have written the rest down. I think you're going to have to either get your machine fixed, or get that new BCTel voice mail, as some of your messages were rather garbled. I put in a new tape, and it seems to be working okay for the moment. Payment—I raided the freezer and Moss and I barbecued a couple of steaks and had a bottle of wine! It was good. Give me a call when you arrive. Love, Deb.*

There was one message since Deb and been there, and it was perfectly clear, so maybe the tape had been worn out. She made a pot of tea, started in to answer her messages, then opened her mail, and set to work to get caught up on her correspondence. Nell, meanwhile, drank her tea, and set out for a walk. When she got back the delicious aroma of home-cooked soup met her, and she saw that Robin was busy making sandwiches.

"I thought an early supper was in order. I'm hungry! I just realized that we haven't had anything since breakfast except that muffin on the ferry. If you want to phone your aunt now, do go ahead. You can use the phone here or in the study. I phoned and got the number for you—here it is."

Nell hesitated, and decided to use the kitchen phone. There was nothing private that she wanted to say to her aunt, but she realized that it would be the first time she had spoken to her aunt since she was a child, and she really didn't remember anything about it.

She pushed buttons carefully, heard the phone ring, and was rewarded to hear a woman's voice answer. She smiled and nodded at Robin and said,

"Is this Eleanor Shaw? It's Nell Maclachlan calling."

Robin could hear the clear feminine tones, rising in pleased surprise, and saw Nell's face flush with pleasure.

226

"Yes, it's me, Aunt Eleanor....you got my letter? Oh good.... yes, we just got to Victoria today......oh we had a grand trip. Banff, Lake Louise, Waterton Lakes, Whistler, what else? We were just three nights in Vancouver...it was raining when we left this morning, but the ferry trip was fabulous—we saw killer whales, and eagles, and had some marvelous experiences.... Dad was fine when we left—-we've been gone nearly three weeks...I guess should have rung him this afternoon, it'll be too late now.......when can we come to see you?" She looked at Robin. "I guess whenever it's convenient for you and Robin.....That's Mrs. Lindsay who I've been traveling with—she stayed with us at Rannoch...may the both of us come? Robin can drive us over, perhaps you had better speak to her and tell her how to get to your house....me too, Aunt Eleanor, do you realize it's nine years since we saw you.....yes, thank you, here she is.." and she handed the telephone to Robin.

Robin picked up the instrument and said, "Hello, Robin Lindsay speaking, Ms Shaw."

A warm smiling voice came down the line. "Please call me Eleanor. I'm so looking forward to meeting you both." And proceeded to explain to Robin where she lived.

"Oh, that's quite clear. I have friends in Ganges, and I know the area fairly well. Are you sure it's convenient? Haven't you just moved in? You can always come to Victoria."

"Thanks, but it's fine. I'm quite settled in—you will be my very first guests. Will Sunday be all right? I play the organ at the local Anglican Church, so I'll expect you for lunch after the morning service." She went on to recommend which ferry to catch, to get them to her house by 12:30, then with a cheery good-bye, rang off.

Robin turned to Nell, and said, "She has asked us to come at lunch time on Sunday. I shall probably visit my friends in Ganges while I'm there, and leave you to have a good visit with your aunt. Meanwhile we can see a bit of Victoria between now and Sunday morning. There's a castle right here in Victoria built by a Scottish coal baron that you might be interested in seeing. It's not as grand as your house, though."

The next morning at ten o'clock Nell telephoned home to Rannoch Castle, timing it so that she would find her father home. Robin could hear his voice as Nell talked to him, excitedly relating the last few days. Then Robin took the phone and smiled as she heard his warm Scottish voice.

"Robin, I've missed you very, very much. How are you?"

"Just grand, hearing your voice, Jamie."

"That's what I wanted to hear. Still considering my offer?"

She laughed, feeling quite like a school girl, and said lightly, "I think of it now and again. Nell has been a wonderful traveling companion, you know, and we've seen a lot of country."

"So she says. I expect neither of you have given us scarcely a thought. Well, your letters of course. Iain has really enjoyed the ones Nell has written, and I yours." He paused. "Iain's here, wanting to speak to Nell. Ring us again soon."

"I will. Good-bye, Jamie."

Chapter 22

NELL AND ELEANOR

Eleanor Shaw sat at the window seat in her sitting room, book on her lap, gazing out to her view of Ganges Harbour. It was a fine October day; the sun was shining on the waves in the water below. Colorful leaves were flying past her window, and high above a solitary raven was circling slowly, turning on the updraughts of the air. The pine and fir trees made a sort of window frame to her scene of mountain and water, and in the east she could see the gathering clouds. This wonderful autumn weather would be coming to an end soon, she thought. She loved her little aerie, and though there were other homes nearby, the trees hid them well, and she had privacy and quiet. It was only a few minutes' drive down to the village and all its amenities.

She arose, and went through to her sunny kitchen where the table was set for lunch. She had chosen a periwinkle blue tablecloth with contrasting serviettes in a gay floral design, and her plain white china with its narrow blue rim made a pleasing contrast. An arrangement of the last fall flowers from her garden stood in the center of the table, and her best crystal gleamed in the noon sunshine. The casserole was waiting to be popped into the oven, the salad was prepared and chilling in the refrigerator, just needing to be tossed with dressing and placed in her blue pottery bowl. Cold white Chablis was waiting in her terra cotta wine chiller, and there was sherry and glasses ready on the sitting room buffet. She checked the main floor bathroom; fresh guest towels were folded neatly in a wicker basket, new soap in the soap dish and the chrome faucets and porcelain bowl shone with her polishing. The upstairs guest rooms, she knew, were ready and tidy, with fresh linen on the beds and fresh flowers on the dressers.

She looked around, and in her mind, again blessed Aunt Effie for her generosity. She planned to enlarge the cottage that her aunt had purchased over fifteen years ago. She knew exactly what she wanted to do in order not to spoil the pleasing lines of the house, and to give her the extra room she desired on the main floor.

Eleanor glanced at her watch, saw that it was nearing twelve-thirty, and at the same time heard the sound of a car coming up the hill. She went to the door to see a blue Toyota come into view, and watched its driver park it carefully behind hers, which was in the small detached garage. She saw the two women emerge, talking in an animated fashion, and as the younger one turned, she waved, and Nell smiled. She would have known her niece anywhere, even without the pictures that had been sent to her over the years, for her golden red curls were the same as she had seen on the eight year old Nell, and the brilliant smile was James'; the smile that once had the power to send her pulses racing and render her legs to jelly.

She came down the steps with her arms outstretched, and enveloped her niece in a warm hug.

"How wonderful that you are here at last!" she exclaimed. "I've been looking forward to this ever since I received your letter." Then she held Nell at arm's length and looked her over. She saw nothing of her sister in the girl, just James' smile and his father's bright blue eyes. She then shook hands with Robin saying, "How lovely to meet you, Robin. Come in and make yourselves comfortable. Do you have suitcases?"

Robin opened the trunk of her car, and lifted out Nell's case. "I have friends that live in Ganges," she said, "and I thought that I'd visit them while I'm here."

"Please stay at least one night," Eleanor urged. "How long can you stay, Nell? I forgot to ask you when you telephoned."

They went indoors, Nell explaining that she hadn't yet booked her return flight. Eleanor led them into the sitting room, saying to deposit their bags in the front hall, and they could be taken upstairs later. As they sat down Nell gravely presented Eleanor with a bottle of fine old sherry.

"Dad thought it would be a good idea to bring you a bottle of this sherry. It is what Aunt Katharine bought and laid down at my baptism," she explained. "You mustn't open it until next August on my eighteenth birthday."

Eleanor took it with a pleased smile. "I remember your aunt bringing a case of this in and saying aside to me that she didn't care for spirits much, and wanted you to appreciate fine wine as well. And Iain figuring out that he'd be an ancient thirty-one when it was due to be opened." She smiled reminiscently. "That was such a happy time, Nell, when I was there for your baptism. Katharine and Roger had just become engaged, and it was my twenty-second birthday. I remember being rather miffed that my sister had forgotten all about it, but I inadvertently told Katharine, and she must have told your father, because there were toasts and flowers later that day."

She put away the bottle carefully in her cupboard, and poured her own sherry for them, saying that it was time Nell developed a wine palate, and then excused herself to go to the kitchen and put the casserole in the oven to reheat. When she returned Nell said, "I think your home is delightful, Aunt Eleanor. You mentioned renovations in your letter. What do you plan to do?"

Eleanor sat down, pleased to discuss her beloved home. "I thought I would have the sitting room here extend out and make a space for my piano, which, as you see, at this moment reposes in the dining room. Aunt Effie had a small dining suite, which I use in the kitchen, and her dining room furniture from the Kirkland house, will, I think, fit in here just fine. At the same time I'll enlarge the downstairs bedroom and add an en suite bathroom. At the present time I have to go to the upstairs bathroom if I want a bath or shower. There's only a powder room on the ground floor. It will be expensive, but Effie's generosity makes it all possible."

"Are you planning to make your permanent home here?" asked Robin.

"Yes. I've been back and forth to Salt Spring with and without Effie ever since she bought this place, and I love it here. The Seattle area has gotten so big and crowded, and I wanted a quiet place to live. I've already received inquiries about piano lessons, and the local church is hiring me to be their organist and music director. I'll miss my friends at my church in Kirkland, but I have one woman friend that I plan to keep in touch with. She's just recently moved to Whidbey Island and starting a bed and breakfast there. I feel at home here," she went on. "I was so touched when they held a memorial service here for Effie. She had a wide circle of friends, and they always included me. I feel very blessed."

"You mentioned something about becoming a landed immigrant," Nell said. "Would that mean giving up your American citizenship?"

"Yes. I feel if I am going to live here that I should become a Canadian. I like Canadians, and I don't feel particularly American, so I'm happy to take out citizenship."

Presently they moved into the kitchen, and sat down to lunch.

"Enough about me," said Eleanor, serving the casserole. "Tell me about your family. How is everyone?"

"Pretty much the same," answered Nell. "Grandfather will never retire, and Dad's full time at the 'Still' now and Iain lives in the Dower House and runs the dairy farm. I've left school, I think I told you that, and I'm overseeing the stables and giving riding lessons."

"Nell said you had stayed at the castle," Eleanor said to Robin. "How long have you known the family?"

Robin smiled. "Not very long at all," she admitted, colouring a little. "I met James quite by chance on my trip over there about six weeks ago, and he invited me to spend the weekend at his home for his birthday. Because of circumstances, I stayed longer, and then asked Nell to come with me for a holiday."

Eleanor noted the blush, and wondered about the 'circumstances', but was too polite to ask. Robin was silent for a moment, and gazed at her hostess. She liked what she saw in her face.

Finally she said, "A man I knew was murdered in St. Andrew's, and I had to talk to the police and go to the inquiry. You see, I had been the last to see him before he was killed." Eleanor made shocked and sympathetic noises as Robin continued. "He had been a friend of my husband's, and I now use that term advisedly," she said, a bitter note coming into her voice. "I met him by chance, and went out to dinner with him. It was a disaster. He was drunk and abusive, made horrible innuendoes about my husband who was killed in an air crash three and a half years ago, and made several rather unpleasant passes at me before I could get out of his car and run away. It was a ghastly evening I would like to forget, but find difficult to do so."

Nell reached over and gave her friend's arm a sympathetic squeeze. "I didn't make it any easier by being rather beastly to her when she first arrived—no, don't deny it Robin, I was quite horrible. I'm *very* ashamed of myself. And she was so kind to me, Aunt Eleanor. The policeman that came had been the investigating officer when my grandmother died in the car crash, and also when my mother died. It was all rather awful, because it triggered some memories that I had buried. Dad and Robin and Aunt Katharine and Uncle Roger have been grand about it all, and I feel so sorry for Grandfather. He is still suffering over Granny's death."

"You two can have a good heart to heart tomorrow after I leave to visit my friends here," Robin said.

Eleanor removed the plates from the table and proceeded to serve the dessert. As she poured coffee a short time later she said thoughtfully, "You know that I knew your father before he met my sister," she said. "I was very young and madly in love, and after their wedding I came back to the States with a broken heart." She smiled at the memory. "I only made two visits to Scotland, one for your baptism, and the other for Claire's funeral. The first visit was simply wonderful; you were such a beautiful baby, I fell fathoms deep in love with you at first sight. Your mother wasn't well—I guess she had what we call post partum depression. I was quite worried about her, but we parted on a positive note, and for that I am eternally grateful. It was so shocking, my mother died just before your brother was born; then your grandmother was killed in that horrible accident;

and then your father telephoned me about my sister. I went from my mother's funeral to Claire's funeral. I wanted to take you home with me, you know. You were so bewildered and lost. Lucky for everyone that Nanny was there. What a grand person she was—is she still alive, Nell?"

"Yes. She's retired now, of course, and lives with her sister in Lossiemouth. I think she looks after her sister, who is quite elderly now. Dad says that Mrs. Ross (that's the sister) has been enjoying poor health for years."

Eleanor laughed. "I remember that Nanny went to see her sister while I was there, and I looked after you. Your mother was very annoyed at me for interfering and telling Nanny that she needed a break."

"Aunt Eleanor, did Dad ever talk to you about how my mother died? He never talked to me. It was if he had closed a door, and locked it tightly, and wouldn't open it. I didn't even know until recently that she had taken her own life. For years I just assumed it was because of Malcolm—complications if his birth, you know…No one set me right." She paused to reflect. "I can't believe how uncurious I was about her—it was though she had never existed. I had Nanny and Aunt Katherine, and Janet, as well as your wonderful letters."

Eleanor looked distressed. "You were barely eight years old, and it had been a horrendous experience for you. Do you remember finding her, Nell? Was that a memory that became unburied?"

Nell nodded. "It was though it had happened yesterday. I came down to Grandfather's room, and he held me and comforted me as though I was a child again. He also said there was no note, and that the police thought it very suspicious."

Eleanor sat back. "I remember James saying bitterly that he was their only suspect." She shivered. "I, also, don't like thinking about that time. I can share James' point of view. My sister and I were never great friends, and I think she made your father very unhappy and bitter. She was your mother, Nell, and I'm sorry! But somehow I wasn't surprised. She had been so queer after you birth, and Fee, your grandmother, wrote to me quite soon before her accident and said she was even worse after Malcolm's. The fact of no note has always puzzled me, though. My sister was rather self-centered, and it really surprised me that she hadn't written reams blaming everyone but herself."

"I find it strange that no one in the village or at your school ever said anything about it," put in Robin. "It must have been common knowledge at the time."

Eleanor thought for a moment or two. "Fee's death was what affected everyone in the area. She was well and truly loved. Claire was always off somewhere—I don't think she had made much of a dent in the community, and you can be sure that if there was any gossip amongst the staff at the castle Mrs. Stevens would have squelched it immediately." She smiled apologetically at Robin. "I am sorry for discussing these unhappy memories!"

Robin set down her empty cup, and said what had been on her mind for several weeks now.

"Forgive me, Eleanor, and you, too, Nell, but I have been thinking: do you think your sister could have been capable of deliberately not leaving a note?"

"You mean the 'you'll all be sorry when I'm gone and you won't know what happened' sort of thing?" Eleanor raised her eyebrows in speculation. "It's possible, I suppose. It had never occurred to me. But maybe that's the answer." She reached for the coffee pot. "Let's not dwell on it now. More coffee, Robin?"

Soon after they all went back into the sitting room with their second cups of coffee, Eleanor saying that she wanted to hear all about the trip and did Nell have pictures? Nell went to her suitcase and pulled out a small album and brought it to her aunt. "I put this together when we got to Victoria. I didn't know that you could get photographs developed in a matter of hours," she said. "It comes from living in a little village in the back of beyond."

"But you wouldn't live anywhere else, would you," said her aunt, smiling.

She looked at the photographs, and heard about the wonderful sights that Nell had seen and her interesting experiences. Nell said, "I wrote to Iain practically every day about what we were doing. It was like a journal. I do hope he has kept my letters. It would be fun to read them for myself."

Eleanor smiled and said, "I wonder if Iain remembers proposing to me when he was fourteen. I told him it was the nicest compliment I had ever had and if he was of the same mind in ten years to ask me again. I guess he decided I was too old for him. He's never married then?"

Nell was rather taken aback. Iain had never mentioned a childish crush on Eleanor. "He still has the picture of killer whales you gave him years ago. It hangs in his living room."

"Ah, then he hasn't completely forgotten me," she smiled.

"He's been seeing Bernice Porter lately, I think," said Nell in contemptuous tones. "She's a Sassanach, and her father is enormously rich."

"Oh. I see you don't approve," Eleanor said with a twinkle. Then she noticed Nell's expression and bent to look at the photograph album.

It had been the only awkward moment, thought Robin, as she drove down to the village to visit her friends the next day. Eleanor was a wonderful hostess, and she had been completely charmed by her. Robin hadn't been prepared for such a beautiful woman, either. James hadn't mentioned her beauty, only Claire's and she could scarcely imagine a woman more beautiful than Eleanor. And it seemed that she had once been in love with James. Perhaps she still was. Robin felt a small chill. How could anyone resist her? It was astonishing that she had never married, but more surprising that she had never returned to Scotland after her sister's death. Robin wondered if she had known then how unhappy her sister and James had been. James had alluded to their unhappiness only once or twice when he was discussing the circumstances around her death to Nell and her. Robin still felt that there was a mystery involved, even more than the one surrounding the lack of a suicide note, just from all the things that hadn't been said. Ah well, James would tell her when he felt it was right.

She had been surprised at how much she had told Eleanor about the events in St. Andrew's. Her mind moved on to the last thing that George Sinclair had said to her when James had dropped him off at his home in Inverness. She hadn't thought about it since then. It would be a good idea to talk to Cameron Jagger about that, and her will as well. If she remarried, (if she was ever sure about herself and James) she would need to have a new will written. She'd phone over to Vancouver when she returned, and make an appointment.

Chapter 23

DEBORAH AND ROBIN

Robin took a Tuesday afternoon ferry back to Victoria. She called Eleanor before she left her friends' home saying that they were just to let her know when Nell wanted to return to Victoria, and she could meet the ferry, if Eleanor didn't want to make the trip herself. She also told them she might be making a quick trip to Vancouver later that week, but thought that wouldn't interfere. Eleanor had indicated she wanted Nell for at least a week or two.

"In case I can't be reached, I'll give you Deb's number; she'll know how to get in touch."

Once home, she checked her answering machine and there were two perfectly clear messages waiting. At least it was working now. One was from Deb, and the other, to her surprise, was from Georgia Morrison.

"Robin, I don't know whether you're back from your trip yet, but if you are, please call me. I really think we should get together and talk. Actually, I'm quite worried about something. Um, please call me as soon as you can."

Robin frowned as she listened to the tape, rewound it, and played it again. Georgia's voice was tense, and Robin thought that she might even be frightened. Should she call her now and hear what she had to say? No, she would book an appointment with Cameron

Jagger first, and work around that. She picked up the phone and punched in her lawyer's number.

"Oh, Mrs. Lindsay, Mr. Jagger is tied up all week in court, and he's booked solid on Friday. What about next week?"

Robin murmured her disappointment. "I'll need more than a few minutes, too," she said.

"Wait a moment; I see there's been a cancellation. I can fit you in first thing Friday morning at nine o'clock. Will that do?"

"Perfectly." Robin gave the secretary her phone number and rang off.

She sat and thought for a few minutes. She had hoped to speak with Cameron personally, and mention Georgia's phone call. She would have to go to Vancouver on Thursday, now, since she couldn't get downtown by nine o'clock taking the seven am ferry on Friday. Should she see if Georgia was free on Thursday? No, better see Cameron before she met with Georgia. Sometime on Friday would work out well, and she could return that evening. She checked Georgia's telephone number that she had written down and put in her call.

The answering machine came on, and she was chilled to hear Charlie's voice giving the message. Her legs felt suddenly weak as the events of that evening came rushing back. She sat down, and in a voice that shook a little, began her message, "Georgia, it's Robin Lindsay calling. I have to be in Vancouver—-" She was interrupted by Georgia's voice, who said breathlessly, "Oh, thank God it's you, Robin. When are you coming over?"

Robin's eyebrows went up, and she answered, "I started to say that I will be in Vancouver on Friday. Are you free that day or evening?" She could stay another night if needs be.

"Let me see, oh no, I'm not, and it isn't anything that I can cancel. My mother-in-law is coming to town on Thursday and is leaving Saturday sometime. Can you come tomorrow?"

"No, I can't, Georgia, I'm sorry; what on earth is the rush? Can you tell me what you want to talk about?"

"Oh God, not over the phone. Can't you stay another day and we can get together on Saturday?"

Robin sighed. "That'll be fine, Georgia. You sound upset. Are you all right?"

"I'll tell you all about it on Saturday. Where will you be staying?"

"I usually stay at the Hotel Vancouver, but if not, I'll let you know."

She rang off then, and made a third call to Vancouver, this time to book her room. That done, she returned her daughter's call, and was fortunate to find her in.

"I was just checking up on you, Mum. Glad the answering machine is working. How was your visit to Nell's aunt?"

"It went very well. I left Nell there with her, and I expect she'll be there at least another week. Look, Deb, I was going to call you anyway to see if we can get together soon. There are a few things I want to tell you. We haven't had a chance to have a heart to heart since I got back."

"You have been very busy with Nell. She's a nice girl. I like her, Mum. What's her dad like?" she asked, with a sly chuckle.

"You can read me like a book, can't you, my dear. Needless to say, all will be revealed—I think. Are you busy tonight?"

"Tomorrow is better for me. Moss is in town and is coming for dinner tonight, but I can put him off if you like."

"No, tomorrow is fine. Shall I come to you? I haven't seen your flat since you did all that painting. Actually, Deb, tomorrow is better than tonight. I shall make myself a tomato sandwich for supper and go to bed early. I'm rather tired and a bit perturbed over a telephone call I had today. I'll tell you all about it tomorrow. Say hello to Moss from me."

Robin rang off and proceeded to tidy her house, remake the guest room bed and clean the bathrooms. She then made herself take a walk, and when she returned she made herself a sandwich and poured a glass of wine, and soon after had a long hot bath and went to bed. She lay in bed, tired but sleepless, and more perplexed and worried about Georgia's call than she had let on to Deborah. She remembered James saying the night they met that more energy was wasted worrying about things you couldn't change, so Robin turned over and deliberately put Georgia and everything connected with her out of her mind. She instead thought about Eleanor and Nell, and wondered how they were getting on. Through her open window she heard the rain begin to fall, and with that soothing sound in her ears she fell asleep.

The next evening she drove to Deb's flat near the university, bringing a bottle of wine and some smoked salmon for appetizers. Over drinks and then dinner she gradually told Deborah all that had occurred in Scotland.

"I remember Charlie Morrison quite well," Deb said candidly. "Frankly, I could never stand him. Dad made a comment to me, oh, three or four years ago—I don't remember exactly what he said, only I got the impression that Mr. Morrison wasn't what he seemed."

Robin was astonished and said so. "Your father never said a word. We saw them socially only occasionally and there was never a hint of a bad relationship, and Charlie only flirted with me, and with all their other women friends, I might add, in the mildest manner. I was completely taken aback by his ghastly behavior and his innuendoes. Now this strange call from Georgia comes. Plus she still has his recording on her answering machine," she went on with a shudder. "It was a nasty experience hearing his voice like that."

"I think it's a good idea to talk with Mr. Jagger about the whole thing, Mum. And what of Nell's father? Are you thinking of marriage?"

"Deb, it's so soon, isn't it."

"Mum, sometimes someone comes along, and if it's right, it doesn't matter how soon it is. Dad would want you to be happy."

"It's funny how we think we know what the dead would have wanted. But you're probably right. Your father was a very unselfish man."

"The other thing — are you willing to take on his family?"

"There's that, too. Nell is a wonderful girl, and I'm sure she wouldn't resent me. Malcolm is a very intelligent and attractive boy, and he seemed to like me. But...."

"You'll find the answer, Mum. Just think of yourself first. You've got to live your life, and we have to live ours. Besides, I've always wanted to go to Scotland."

On this pleasant note, Robin finished her coffee, and said she should be going, as she hadn't yet packed a suitcase for her two days in Vancouver, and she had promised to volunteer at the church the next morning helping set up for their annual Fall Fair. "I'll be at the Hotel Vancouver tomorrow night and Friday," she said, as she went out the door.

It was nearly five o'clock the next afternoon before Robin got home. Her weekend case was ready in the hall, and she had decided to leave for the ferry no later than at six. She had spent much longer at the church than she had planned, afterwards had run a few errands, and before she knew it, it was getting dark. The light on her answering machine was flashing, and she turned it on. To her dismay it was completely garbled, only a few words were decipherable. She knew at once it was James who had called, but she could not make out what he was saying. She heard Nell's name, and then Eleanor's, and something about 'coming home', and that was all. She glanced at her watch, and knew there was no point in telephoning now. It was one o'clock in the morning in Britain. Instead she looked up Eleanor's number, and put in a call to Salt Spring Island. She was not really surprised to hear Eleanor's answering machine, as she knew they had been planning to go away for a few days. So she left a message.

"Eleanor, this is Robin Lindsay calling. It's Thursday, just after five PM. James has called, and my machine has quit working again, so I was unable to hear what he had to say. I think Nell had better call her father as soon as possible. I am going to Vancouver tonight, and should be back Saturday evening. I'll call you then. Sorry to be in such a rush, but if I leave now I'll be able to drop this infernal machine off at Radio Shack for repairs on my way to the ferry. Talk to you later. 'Bye."

She unplugged the 'infernal machine', bundled it under her arm, and picked up her suitcase. She left the outside light on, got into her car and drove away.

On the ferry, she sat down at one of the workstations and made a schedule for her two days in the city: Thursday—arrive at hotel Friday——-9am appointment with Cam Saturday-lunch with Georgia?

Friday was empty all day after her talk with Cameron. She would call Marilyn Baker, a long time friend, and see if she were free tomorrow, she decided. She quite often had been in touch with her when she was planning a trip across the "pond", as locals called the stretch of water between the mainland and the Island. She got out her calling card, and proceeded to put in a call to her friend.

"Robin! What a coincidence! I was just sitting here wondering whether to change my concert tickets for tomorrow night. Gene has to go out of town. It always seems to happen on symphony nights. I'm beginning to think he dislikes classical music. How about dinner and a concert at the Orpheum tomorrow night?"

"Sounds great, Marilyn. I'm at the Hotel Vancouver for two nights, so I'll meet you at El Caravan at six o'clock. I've got lots to tell you." The little Middle Eastern restaurant near the theater had always been a favorite of theirs. Marilyn agreed, and they both rang off. Robin, pleased, added this to her list, and thought that if it wasn't raining tomorrow, a long walk, lunch on the waterfront somewhere, and some shopping would adequately fill in the day. She considered how much she should tell Marilyn. She would want to hear about her trip, but Robin hoped the local newspapers had not picked up the story of Charlie's death. True, it had occurred three or four weeks ago, and most people had short memories. No one had questioned her about it, so she came to the conclusion that it had not made headlines. Certainly Deb had not read anything about it. Robin and Marilyn had been close friends for a long time, and they had confided in each other before. She would probably play it by ear. She gathered up her notepad and pen, slipped them into her bag, and strolled into the forward lounge to buy a cup of coffee and find a comfortable spot to read her book. It was dark and windy outside. She would save the walk around the decks for her return trip Saturday afternoon.

The next morning she sat in Cameron Jagger's paneled, book lined office, and told her story over again. Her lawyer nodded, asked a few questions, all the while taking notes. When she had finished, she handed him George Sinclair's card.

"This is James' solicitor who advised me. He was very kind, and suggested that I come to you and let you know what had happened."

Cameron Jagger was a tall, thin man in his early fifties who wore old-fashioned horn-rimmed glasses. He leaned back in his swivel office chair and regarded his client, chewing thoughtfully on his pen. He uncrossed his long legs and got up and went over to the window.

"I'm glad you came to me, Robin. I don't remember reading anything about it in the local rags. Certainly your name was never in print, as far as I know. I usually read the papers thoroughly. You said his widow had contacted you."

"Yes. She had asked me, after the inquiry was over, to come and see her when I got home. We weren't especially good friends at all, but she had been very kind to me after Tim's death, and although I really didn't want to talk to her about her husband, I was thinking of calling her. But then yesterday I got this very peculiar call from her. Maybe I'm suffering from an overactive imagination, but she sounded almost frightened. So I agreed to see her tomorrow."

"Be careful, Robin. This may not have been a random killing in St. Andrew's. She may know something dangerous, and that could put you in peril."

Robin hadn't thought of that, and she bit her lip and frowned. "What should I do?"

"See her, by all means, but urge her to see the police if she knows anything. Now, you mentioned to my secretary that you also wanted to discuss your will."

"James wants to marry me, Cam."

Cameron smiled and congratulated her. Robin quickly pointed out that they weren't officially engaged, nor was there any sort of understanding yet. "I'm not sure of me or him," she said frankly. "But I did want to see when I should renew my will." They discussed the possibilities of revising the will if and when she should be remarried, and after a cup of coffee with Cameron, she left his office and went across the street to her hotel. There she changed into walking shoes, and left for a long walk. Her mind was busy the whole time, and she felt better for the exercise, but she still hadn't come to any conclusions regarding James, or what to say to Georgia when she saw her tomorrow. It started to rain after lunch, so she headed back to the hotel, took a long bath, and curled up with her book.

Her friend Marilyn, a short, plump dark-haired woman with a smiling countenance, was already seated and had ordered a bottle of wine when Robin came into the restaurant at 6:00. Marilyn got up and gave Robin a hug and exclaimed how good it was to see her.

"I've missed you, Robin," she said candidly, after Robin had hung her coat up and sat down opposite her. She poured her a glass of wine and said, "Now tell me all your news."

Robin looked at her friend and laughed. "Where shall I start?"

"Well, you've been away for a few weeks, haven't you? You went to Britain, didn't you?"

Robin gazed at her friend, and knew she would have to tell her the whole story. Marilyn was a safe confidante, and she would be unbiased.

"Well," she began, "I went to Scotland in September, and I'd been there about a week, when I got lost in the Highlands and got stuck in the middle of a tremendous thunderstorm."

Marilyn grinned and leaned forward, cupping her face in her hands, elbows on the table. "That's a great beginning. Please don't keep me in suspense."

"I took refuge from the pouring rain in a house which turned out to be a bed and breakfast, and the lady who lived there had her nephew visiting her." Robin's expression grew softer, and she said simply, "He's wonderful, Marilyn. His name is James Maclachlan, he's a widower and has two children, ages nine and seventeen. His marriage ended over eight years ago just after his son Malcolm was born when his wife committed suicide."

Marilyn said nothing.

"There actually was a double tragedy—his mother had been killed in a car crash a few weeks before that. I gather that the marriage was unhappy. He hasn't told me anything about his wife except that she was beautiful and self-centered. The children are surprisingly well adjusted. Nell, his daughter, came home with me. We flew to Calgary and have spent about ten days on the road, sight-seeing. We were very lucky that we've had such a mild autumn. Right now she's visiting her aunt, her mother's sister, who lives on Salt Spring Island. Her mother was an American.

"James lives in an enormous house in the Highlands, they own a small distillery and make very good single malt whisky, have a dairy farm, and you won't believe this, but his father is an earl, and James will inherit the title one day. His father is a lovely man, but I think he has never gotten over losing his wife."

The waiter was hovering, so they ordered their meal. Marilyn shook her head wonderingly. "I thought this sort of thing happened only to people in books. Are you going to marry this Prince Charming? It sounds too good to be true."

"Marilyn, I don't know! There is so much about him that I don't know, but when I was with him, it didn't seem to matter. There's more, too. I guess you could say that I got mixed up in a murder while I was there."

"Good heavens, Robin! You don't do anything by halves, do you? Tell all to Auntie Marilyn."

Over their tabbouli salad Robin related the events that took place in St. Andrew's, then her subsequent discovery of the newspaper story. She left nothing out this time. "You're the first person except for James' solicitor that I've told everything to. I have told Deb some it, leaving out some of the more unpleasant details, and I was at my own lawyer's office today. Mr. Sinclair, that's James' solicitor, advised me to 'apprise your own solicitor of these events' is how he put it in his dry way. I was good advice. Cameron intends to write to him, I think. But it's Georgia's phone call that really bothers me. I'm only going to see her because she was so kind to me after Tim died. I really don't want to talk about Charlie Morrison at all."

"He sounds like a right sleaze."

"You said it, Marilyn! I still find it puzzling that Tim never said anything about him to me. He apparently warned Deb, though, so she was telling me."

"Tim kept his own counsel, though, didn't he, Robin. Some men gossip, but I never heard Tim say a bad word about anybody. He probably thought it wasn't necessary to say to you, 'Look, old girl, don't ever be alone with Charlie, he'll try to get into your knickers,' because probably Charlie, like most lechers, was a coward and would know that Tim would have his balls cut off if he had tried anything with you."

Robin grinned at Marilyn's colorful language, and agreed with her assessment of Tim.

Over the rest of dinner she told Marilyn about Glen Rannoch, the village, and the interesting people she had met. She went on to her holiday with Nell, and meeting Eleanor Shaw.

"She is gorgeous, Marilyn, but so natural and charming. It's as though she doesn't even realize that she's beautiful. She was in love with James when she was young," she continued, as they walked down the street to the theater. "I can't figure out why there isn't a line of men at her door."

"Sometimes men are afraid of a really beautiful woman."

The musical presentation was just what Robin needed. She relaxed for the first time in several days, and afterwards Marilyn refused coffee, saying she needed her beauty sleep. "My news pales in comparison to your doings," she remarked as they walked to her car. "Katie is getting married at Christmas to the nicest guy. I can't imagine why he wants to marry her. She's been god-awful to live with at home," went on Katie's mother. "Good luck to him. You'll be getting an invitation, of course," she added.

Robin laughed. She knew more than anyone that Marilyn adored her daughter, and that they both enjoyed their rows.

"Give her my very best wishes, won't you," she said, kissing Marilyn fondly, "and also to that great bear of a husband of yours. You realize that if it wasn't for our friendship, I would have stolen him from you long ago."

"Right, I'll tell Gene that. It'll make his day. Bye-bye, darling. Let me know any pertinent developments, romance-wise as well as crime-wise."

When she got back to the hotel, she discovered that Deb had called, but since it was nearly midnight she decided to leave it until the morning. She climbed into bed, and for the first time in a few nights fell immediately into a deep sleep and didn't stir until morning.

She was awakened by the telephone, and thought it must be Deb, but it was Georgia, asking her when she could come to her house. It was nine o'clock, much to Robin's surprise.

"I'm still in bed. I'll have my breakfast and check out and drive right over. I'll be there before eleven."

She was half way to Georgia's when she remembered that she hadn't phoned Deb. Ah well, she'd phone from Georgia's.

Georgia's home, a large house overlooking the river on Southwest Marine Drive, was surrounded by hedges fifteen feet high and a locked gate. There was a 'For Sale' sign on the boulevard. She rang the bell, and a voice over the intercom asked for her name. The gate opened noiselessly, and she got back into her car and drove up the driveway and parked the car. Even then she had to ring the doorbell, and was scrutinized by someone within. Finally the door opened, and a woman showed her in. Georgia was in the living room, impatiently waiting for her.

"Robin, oh I'm so glad to see you!"

"Georgia, what's all this about? Were you expecting someone else? Why all this secrecy and security? Is that your housekeeper?"

"Robin, I am so frightened. Maria has given her notice, and I'll be all alone here!"

Robin took one look at her and said, "Sit down, Georgia." She left the room and went to the kitchen, where Maria was preparing to leave.

"Mrs. Morrison needs a cup of tea; could you make us a pot, please?"

"I'm on my way out, Miss. Everything you want is right here. I am sorry, but this is not a good house to work in. Good-bye." She put on her coat and quickly went out the kitchen door, leaving Robin to stare at her retreating back.

She plugged in the kettle, found tea, and china, made a pot of tea, and then went back to the living room and found Georgia where she had left her.

"Come on. Georgia," she said kindly. "Drink some tea and tell me what this is all about."

Georgia looked as though she hadn't slept all night. Her face was thin and drawn, and she hadn't put any makeup on.

"It's Johnny Eden. He's been phoning me and making threats."

"Eden? Charlie's friend?"

"He wants money. Charlie took out a huge life insurance policy last year, and he must have told Johnny."

"But what is he threatening you about?"

Georgia didn't answer, but only said, with a sly look in her eyes, "I wanted to know whether or not you really killed Charlie."

Robin sat back and laughed. "Really Georgia, that's nonsense and you know it."

The frightened look was back. "I know, Robin, I'm sorry, it's just that I can't think about what to do."

"Georgia, if you don't tell me simply and clearly what is going on, I am going to walk out that door, and catch the next ferry home!"

"Johnny has been calling me and saying he'll go to the police if I don't pay him money."

"What will he tell the police?"

"Where I was when Charlie was killed."

"What do you mean? Weren't you in London?"

"Well, yes. Linda and I were in London while Charlie and Johnny were playing golf. We were going up on the train on Friday to Edinburgh where they would meet us. She must have told him that I went up early."

"So where were you were on that Tuesday?"

"St. Andrew's."

Robin was dumbstruck. She just sat there and stared at Georgia. "Whatever for?"

"I was sick to death of Charlie's philandering. I thought he had a woman with him."

"So you took the train to St. Andrew's on Tuesday, and then what?"

"I didn't kill him, if that's what you mean," she protested. "I didn't even see him. I got as far as the outside of the hotel, and I lost my nerve. I went back to Edinburgh, and stayed there until Linda joined me the next day. She told the police we were together all the time. Johnny must have seen me, and made Linda tell him."

The phone rang in the hall at that moment, and Georgia jumped. "Don't answer it! It might be him."

The answering machine came on and a prerecorded message in Charlie's voice asked the caller to leave a message. Again it gave Robin an eerie feeling to hear his disembodied voice. The caller said, "You know who this is, Georgia. Phone me."

"No way, no way," muttered Georgia, rocking back and forth.

"Georgia, pull yourself together. The first thing we'll do is call the telephone company and request an unlisted number. Then you just give whatever friends you want that number. When Johnny calls the old number, he'll just get 'that number is no longer in service.'" She went to the phone. "Where's your telephone book?" Very soon she was talking to an agent, and explaining that Mrs. Morrison had been having some unpleasant phone calls. She returned once and asked Georgia what her mother's maiden name was. In a little while she came back with a number written on a piece of paper. "Here's your new number. It is unlisted; they won't give it out to anyone."

"Oh thank you, Robin. What shall I do about Johnny?"

"I think you should call the police. Blackmail is a crime."

"What if they think I had something to do with Charlie's death?"

"I'd trust them to find out the truth."

"I don't want the police."

"Look, Georgia, you can't stay a prisoner in your own house. What about your lawyers?"

"They were Charlie's friends. I don't like them at all."

"How about Cameron Jagger? He's a friend as well as my lawyer. You could talk to him."

She was wavering. "Well, maybe..."

"Look, I'll call him at his home, and hope he is in. You shouldn't waste any time."

Fortunately, Cameron was at home, and listened while Robin told him what she had learned.

"He'll see you tomorrow," she said, hanging up the phone. "He's doing me a great favor, and will come here. Luckily, he lives not too far away."

"You'll stay with me tonight, won't you? I'm afraid to be alone."

"I really should be going home. Good grief, that reminds me, I haven't returned Deb's call. May I phone to Victoria?"

Georgia waved her hand in an assenting gesture, and Robin went out to the telephone. There was no one at Deb's, so she left a message that she was at Georgia's, and that she'd be home tomorrow instead of today.

"Don't give her my number!" Georgia called out.

Robin shrugged, and hung up the phone, and prepared to put on a long day and evening.

Chapter 24

COMPLICATIONS

Robin took the 3pm ferry the next day. Cam had come to the house, interviewed Georgia, and talked to her for a long time. She finally agreed to talk to the police, and Cam assured her he would go with her the next day. He advised Robin to help Georgia to check into a downtown hotel. He asked her if she had a trustworthy woman friend nearby who give her some support. Georgia shook her head dumbly. Linda Eden had been her closest friend, now even she couldn't be trusted. She had called her real estate agent, to tell her that she would be away from the house, and could show it any time. A cleaning service was coming the next day to go through the house, and could she open the house for them? Her agent agreed, and Robin left Georgia packing her bags, focused on something at last.

"Thank you, Cam, for sacrificing your Sunday morning," she said as she went to the door with him.

"I just hope Mrs. Morrison appreciates your efforts on her behalf."

"She was kind to me after Tim died. Also, she can talk to me about her husband more easily than with someone else, perhaps."

"You're a nice woman, Robin. Would you object if I made some inquiries about the Maclachlan family?"

Robin was taken aback a little, but said slowly, "No, I guess not, Cam. I know you have my best interests at heart. I don't think you'll find any skeletons that I haven't heard about already."

"His wife's death concerns me for several reasons. If it was indeed suicide, it might indicate a pretty poor relationship between him and his wife. If someone else administered the poison, that's another ball game."

"You mean murder, Cam. That's a grave accusation. It's been my thought that she might have deliberately not left a note in order to muddy the waters. 'I can still cause trouble when I'm gone' sort of attitude. I'm sure the police investigated that aspect, in fact James intimated that he had been a suspect for a while."

"The spouse is always the prime suspect. Husbands can be driven to murder, you know." He got into his car and started the engine. "Take care, Robin. You'll hear from me soon."

There's darkness in him, Robin. Take care.

"I don't know whether to thank you again or not, Cam. However, I know that James couldn't have done such a thing."

He waved, smiling, and drove away.

Soon after, she followed Georgia downtown and helped her check in and settle at a small hotel that Cam had suggested. Robin had an afterthought as she was leaving, and she asked to speak to the manager.

"Mrs. Morrison is being harassed by a man," she explained. "That is why she's here. If anyone phones or comes around asking if she is registered here, please deny it. No matter what he says—or she— he could even get his wife to make inquiries. Those that she wants to know her whereabouts, she'll tell herself."

The manager promised to put a notation next to the name in the computer to alert clerks not to answer such inquiries. Trouble was the last thing they wanted for their guests, he declared as he shook hands with Robin. Robin hurried away, satisfied that Georgia was safe and that Cam would take over from now on, she got into her car and headed out to the ferries.

As she drove into her driveway three hours later she was surprised to see Deb's small car sitting by the front door. She had phoned her daughter from the ferry, but got the answering machine again. She had walked the deck in the afternoon sunshine grumbling to herself about people who leave messages, and then don't stay home to take the return call. She let herself in, calling out her daughter's name. Deborah appeared in the door to the living room.

"Mum! Where have you been? Didn't you get my message to call me?"

"I've made several calls, but you weren't there. Don't tell me you've been here all this time! Why?"

"I did leave this number with the hotel..."

"When they told me my daughter had called and started to give me the number, I said I knew your number, just assuming you'd be at home. I'm sorry, dear." She took off her coat and hung it in the closet.

"I picked up my messages over the phone and got your call, but Mrs. Morrison's phone number had been changed, and I didn't know how to get in touch." She watched her mother go to the bar in the living room and pour herself a stiff drink.

"I need this after spending twenty-four hours with Georgia Morrison," she confessed, sitting down and putting her feet up. "It's a long story. What's up, Deb?"

"Nell has gone home."

Robin felt as if her face had been slapped. "Gone home! When? Why?"

"Nell called Scotland as soon as she got your message. Her grandfather has had a stroke, and her father wanted her to come home. In fact, she said that her grandfather was asking for the three of you, he was very urgent, very distressed. Eleanor went with her."

"She did? Do you know how he is?"

"No. They left last night. I guess they should be nearly there by now. Nell was *very* upset that she couldn't say goodbye to you. They came to pick up the rest of her luggage, and caught a noon plane to Vancouver yesterday. They were flying to Glasgow and taking the train to Inverness. Mum, I think you should go too."

"You met Eleanor, then."

"Yes. Stunning! Very dangerous to let her loose around Nell's father. If you're serious about him—should I call him Mr. Maclachlan or James or what? —I think you had better get going. Besides, Lord Rannoch was asking for you."

"Was James asking for me?" she said quietly. "That's more to the point."

"I almost forgot: Nell dashed off a note to you while she was here." Deb produced a folded sheet of paper and handed it to her mother.

Dear Robin, (she wrote) *I am sorry we couldn't get in touch with you to let you know what has been happening. Deb has probably told you that Grandfather has had a stroke, and he has been asking for you, Eleanor and me. Dad said he's holding his own, and will probably settle down once he knows we're on his way. Please come as soon as you can. The dear knows it's been an expensive time for you, but I know Dad wants you to be there. I do too! Thank goodness Eleanor has agreed to come. We made a tentative booking for you, but cancelled it just now.*

Thank you so very, very much for your company and your kindness. I thought of leaving my luggage so you would have to come and bring it home with you, but I wanted to wear my gorgeous coat. (Are my priorities skewed?) Darling Robin, please, please come. So I won't say goodbye, but only au revoir. *Love, Nell*

Robin looked up with tears in her eyes. "I feel as though someone has died."

Deb looked her mother straight in the eyes. "Mum, you should go. If you hurry and get packed, I can get you to an eight o'clock flight to Vancouver. There is a flight that leaves at ten PM that goes straight to Glasgow. You're booked on that."

"Deb! I just can't leave like that!"

"Yes you can, and you will." Robin had never seen her daughter so determined. She finally allowed her to help her pack, and drive her to the airport. On the way Robin sketched the events that took place in Vancouver, her interview with Cam, her evening with Marilyn Baker ("That reminds me, Katie is getting married at Christmas"), and Georgia Morrison's problems. "Cam Jagger will probably be in touch, Deb, just tell him you packed me off to Scotland and that I don't care what skeletons he unearths. This is one time I'm glad that Den is away. He would fuss so." She kissed Deb. "I will phone you. You'll be at the house, won't you? Goodbye, darling, and God bless."

Eleanor and Nell sat in the swaying coach as the train to Inverness rumbled north. Eleanor had been thinking long and hard about her relationship with all the Maclachlans.

"I have been very selfish," she said aloud.

"What on earth do you mean?" asked Nell, turning in surprise to her aunt.

"When I agreed to be your godmother, I made some promises, which I haven't been very good at."

"But what about all your wonderful letters, and the gifts, and the books? I have always known that you loved me," she declared passionately.

Eleanor smiled at her niece and took her hand. "Thank you for that," she said.

Nell moved closer to her aunt. "Tell me about my mother. I've wanted to ask you all week, but never had the courage. You said that first day at your place that Dad met my mother through you—that you had met him first."

"Yes, they met at my parents'—I had invited him there for tea." She paused and thought a moment. "You will have guessed that my sister and I had a very uneasy relationship. She was older, beautiful, talented, and my mother spoiled her. She was very insensitive too— no empathy for a teenager in the throes of first love. She just saw James and whisked him off from under my nose. I couldn't do a thing. You know that I wasn't even going to go to their wedding? My father made me see that I must, but I went very reluctantly. She didn't ask me or your aunt Katharine to be her bridesmaids—she wanted ones that 'matched'—all pretty, but not as pretty as she," she added, a bit bitterly. "However, I was glad in the end that I went because I met your grandparents, and found a wonderful friend in your grandmother."

"Why was my mother so unhappy?"

"I don't know, Nell. Perhaps she was one of these people who are incapable of happiness because the whole world revolves around them and how they are feeling. I'm sorry to say this about your mother, but it was true. She could be charming if she wanted, and she was very beautiful. Have you seen that portrait of her that used to hang in your father's study? It was exquisite."

"I actually forgot about it, so I haven't seen it since I was small. Perhaps Dad put it away after she died."

"I'll ask James about it. It might be good for you to know more about your mother. I'm afraid I am biased. Though I've always been glad the last time I saw her we were pleasant to each other—that was just after your baptism. I was worried about her mood swings, and she promised to see her doctor about it. I didn't see her when she came to look after my mother when she was ill, and of course she didn't go to the funeral—she was busy having Malcolm."

"She never went to see you when she went to America?"

Eleanor shook her head. "Washington D.C. is a long way from Seattle. And I didn't go to Washington either. I had come home from visiting my mother before Claire arrived. I guess I could have stayed—but remember that my mother and I have never been close. All she could talk about was Claire—when was she coming and how long was she staying. I finally booked a flight home before Claire was due. I think Dad was a little disappointed in me, but I couldn't stand it any longer. I promised myself that I'd come for a visit in the spring—I never went, of course—who knew I'd be coming to her funeral? And I still feel badly not visiting you more often, Nell. I could have sent for you to come for a visit. Now here is Robin, who has only known you for a few weeks, doing what I should have done long ago."

"But we're together now, and we'll get well acquainted. I just hope Grandfather is going to be okay. He's at home—wouldn't he be in hospital if he was in danger of dying?"

"You're quite right, Nell, and we must hope for the best."

Nell settled down and closed her eyes. Eleanor did the same, but couldn't sleep. She kept thinking about herself and Claire and James. She had been horribly jealous of her sister, because she had

had everything that Nell wanted: James, a beautiful baby, a gracious home to cherish, wonderful in-laws. Why couldn't Claire realize how lucky she was? And when Claire died, Eleanor had allowed herself to dream. Hadn't he kissed her with such longing the night she was looking after Nell? James should have seen that it was Eleanor who cared for him—he should have seen her for what she was—but the visit was a disaster when she travelled there to her sister's funeral. Fee was gone, James' father was prostrate with grief, and James was unreachable. He barely spoke to her during the few days she was there, and as soon as she could she fled back home to America. Aunt Effie had been a wonderful support, and Eleanor busied herself in her music, and was reasonably happy. Now that James had found someone to love, she must put away her dreams forever.

She turned and twisted restlessly in her seat.

Yes, she had been very selfish. She was glad that Nell had not persisted in asking her just now, exactly why she hadn't come to visit while she was growing up. Would she have answered and said that she had been deeply in love with James, but he only thought of her as a sister? That she couldn't bear the thought of seeing him only as a friend? That her feelings were more important than Nell's well-being? Oh, she had told herself what a wonderful aunt she was to Nell, sending letters and gifts. Of course she loved Nell, but apparently not enough to put aside her wounded feelings, and do what was right. And was she really happy for James, now that he had fallen in love with someone else?

Eleanor despised herself.

Nell and Eleanor arrived at Rannoch Castle in the pouring rain. James had met the train and couldn't conceal his disappointment when Robin was not with them. He greeted Eleanor with great enthusiasm, giving her a warm brotherly kiss, and hugged Nell until she begged for mercy.

"It seems years since you left, Nell. We've all missed you."

"How's Grandfather?"

"About the same. He'll be glad to see you."

"There is something on his mind," he said later as they drove south to Glen Rannoch. "Aunt Sarah is with us and Malcolm phones every day from school. Katharine and Roger have worn a path between the Manse and the Castle. Roger says the whole congregation is praying for him."

It was dark when they reached the big house, but lights were burning in many windows. Janet was there with tea and hot buttered toast for the weary travelers. Iain had been sitting with the earl and he came downstairs to the morning room where the new arrivals were refreshing themselves. He shook hands with Eleanor.

"Iain, it's lovely to see you." she said with a smile. "It's been too long."

Nell had jumped up when he came in. She didn't know how she looked. Her curls were awry, and she had no make-up on, though why she should worry about that, since Iain had seen her in a mess many times in the past. He smiled down at her, and said, "I missed you, Nell," and hugged her.

He said to James, "Uncle Robert is awake."

"The doctor is restricting visitors to two at a time," James said to Nell and Eleanor. "Why don't you take Eleanor up to see him, and you can explain why Robin didn't come with you."

As Nell led the way up the broad staircase, Eleanor thought that the house hadn't changed at all. The double mahogany doors to the earl's suite were open, and the nurse was in the kitchen. She came to the door and motioned them to go in.

"How is he really?" whispered Nell.

"He's doing fine, though he's restless waiting for 'Eleanor' to arrive. He's been talking about nobody else since your father went to meet you," she answered. "I know, if Dr. Rennie was at all worried about him, he would have him taken straightaway to the hospital in Inverness."

The two tiptoed through the sitting room and into the earl's bedroom.

"I'm home, Grandfather. What a fright you've been giving everybody. Look who I brought from Canada. It's Eleanor!"

Eleanor sat down on the other chair and took his hand. "Here I am. Nell and I came as soon as we heard you were ill."

The earl turned his head from side to side, smiling at them both. His voice was faint, but quite firm. "You both are a beautiful sight. Thank you for coming all that way." He looked around the room. "Did Robin come, too? I want to see her as well."

"She was away when Dad called. I'm sure she'll come as soon as she can get a flight."

"Where is Roger?"

"I think he was taking Aunt Katharine home and coming straight back."

He closed his eyes, and they thought he had fallen asleep. But then he spoke, and his voice was quite strong.

"It was your twenty-first birthday, wasn't it?"

"What's that, Grandfather?"

"Eleanor. When she came to see you when you were baptized. It was your twenty-first birthday, wasn't it, Eleanor?"

Eleanor smiled. "Actually, it was my twenty-second. There was a lovely dinner, and Katharine and Roger had just gotten engaged. We toasted them, and the baby (that was you, of course, Nell) and you toasted me as well. I'm sure you opened a bottle of champagne."

A little while later, the door opened, and the nurse said, "Mr. Perry is here."

"Nell, darling, will you excuse us?" the earl said. "I do want to talk to Roger and Eleanor."

She bent and kissed him. "I should go and get Eleanor's bags taken to her room. I'll be back."

Roger came in as Nell slipped out, and he closed the door behind him.

"Here I am, and here is Eleanor at last. How well she looks, don't you agree, Robert?"

The old man said gallantly, "I always said she was just as lovely as Katharine. But I have things to tell the both of you. Do I have your word that it will go no further? Not to James or Katharine or anyone?"

Eleanor looked bewilderedly at Roger, and then said to the earl, "Yes, I promise."

Roger said, "I'm your pastor, Robert, and you know that what you tell me stays with me."

Roger's father-in-law leaned back into his pillows and gave a long gusty sigh. "It was when Claire was expecting Malcolm..."

Chapter 25

ROBERT 1987

Fiona, Countess of Rannoch looked gravely at her daughter-in-law. "Claire, you'll have this child because it is the right thing to do." Her voice was cutting and her eyes, usually sparkling with humor, were flat and steely.

"I nearly died with Nell."

"I know you were very ill, but we'll have the specialist, and if there are any complications we'll be on to them straight away."

Claire sat down. "You don't understand how wretched I feel."

"You don't have an abortion because you feel wretched."

"Rape victims can."

Fee frowned at her daughter-in-law. "What's that got to do with it?"

Claire said defiantly, "Your precious son raped me, that's what it has to do with it, and this is the result." And she looked down at her abdomen with loathing.

Fee was speechless for only a moment. "I don't believe you."

"Of course you don't. He can do nothing wrong in your eyes."

He married you, didn't he? Fee clenched her fists, kept her mouth firmly closed on that thought, and only asked curiously, "and what do you call rape?"

"He forced himself on me. We were in the hotel in Edinburgh. I was tired from my trip."

"He wanted sex, and you didn't. Good God girl, you'd been away for six weeks. Isn't a husband entitled to...?"

"I knew you'd see it only from his side," interrupted Claire, glaring at her.

Fee forced herself to speak calmly. "I know that you're frightened that you'll go through the same awful time as before, but it doesn't necessarily follow. We'll have the best of doctors..."

"No. I went through it once, and I'm not going to do it again. It wasn't my fault that Nell wasn't a boy."

"Claire. You will have the baby because it is the right thing to do," repeated Fee calmly.

Claire burst into tears. "Nobody understands."

"What do you want from us, Claire?"

Claire looked up at her mother-in-law, her violet blue eyes streaming. "Not another baby, that's for damn sure."

Fee related all this to Robert later that evening. "I'm afraid she might do something foolish, Rob."

"Have you talked to Jamie?"

"I'm not about to cross-examine my son on his sex life."

"Why on earth do you suppose she married Jamie?" he asked wearily.

Fee shook her head. "I really think that she liked the idea of being a countess one day." She leaned over and kissed him affectionately. "I've never withheld sex from you, have I, Robin?"

"I always know when you're not in the mood, Fee darling, so the situation has never arisen." He grinned at her wickedly. "For example, at this moment, you just might be willing." He nibbled her ear affectionately, and with one hand began to unbutton her shirt.

Fee went into his arms with a throaty laugh. "You're a right randy old man, my lord," and kissed him soundly.

Time went by, and there was no more talk of abortion. Claire sulked for a few days; Nell crept around like a mournful shadow.

"Is Mummy going to die, Grandfather?" she asked one evening after their bed time reading session.

"What makes you think that, Nell?"

"I heard her say that we'd be sorry when she was dead."

"Nellie, darling, sometimes Mummies have a bad time when they're having babies. They very seldom die."

"Is that the honest truth?"

"Yes, Nell, it is. Look at your Auntie Kath. She feels grand, and she'll be having a bairn a month later than your mum."

"I know. Isn't it wonderful? They will be cousins and almost the same age. You know, Grandfather," she said seriously, "Maybe it's because she wants one ever so much, and Mummy doesn't."

Robert was speechless.

"I prayed *very* hard for Auntie Kath and Uncle Roger to have a baby. I hope they're both boys. Won't they have fun playing together! I'll never tell my wee brother that Mummy didn't want him at first. I expect she'll change her mind when he arrives, don't you think?"

"I'm sure she will, sweetheart," he answered huskily.

The months following were relatively calm. It was that spring that Robert was asked by the Glen Rannoch villagers to join their darts club at the Crow and Gate, the local pub. Robert was a modest man, and the locals were very fond of the family 'up at the Castle', especially the current head of the Maclachlan clan, whom they considered their Laird. In Robert's eyes they had conferred an honor upon him, and that was his attitude among the men there. They loved him for it, and were also glad to have his prowess in darts on their team. So began a weekly ritual: Tuesday afternoons he took the station wagon and drove down to the village at two o'clock. He got into the habit of doing household errands, then stopping in at the Manse for a wee crack with Katharine on his way home.

He watched his daughter bloom and grow more beautiful (if that were possible) as her pregnancy advanced. Her hair, skin and eyes shone with health. She was in direct contrast to Claire, whose hair and complexion suffered, and whose moods swung wildly. Now that it was far too late to end the pregnancy she endured her discomfort with bad grace. Even though the specialist had pronounced her fit, her blood pressure being only slightly elevated, Claire took to her bed and made life miserable for anybody foolish enough to stay around her.

Fee even begged Eleanor to come for a visit, remembering how good she had been with Claire after Nell was born, but Eleanor was back in Washington with her mother, who was dying of cancer. Claire had not been told that her mother was now terminally ill. James, rightly or wrongly, felt that the knowledge would cause more stress than she could handle. Mary Rose was the only person who seemed to be able to cope with Claire. She was firm and took no nonsense from her mistress. Every day she had her walking in the garden that Claire had designed, she gave her soothing massages, and shampooed and set her hair frequently, and brought her a jug of hot chocolate at night. When word came in June that Mrs. Shaw had died, it was Mary that broke the news. Claire wept stormily, grief-stricken and angry that she hadn't been told that her mother had been dying. She went into labor soon after that, and to everyone's surprise she had a quick and relatively easy labor without the assistance of surgery or the benefit of an anesthetic. Malcolm was born at home in his mother's bed with only the local doctor and Mary Rose in attendance. Nell had been hustled off to the Manse when it became clear that there would be no time to get Claire to the nearest hospital, let alone into Inverness. Claire was frightened, not knowing what to expect (she had refused to attend prenatal classes, and Nell had been born under a general anesthetic), but Mary had calmed her down and helped her to do the proper breathing. She told the doctor she had helped two friends during the births of their children, as the fathers had been squeamish about entering a birthing room.

"You should take up nursing," he advised her.

"Not me," snorted Mary Rose. "I prefer people who are well."

The family welcomed the new son and heir, but it soon transpired that he was allergic to cow's milk, and Claire found it difficult to nurse him. The whole process she seemed to dislike intensely, so they tried a breast pump, and then bottle feeding Malcolm, but Claire wasn't able to extract enough milk.

"I feel exactly like one of James' cows," she said in disgust.

Fee, unexpectedly, was her ally. She had attempted to nurse her babies even though the trend in the fifties was to bottle-feed. When she had to give up breast feeding, she felt a vague sense of failure; that she had fallen short of ideal motherhood. She now defended Claire against the district nurse who kept exhorting Claire to 'try harder' and from Nanny's silent disapproval.

"It's not easy for some," she said, taking the screaming infant. "Where, oh where is Eleanor, when we need her to soothe the baby? Remember her with Nell, Nanny?"

They tried goat's milk, and soya milk, but nothing worked, so finally had to get in touch with the hospital where there was a mother's milk bank. So after Robert's darts on Tuesdays he would drive into Inverness and pick up a week's supply of milk donated by various mothers in the district.

Malcolm was baptized when he was three weeks old. He wore the gown his sister had worn eight years before, and the family gathering took place, but it didn't seem to be the happy celebration as it had been for Nell. Katharine, hugely pregnant, was nevertheless radiantly beautiful as she stood with James and Claire as Godmother to her small nephew. Claire was thin and her face was drawn, and there were lines between her eyes that hadn't been there before. Afterwards folks remarked that Mistress Maclachlan hadn't looked at all well, and wasn't she also in mourning for her own mother? Mary Rose had told her mother that she had been wild with grief when they told her of her mother's death. She also had terrible tantrums; Mrs. Rose didn't know how poor Mr. James put up with it.

It was a warm July day that Sunday, and they took pictures in the Manse garden, and a lunch was served for the family. Mrs. Stevens inexplicably had given the cook the day off and she was finding it hard to cope. Mary Rose was helping out and had asked her mother to come in at the last minute to help out in the kitchen. Mrs. Stevens had let the soup burn, so Mrs. Rose whipped up a cold tomato soup in no time at all. Mrs. Rose opined in a loud voice that it was time for Mrs. Stevens to retire.

The next day Robert drove the aging Jaguar into Inverness for its regular servicing, and young Charlie the garage assistant drove him back to Glen Rannoch. The earl was intending to have Charlie drop him off at the fork in the road and he would walk to his office at the distillery, but he changed his mind as they were approaching the turn.

"Would you mind driving me up to the house, Charlie?" he asked. "I've had a sore throat all morning, and I think I'll take it easy today. Now that Iain is back James is spending more time at the Distillery. They don't need me today."

As they turned up through the trees a car appeared around the bend, and with tires squealing, barely squeezed by them. It was Claire in her sports car, and she was driving rather recklessly, thought the earl, for this narrow and twisting track. Charlie braked and almost went off the road. He swore loudly and asked who the hell was yon crazy woman?

"My daughter-in-law," said Robert shortly. "She'll crash that car one day."

He dropped him off at the front door with a cheery wave and a suggestion to have a hot toddy and go to bed. "We'll call ye when the Jag is ready, and someone will be out to collect you. You're no' in a rush for her, are ye, my Lord?"

"Not at all, Charlie. The station wagon's been giving us a wee bit of trouble lately; we'll bring it in next week, and my son has his own car. If it's not ready tomorrow, that's fine."

He found Fee vacuuming their suite furiously. She switched off the Hoover as he came in and put it away in the kitchen closet. She washed her hands at the sink and came out and kissed him.

"I've just had a thundering row with Claire. She has said some things I cannot forgive. I also said a few things myself."

"Charlie and I met her coming down the hill at a furious clip. I thought she looked pretty grim. We were practically forced off the road. I've never heard Charlie swear before."

"Mary Rose must have told her about the luncheon fiasco in the kitchen yesterday. She wants me to get rid of Mrs. Stevens."

"What happened yesterday?" he asked. "There was nothing the matter with the lunch."

"Oh, Rob, you never notice things like that. For one thing, she forgot to tell Cook that we'd need her for the lunch and gave her the day off. Then she put the soup on while we were at the church and practically burned down the kitchen, if you can believe Mary Rose. No, I've noticed that Mrs. Stevens isn't coping as well as she used to, but I'm not having Claire tell me to fire a staff member who has been with us for over thirty years and is like family. I wrote to her daughter Janet last week and asked her to come and see her mother. Poor Janet has had a bad time of it lately. Her husband has walked out on her with another woman, and she's divorcing him. I told her if she needed a job there was always a place here for her. You remember how she practically grew up with the children. I'm very fond of Janet, and I am worried about her mother. But for Claire to march in here and demand we send her away...I was plain furious, let me tell you, Robin. Then she berated me for comparing her with Eleanor. I asked her what the devil she was going on about and she said she heard me moaning about how I wished her sister were here to soothe the baby—and to say this after I'd been defending her about breast-feeding. The district nurse was the one who was going on about her not trying hard enough." Fee got up and paced the sitting room. "Then she went on and on about James, and from now on it was separate bedrooms. 'I hope you're satisfied with the son and heir,' she hissed at me'—she did hiss, Rob—'because there will be no more babies.' I accused her marrying James only because of the title, and of being frigid and needing psychiatric help, and I thought she was going to hit me! 'Talk about Randy Andy, it's Randy Jamie here,' she said. And then she insinuated that *you* had made advances at her, Robin! I was speechless. 'It'd be Randy Robby if I let him,' she said, and whirled and left the room. I saw her stride across the lawn to the garage and take her car."

Robert got up and enfolded his wife in his arms. "She'll be over her tantrum in a while. I think that's one of the things that infuriates her about James. He won't fight with her. He just leaves the room."

Fee kissed him. "I won't be speaking to her for a while, I can tell you that."

"I thought I'd make myself a hot toddy and go to bed," he said presently. "My sore throat hasn't gone away."

"And here I am going on and on about Claire, and you're not feeling so well," Fee exclaimed, contrite. She gave him her melting smile. "You go and have a hot shower and I'll make the toddy. I'll even join you in bed if that would make you feel better."

Robert kissed her in return. "I'll take that offer under advisement," he answered with a grin, and turned and went into the bathroom.

A little while later he appeared in his enormous terry cloth robe and he sipped his hot drink while he gazed out the window. He saw Claire drive into the garage, come out the side door, and then turn and go back in. At that moment Fee called to him from the bedroom, and forgetting Claire, he joined his wife in their big, canopied bed. Her black hair was tumbling down around her bare shoulders, and her dark eyes were sparkling. She held out her arms, and he crawled into bed and wrapped his arms around her.

The next morning James joined them for breakfast. He was very quiet, and finally he said, "Claire is insisting on separate bedrooms. I've asked her if she would go with me and see a marriage counselor, but she's adamant she won't. She was outside last night wandering around after dark in her night things. I saw her come up the stairs quietly and when I asked her what on earth she was doing, she just shrugged. She's left Nanny to look after Malcolm most of the time, and she hardly says a word to Nell. Though Nell's usually in the nursery with Nanny and Malcolm. I must say she loves her brother." He was thoughtful. "I'm even considering divorce, Mother. This can't go on much longer if she won't get help. I wish Eleanor were here to talk to her."

Fee was visibly upset. "Jamie, dear, I had a horrible row with her yesterday. We both said some awful things to each other."

"She said to me, 'You can't make me leave here, you know. I'm staying whether you like it or not.' I hadn't even mentioned separation, let alone divorce. I've packed a few things and moved them into one of the guest rooms." He sighed. "The whole village will know, of course; Mary Rose will tell her mother, and Mrs. Rose will broadcast our affairs to everyone."

Fee got up resolutely. "I will speak to Mary Rose, and appeal to her better instincts, if she has any. She's loyal to Claire; I'll say that much for her. I'll just have to convince her that it would harm Claire for gossip to be spread," she said firmly, and went out in search of the girl.

Robert walked down to the office at the Distillery, more to get away from the unpleasant atmosphere in his home than for any need to work. Later James dropped him off at the house for lunch, saying he would spend some time with Iain at the farm, and they would find their own lunch later. Robert went slowly upstairs after his meal, feeling worse than he had the day before. He had a drink, which was unusual for him at that time of day, got undressed and crawled into bed. Fee found him there a short time later.

"I don't think I'll go to the darts club today," he told her. "Oh blast, Malcolm's milk! I should fetch it today, shouldn't I?"

"Don't worry, darling, I'll do it for you. I'd ask James, but he and Iain are busy at the farm getting Iain organized—it's wonderful having Iain back, isn't it—I could do a little shopping in Inverness and kill two birds with one stone..."

"Are you sure, my dear?"

"I'll go, Robin, it's no problem." She kissed him warmly, admonished him to have a good rest, and went out of the room. She looked over her shoulder at him and smiled. "Be back soon, darling."

He didn't sleep, but got up, inexplicably restless, and went out into the sitting room and looked out the window. He saw the station wagon emerge from the garage and pass through the gates. He put on his robe over his pajamas and went out on to the landing. Claire was standing with her back to him, halfway down the stairs looking out the window. She turned, and Robert saw her brush her hands together in a 'that's that' gesture. She started up the stairs, and Robert backed in to the doorway. A smile curved her lips. It was a cruel smile, Robert thought. She paused, not seeing him, and turned to go into the gallery. Robert said quietly, "Claire."

She jumped in surprise, and turned with a gasp. He eyes were wide with shock and the color drained from her face, leaving two patches of red where she had applied rouge. She backed away. "You! You should be going to the village." She took a step toward him. "Who's in the station wagon?"

Claire coming out of the garage the day before, then turning and going back in. James saying this morning that she had been out last night in her night attire and not saying what for.

A sense of impending doom was upon him. He took a couple of steps toward her and said. "Claire. What have you done?"

She backed away from him, suddenly angry. "I don't know what you're talking about," she declared.

"I don't believe you. Fee is in that car. What have you done to it?"

"Nothing! Nothing."

He took her by the shoulders and repeated desperately, his face close to hers, "What have you done, Claire?"

"Take your hands off me!" She twisted away from his grasp and ran up the stairs. He heard the big doors slam and the key turn in the lock.

He walked down the stairs as though in a trance, and went to the front door. As he stood there he heard an explosion in the distance. All was quiet for a short time until he heard voices in the distance, shouting. Presently he heard sirens wailing. He was in his study when James and Mrs. Stevens, her face streaming with tears, came to tell him what he somehow knew, that his wife had been killed.

The next few days were a blur of police and doctors, incessant questions. He said nothing of his encounter with Claire. Someone said that she was in a hysterical state. Sarah came and shared his grief. She was the one who told him that Simon had been born. Katharine was fine, she said, and was bearing up well. The bairn was healthy.

"Thank God," was all he said.

He called Eleanor in America. "I understand that you can't be here. I know your thoughts will be with us all. She was very fond of you, Eleanor." Claire's sister had been hardly able to speak.

The inquiry a week later ruled it an accident. There had been nothing left of the car to examine. The gas tank had been full and the car had exploded upon impact thirty feet down the steep slope from where it had gone off the road on the first sharp curve. They said a pillar of smoke a hundred feet high could be seen all over the valley.

The church was crowded with people from all over. There were flowers and cards and telegrams from far and wide. Katharine brought Simon with her in a carrying cradle. Nell was dazed with disbelief. She clung to her grandfather. He was glad of her warm person next to him. Claire was stony faced; James, the reserved one, wept openly. Sarah sat next to her brother, lips firm, trying to keep tears back.

The last hymn was 'Now Thank We All Our God' and Robert found himself, to his surprise, singing. It had been Fee's favorite hymn. He held his emotions in check until the last guest had left the reception after the service, then he went upstairs and wept noisily.

One or two days later he found himself in the stable, comforting Fee's gelding Kinsale. The horse had been restless, missing his mistress. There was nobody else there, and he poked around aimlessly, not really knowing what he was doing. It was on a shelf, back in the tack room that he found the can of rat poison. Almost in a daze, he dumped a portion in a plastic bag, and put it in his pocket. Then he walked back to the house. He remembered it was evening, and the sun had just set behind the mountains. There was a fresh breeze blowing, warm and fragrant with the scent of the pines. No one saw him go into the kitchen. There was Claire's jug in which Mary Rose made the hot chocolate every night. It was sitting on a tray in the pantry. Mrs. Shaw had sent it last year. It was of doubtful taste, with a picture of the Princess of Wales on one side and one of the Prince of Wales on the other. Claire not only liked it because her mother had chosen it, but also because she greatly admired Diana. She insisted that Mary take the jug and china down to the main kitchen every morning so they could be washed properly in the dishwasher. Mary Rose usually mixed the chocolate down there as it was just as easy to do so as up in Claire's kitchenette. Robert unscrewed the lid. He could smell the steaming beverage.

The old man in the bed sighed as he looked at Eleanor's shocked face, and Roger's impassive one. "It was so easy," he said quietly. "I just dumped most of it in, stirred it with the spoon that was there, wiped the spoon, and replaced the lid. I walked out and went upstairs. No one saw me. I don't know where Mary Rose was. It was easy the next day, in all the confusion, to drop the bag amongst Claire's things in the bathroom." He paused and his face wrinkled with distaste. "I didn't know what arsenic did to one. I never meant Nell to find her. I was horrified when I realized what had happened the next day. I only knew that Claire had somehow altered something in the station wagon and caused that crash. It should have been me, but it instead it was my darling Fee."

He was very tired, now. He looked at Eleanor, whose expression was still one of love and compassion. "I need your forgiveness for taking your sister's life." The tears in her eyes were for him, and she took his hand and held it to her cheek. "Of course I forgive you, Robert. How could I not?" She had never used his given name before.

He closed his eyes. "I was sure you would forgive me, but will God?"

Roger said slowly, "The God I believe in is a loving compassionate being and eager to forgive us if we can forgive others."

There was a long silence. Finally the earl spoke. "You mean I should be able to forgive Claire for taking Fee's life?"

Roger nodded. There was another long silence. Finally he spoke. "Roger, thank you for showing me another point of view. But how can I forgive? How can I? No, no, I canna!"

Eleanor thought her heart would break. She whispered, "I don't know if I can forgive her either. I also loved Fee."

Robert gazed up at her. "So you did. And she loved you, Eleanor. My sister once said that I was selfish in my grief when Fee was killed; that I wasn't the only one to have loved her. Roger, can you pray for both of us to find forgiveness?"

The three joined hands and Roger prayed. When the prayer was over Roger and Eleanor stood up.

"We'll leave you to sleep," she said, stooping to kiss him on the cheek.

She made her way out of the suite and stopped at the top of the wide staircase that led down to the front hall.

"Roger, I can't face them tonight—they'd know something happened. I can't bear it!"

Roger took her arm. "Knowledge can be a dreadful burden at times. I think you should just go to your room. I'll tell the others you have a headache and are going to bed."

"I don't even know what room is mine."

"When I came up a little while ago I met James who was returning from taking your bags to your room. Let's just go and look for them."

He led the way through the gallery and into the guest wing. They found her bags in the first room they looked into. Eleanor suddenly found herself shivering uncontrollably. Roger sat her down in the chair by the fireplace, while he lit the fire for her. Then he came and sat on the big ottoman at her feet. He took her hands in his and searched her face compassionately.

"Roger, how can you bear hearing confessions like this? I just can't believe it."

"I just turn it over to God," he replied simply. "It's not that I forget, but it is no longer my burden." He smiled gently and rose to his feet. "I'll go and find Janet. She's the soul of tact and would never speculate or ask questions. Good night, Eleanor. Have a good sleep and you'll be surprised how differently you'll feel in the morning."

Eleanor smile up at him. "Thank you, Roger. You've been—wonderful. I shall pray for us all—especially Robert."

Roger went away, closing the door behind him. Eleanor sat in silence for a few minutes, reflecting on Robert's story. Why was she able to forgive Robert's actions so readily, but like him, not able to forgive her sister? Had she ever come to terms with what her sister had done to her? Claire had stolen James away, made him unhappy, neglected her daughter, and then taken the life of one the few people Eleanor truly loved. She remembered her thoughts on the way north in the train earlier that day, about how she had wanted James to see her as she was. Perhaps he had seen her as she truly was: *a monster that was happy only when her sister died?*

Eleanor put her face in her hands and wept quietly—for herself, for Claire, for James, and especially for James' father. And also for what might have been.

Chapter 26

ROBIN AND JAMES

D eb had seen her mother off on the flight to Vancouver, and the phone was ringing as she came in the door of Robin's house. It stopped just before she lifted the receiver. Robin had forgotten to go to Radio Shack and retrieve her answering machine, so there could be no messages. Darn. She'd pick it up tomorrow on her way to classes. It was midnight before she got to bed, and she immediately fell into a dreamless sleep.

She was getting ready to leave for classes the next day at eight o'clock when the phone rang.

"Hello, Lindsay residence..."

"Robin! I've got you at last! Where on earth have you been? Why didn't—"

"This isn't Robin, it's her daughter Deb." It was a warm voice with a distinct Scots accent. "Is this James Maclachlan?"

A few seconds of silence went by. "Hello?" said Deb.

"Yes, this is James Maclachlan. Your mother has mentioned me, then."

"You might say so," answered Deb dryly.

"How can I get in touch with her? I've been trying and trying."

"She's not here, Mr. Maclachlan. She left last night on a direct flight to Glasgow, and should be on her way north as we speak."

"Pardon me? Did you say she is in Scotland now?"

"Yes," answered Deb patiently.

"Why didn't she telephone? I could have met her...."

"She was over in Vancouver for several days, and didn't return until late yesterday afternoon. When she heard about your father, she just packed and left. How is your father?"

"He's about the same...and Robin? Is she well?"

"She's fine. She went to see Georgia Morrison in Vancouver, and there were some complications. She'll tell you all about it."

"Georgia Morrison—oh, aye, the man's widow. She told you about that, too, I presume?"

"I think she spared me some unpleasant details, but yes, she did. Thanks for being so supportive."

"Oh, aye, dinna mention it. Did she also tell you I want to marry her?"

"Yes, she did."

"And?"

"Mr. Maclachlan, you're going to have to ask her again yourself."

"Please call me James. Do I have your permission to marry your mother?"

Deb laughed. "Oh, aye—I mean yes." His turn of speech was infectious. "You'll both have to sort out your feelings for yourselves."

"While I've got you on the line, tell me a bit about yourself."

Deb looked at the clock and realized that she was going to miss her class, so she shrugged off her jacket, sat down and prepared to chat with the man who seemed destined to be her stepfather. Eleanor was still an unknown quality, but there was no way to bring her into this conversation. Surprisingly, James did himself.

"Your choice of career sounds very interesting. Did you meet my daughter while she was there?"

"Yes, of course, she stayed with mum for several days before she went over to Salt Spring Island."

"Did you meet my sister-in-law Eleanor as well?"

"Just briefly, before they left for Scotland the other day. She's very beautiful."

"Yes, she is. I hadn't seen her since my wife's funeral, but she's kept in touch with Nell since she was a baby. I've always felt as though I have another sister in Eleanor. I've known her since she was eighteen."

"James, will you tell that to my mother? About Eleanor being like a sister?"

"Dinna tell me that she was worried about Eleanor? I love her dearly, just the way I love my sister Katharine."

Deb repeated her request.

⚬⚬⚬

"*Love is lovelier the second time around, just as wonderful with both feet on the ground,*" warbled Robin as she gently put her foot down on the accelerator and steered her rental car expertly around a curve. The sun had been shining for the first hour or so of her drive north, and the road was dry and visibility good. However, it was now clouding over, and the flat leaden sky ahead of her made her think that snow might be in the forecast. As she turned to Nethy Bridge the first flakes swirled by her windshield. She drove slowly through the town, looking for the turnoff to Glen Rannoch Village. What she wanted more than anything was a cup of tea and a visit to the ladies' room. It would never do for her to rush to the bathroom upon arrival at Rannoch Castle, so she stopped at a small cafe that advertised 'Teas and Coffees', and parked the car. In the lavatory she washed her face and hands, combed her hair, and brushed her teeth. She should have been very tired, as she had not slept well on the flight over. She had been able to find three empty seats together and was able to stretch out, but her thoughts had whirled around in her head, and she had not been able to turn them off. Was she doing the right thing? Did James really want her to come, or was that just Nell's interpretation? Now that Eleanor was there, had he changed his mind about her? What of Georgia Morrison and that odious man Eden? She dozed fitfully, and arrived in Glasgow stale and tired, with a bad taste in her mouth. The next two hours or so was taken up with getting through Customs, finding her rental car, and negotiating her way out of the city. Once she had found the motorway to Perth she fairly zipped along. She opened the window and let the wind blow through, and she felt immeasurably better. The further north she got, the better she felt, and she sang 'Road to the Isles' and 'Bonny Dundee' at the top of her voice. *"Come fill up my cup, come fill up my can, Come saddle my horses, and call out my men, Unhook the west port and let me gang free...."*

Now she grinned at herself in the mirror, applied lipstick, and went out and ordered a pot of tea. She only lingered long enough to drink the scalding brew, and then was on her way again, up into the hills to Glen Rannoch. The road was familiar, now, and how the scenery had changed since her first visit in September! The leaves were off the trees, only the pines remained green, and the hills were no longer purple with heather, but dull and brownish. Dead leaves were caught up in the whirlwind as she passed, and the snow was coming down more heavily than ever. Glen Rannoch Village seemed to smile at her in a familiar manner as she crawled through it. Somebody waved at her, no doubt mistaking her for someone else, but she returned the wave cheerily, and started up the hill to the church. Lights in the houses were coming on; it was getting dark, and she almost turned into the Manse. Katharine's kitchen would be warm and bright, but she shook her head and sped by, thinking maybe she shouldn't have stopped in Nethy Bridge. She had a sense of time running away from her. What if the earl—she would never forgive herself if...? She gripped the steering wheel tightly, changed gears, and began the second descent up past the Glen, past the farm, the Dower House, and so through the gates home. Home! Yes it was like coming home, the castle was aglow with lights, and it seemed as though she had never been away.

The front door was unlocked, and she pushed it open and was once more in the large entrance hall. Janet Stevens came out of the dining room and stopped in her tracks.

"Mrs. Lindsay! You're here at last! James and Himself will be glad to see you, I can assure you." She paused and came forward and helped Robin take off her warm coat and scarf. "I didn't say anything to them about your coming—I didn't want to worry them, with the weather deteriorating like this."

Robin said wonderingly, "How did you know, Janet? I didn't phone, I just came."

"I saw you driving up the motorway. You were singing, and with window open because your hair was blowing wildly."

Robin eyes were wide with amazement, but she thought she wouldn't pursue the matter further. She nodded. "How is the earl?"

"Still holding his own. I heard the car, but thought it must be Nell and Miss Eleanor. They've been to Lossiemouth to visit Nanny Markham. Is it snowing much, then?"

Robin nodded. "Is James at home?" she asked hesitantly.

"He's in his father's study, on the phone still, I believe. You know where it is, down the corridor past the drawing room. I'll take your bag—is this all you brought?"

"I came away in rather a hurry."

Janet's eyes sparkled. "Indeed, it's grand to see you."

Robin's heart lifted, and she hurried down the corridor. As she drew nearer, she could see the door ajar, and hear James' voice. She shyly opened the door and hesitated in the doorway. James turned and saw her, and almost dropped the phone.

"She's here!" he said into the phone. He motioned her to come in, a broad smile on his face. "I'll put her on, but only for a moment, mind."

He held out the telephone receiver to her. "It's Deb. We've been having a grand chat." He moved over to the sofa, and perched on the arm.

"Deb, is it really you?"

"Yes, Mum. James telephoned a while ago—he just caught me before going to classes. Is everything all right?"

"I just got here." She was smiling at James, who was mouthing, "I canna' believe you're here!"

"Mum, he sounds wonderful. You both have my blessing. I won't keep you, you must be longing to—well, whatever you're longing to." There was a small giggle at the other end of the line.

"Yes. Yes, I am. Darling Deb, thank you for everything. I'll phone you tomorrow. Bye, dear."

She hung up the phone and turned to James. He held both his arms out to her, and with his foot he nudged the door to the corridor shut. She caught her breath and walked into his embrace.

It was some time before they disentangled themselves. Robin murmured that they should be sensible, and what if someone should come in? James laughed.

"No one would dare, with the door closed. Shall I lock it?" he asked with a wicked grin.

Robin sat up and rearranged her clothes. How came they to be on the sofa? "I came to see your father, James."

His hand, still on her shoulder, crept to her neck and was gently caressing it. "Just to see Dad?" he asked teasingly. "What about me?"

She turned her face to kiss him in answer, and a few more minutes passed agreeably.

"This is indeed lovely, but you're right, my love, we should go up and see Dad. Before we go, though, Deb has ordered me to tell you something about Eleanor. I want you to know that I've never been the slightest bit in love with her. We were friends when she was young, and I love her like I love my sister Katharine. Deb seemed to be worried that Eleanor would return and sweep me off my feet."

Robin colour rose. "She is so beautiful, and she was once in love with you, you know."

James shook his head. "Maybe so, but that was twenty years ago. It's you I love, Robin. Now. Today. Will you please marry me?"

"Yes, Jamie," she sighed happily.

They kissed again, and presently Robin said, "I have things to tell you."

James sat up and said, "Deb said you'd seen Mrs. Morrison."

Robin told him of her visit to Georgia, and the things that she had learned.

"And she was in Saint Andrews at the time! I remember we said, half jokingly, that it was a good thing she was in London; we wondered whether that had been checked out. Strange that it never came up at the inquiry." James yawned suddenly, and got up. "I think we had better go and see Dad. He'll be pleased at our news."

Upstairs, the earl was looking better than he had the previous day. He had more colour, and his blue eyes were clearer. He was delighted to hear that Robin had agreed to marry James.

"I wanted to tell you that you shouldn't worry that James was involved in Claire's death."

Robin smiled. "When Nell told me what she had remembered about that morning, I knew at once that James knew nothing about her death. He would never have allowed Nell to go to her mother's room. I hope you didn't think I ran away when I went home a few weeks ago. Nell and I had a wonderful time getting acquainted, and she was able to spend some time with her aunt, too."

Nell's grandfather nodded. "She told me all about it this morning. She wants you for her mother, you know."

Presently James and Robin left him and went into the suite's small sitting room. His heart was full to the brim with love for her.

"Lass, thank you for saying that about Nell and her mother. I was worried——why was I worried? I'm a fool!" He took her hand, and drew her up into his arms once more. "Oh, Robin, let's not wait too long! I ache for the wanting of you."

<hr />

Nell and Eleanor left Nanny Markham's home in Lossiemouth as the first few snowflakes were beginning to fall. They had had a splendid visit with her; she had been delighted to see them, especially her 'dear Miss Eleanor'. The elderly nanny was just the same, interested in Eleanor's activities and work; there were no reproaches to either of them for not visiting more often. Eleanor had brought her camera, and Nell her holiday pictures, so after descriptions of places seen in Canada, Eleanor took some photographs, and then Nanny demanded they take one of Nell and Eleanor together. Eleanor showed Nanny how to focus and what button to press, so several pictures were taken and a promise given to send them to Nanny if they 'turned out'. For

Eleanor it had been a respite, a time in which she didn't have to think about what James' father had told her.

"That was a lovely visit, Nell, thank you for bringing me. It's a fair distance in this weather."

"Yes, it looks as though we are in for a serious snowfall. Don't worry; this vehicle will get us back safely. It will be snowing in earnest up in the hills, though, so we had better not linger."

They drove in comfortable silence for a few miles. It was now snowing a little harder, the flakes coming at them in the headlights like a flurry of moths attracted to the light. Eleanor always found it rather mesmerizing.

"Penny for your thoughts, Aunt Eleanor."

"Oh." Eleanor came back to the present with some difficulty. "I was just thinking of my mother, my sister, and Fee. Do you remember your Grandmother Shaw at all, Nell?"

"No, I don't think so."

"I know she visited your mother before you were born, but I also think she paid another visit; you were probably too young to remember. She never came back to Scotland because she was diagnosed with cancer a year or so after that, so it was Claire and I who went to see her. I was in Washington with her when she died, and then we heard from your father that Malcolm had been born. There were all the funeral arrangements to make, and people to notify, so I didn't get back to Kirkland for nearly three weeks, just in time to hear from your grandfather about Fee's accident.

"My mother's death; Fee's accident; Claire's death; three deaths in a matter of a month or so. I felt shell shocked. I think I grieved your grandmother's more than either my mother or my sister. Is that an awful thing to say? The truth is I probably loved Fee more than either of them." Eleanor sighed. "And if I had any shred of hope for any kind of relationship with your father, it vanished when I came for your mother's funeral. It was the most depressing experience I've ever had. Your grandfather was still numb with shock over losing his wife—and James—well he wasn't the James I knew. We'd always been friends, he'd write in a friendly way, and I had enjoyed his company immensely when I was there before; this time he shut me out. It was though he was enveloped in a black fog. I couldn't reach him in any way. The atmosphere in your home was just ghastly, Nell. I couldn't wait to get away."

"Are you still in love with dad?" She glanced at her aunt. "Don't answer if you don't feel like it," she added hurriedly.

Eleanor really wasn't ready to answer that one yet, but still she smiled and said firmly, "No, I don't think so. I'm fond of him in a different way. He seems to be more like his old self now, in spite of your grandfather's illness."

"I think it's because of Robin. I do hope he has telephoned her. Do you like her, Aunt Eleanor?"

"Very much. I think they could be very happy together if they can sort things out."

Nell now concentrated on her driving, as the highway steepened as they left the valley of the Spey and neared Nethy Bridge. It was well after six now, and it was quite dark. The snow was still a flurry of white in the headlights, and they passed two cars, abandoned at the side of the road.

"Thank goodness for snow tires and four wheel drive," murmured Nell, as they turned on to the road to Glen Rannoch. A half hour later they crawled through the village and up past the Manse, to begin their final ascent to Rannoch Castle.

"Made it!" laughed Nell as she steered the car into the garage. The house was ablaze with lights, and there were two cars in the drive. The two women hurried across the drive to the side door leading to the kitchen; it was closer than the front door. Janet was busy preparing the evening meal. The delicious aroma of stew simmering on the stove filled the kitchen.

"Thank the Dear you made it back," she exclaimed, worried looks changing to a relieved smile. "It started to really snow a little while ago. There must be two or three inches already."

"No trouble at all, Janet. It's getting cold out there, though. How's Grandfather? Where is everybody? Is Iain here? The Dower House was dark as we came by."

Janet smiled broadly. "Himself is about the same, I think. Iain came in a little while ago, and asked himself to dinner. He's in the library with your Aunt Sarah. The big news though is that Mrs. Lindsay arrived about an hour and a half ago."

"Robin's here! I knew she'd come! Where's Dad?"

"They've been up with Himself for a time. He's been a bit worried about you two."

Nell didn't wait to hear any more, but hurried out into the corridor in search of her father. Eleanor followed slowly, her mind in a whirl. In spite of her assertions of the contrary to Nell, she knew there would always be a small piece of her heart that belonged to James. She wondered now, as she had wondered many times in the past, that if James' and Claire's engagement had been longer whether things would have been different. Claire might have revealed her true nature in time for James to have second thoughts. Who know what would have happened if that had occurred? Would he have grown to love her instead? Or he might have gone back to Scotland, fed up with the Shaw sisters and she would never have seen him again. Never carried on a cheerful correspondence with his mother. Never seen Nell, as she wouldn't have been born. Eleanor shivered. It wasn't to be, of course. Her parents were moving to New Zealand, and it was more practical for the wedding to take place sooner rather than later. *We can't go back, can we*, she thought.

<hr />

Nell met James and Robin as they were coming down the stairs hand in hand, faces radiant. She didn't have to ask any questions, but just hugged them as hard as she could. Eleanor joined them at the bottom of the stairs a moment or so later, smiling bravely and wishing them happiness. Sarah and Iain came out of the library at that moment.

"I'm glad to see you two have finally made up your minds about each other," she remarked tartly.

James smiled broadly at his family. "We haven't said a word. Is it as obvious as all that?"

"Yes," said Sarah, regarding them fondly. "It's written over both your faces. How is Robert?"

"Sleeping now. He was so happy to see Robin. He could hardly wait to give us his blessing."

"Aunt Katharine will be so happy. May I phone her, Dad?"

James glanced at Robin and she nodded. Nell and Iain went back into the library and presently emerged together. "She's ecstatic," Nell said gaily. "Iain and I are going to fetch them in the four wheel drive. They're coming to dinner. They can't wait to see you!"

"Tell Janet!" he called after them as they disappeared down the corridor, donning jackets and gloves.

After dinner the whole family sat in the library, drinking their coffee and chattering happily. Eleanor was so glad that nobody else knew what really had happened to Fee and Claire. It would have spoiled the atmosphere, and who knows how Robin would have reacted? Perhaps one day Robert might tell James of his part in Claire's death, but until then it was a secret she would have to keep buried deep in her heart, never to discuss it, even with Roger. Knowing the truth wasn't always the best thing, she reflected. The family would only be harmed by such knowledge. She sighed. It was best for her to go away again, and continue her life apart from the Maclachlan family; but she would make sure that Nell came again for a proper visit. Perhaps they could even meet in London sometime. She also should have visited Sally and Peter long ago. They were now in the West Country, enjoying the life of a country vicar and his wife. She would enjoy taking Nell on a visit to Cornwall; it would be good for her to see other parts of Britain. No, she would not put this off as she had done in the past.

<hr/>

Robin got up and went over to the window, and watched the snowflakes swirl and tumble outside. She couldn't believe how happy she was. She would phone Deb in awhile with their news and thank her humbly for insisting on her going back to Scotland. She would write a long letter to Marilyn Baker in Vancouver. Soon she would get in touch with Celine and invite her to come here to see them married. Yes, she thought, she would like to be married here—in the drawing room at Christmas and Roger performing the service. She felt James at her side and his arm slip around her waist.

"Penny for them."

"A Christmas wedding, James," she said softly. "A wedding in your beautiful drawing room with the Christmas tree and candles. Celine here, and Deb and Den, all your family and Roger making us husband and wife. What do you think?"

James thought that of all the happy times in his life, this moment was the best. Yes, there were problems that had arisen: Robin's innocent involvement in the killing of Morrison and the ensuing complications; these, however, would not come between them. Together they would see them through. He put his cheek against her hair.

"I think my cup is overflowing," he said.

Finis

9 781643 671116